Revolution and Intervention
in Grenada

Westview Special Studies

The concept of Westview Special Studies is a response to the continuing crisis in academic and informational publishing. Library budgets are being diverted from the purchase of books and used for data banks, computers, micromedia, and other methods of information retrieval. Interlibrary loan structures further reduce the edition sizes required to satisfy the needs of the scholarly community. Economic pressures on university presses and the few private scholarly publishing companies have greatly limited the capacity of the industry to properly serve the academic and research communities. As a result, many manuscripts dealing with important subjects, often representing the highest level of scholarship, are no longer economically viable publishing projects--or, if accepted for publication, are typically subject to lead times ranging from one to three years.

Westview Special Studies are our practical solution to the problem. As always, the selection criteria include the importance of the subject, the work's contribution to scholarship, and its insight, originality of thought, and excellence of exposition. We accept manuscripts in camera-ready form, typed, set, or word processed according to specifications laid out in our comprehensive manual, which contains straightforward instructions and sample pages. The responsibility for editing and proofreading lies with the author or sponsoring institution, but our editorial staff is always available to answer questions and provide guidance.

The result is a book printed on acid-free paper and bound in sturdy library-quality soft covers. We manufacture these books ourselves using equipment that does not require a lengthy make-ready process and that allows us to publish first editions of 300 to 1000 copies and to reprint even smaller quantities as needed. Thus, we can produce Special Studies quickly and can keep even very specialized books in print as long as there is a demand for them.

About the Book and Authors

In Part 1 of this book, Dr. Schoenhals places the Grenadian Revolution and its aftermath in historical perspective. He explores the Anglo-French rivalry over the island, the period of slavery, and the British colonial administration and gives particular emphasis to the Gairy decades (1951-1979). His discussion of the People's Revolutionary Government is based on extensive interviews with the leadership of the New Jewel Movement, foreign diplomats, and Grenadian citizens, and on a review of documents captured by the United States during occupation of the island. In Part 2, Dr. Melanson, after briefly reviewing the nature of U.S. interests in the region and U.S.-Caribbean relations during the Nixon years, focuses on the Carter and Reagan administrations' policies in the Caribbean and relations with the Grenadian government. He examines the justification offered by President Reagan for the 1983 intervention, domestic responses to the action in the United States, and its implications for Reagan's Central American policies. Finally, he considers whether the action will prove to be a prelude to a new domestic consensus about the use of U.S. military power in the Third World.

Kai P. Schoenhals is an associate professor of history at Kenyon College, Gambier, Ohio. *Richard A. Melanson* is an associate professor of political science at Kenyon College and director of its international studies program.

To
Edward Lamb
in
friendship and admiration

Revolution and Intervention in Grenada
The New Jewel Movement, the United States, and the Caribbean

Kai P. Schoenhals
and Richard A. Melanson

Westview Press / Boulder and London

Westview Special Studies on Latin America and the Caribbean

Copyright © 1985 by Westview Press, Inc.

Published in 1985 in the United States of America by Westview Press, Inc.;
Frederick A. Praeger, Publisher; 5500 Central Avenue, Boulder, Colorado 80301

Library of Congress Cataloging in Publication Data
Schoenhals, Kai P.
    Revolution and intervention in Grenada.
    Includes index.
    1. Grenada--Politics and government. 2. Caribbean
Area--Foreign relations--United States. 3. United States
--Foreign relations--Caribbean Area. 4. United States--
Foreign relations--1945-   . I. Melanson, Richard A.
II. Title.
F2056.62.S36   1985   972.98'45   85-3332
ISBN 0-8133-0225-0

Printed and bound in the United States of America

10 9 8 7 6 5 4 3 2 1

Contents

Preface

The murder of Grenadian Prime Minister Maurice Bishop
along with some of his closest advisers on October 19,
1983, and the invasion of the island six days later by the
United States and several eastern Caribbean countries had
significant implications not only for tiny Grenada but also
for the Caribbean area and U.S. foreign policy. What had
become of Grenada's revolution? What had reduced the
revolution's bright hopes of 1979 to the bloodbath of 1983?
Why had Bishop been killed? What roles, if any, had Cuba
and the Soviet Union played in his overthrow? Had U.S.
citizens really been endangered by the situation? On what
grounds did the Reagan administration justify the
intervention? What, if anything, did the action imply
about President Reagan's wider foreign policy goals? What
would become of post revolutionary, post invasion Grenada?
In this volume we attempt to answer these questions both by
closely examining the events and decisions of October 1983
in Grenada and Washington and by placing them in the
broader contexts of Grenadian history and recent U.S.
foreign policy.

The rather unusual format of Revolution and
Intervention in Grenada—two juxtaposed essays, one from
the Grenadian perspective, the other from that of the
United States—deserves explanation. Kai P. Schoenhals is
a Caribbeanist who lived in Grenada from mid-1982 until
shortly before Bishop's demise. He came well acquainted
with the prime minister and members of the People's
Revolutionary Government (PRG) and also conducted
interviews with some of the soldiers who were later to
constitute the Revolutionary Military Council. As his
section makes clear, Schoenhals maintained an ambivalent
attitude toward the PRG: Although he respected many of its

socioeconomic goals and achievements, he was disturbed by
its handling of dissent and by its provocative rhetoric.
His section represents a "worm's eye" view of the Grenadian
revolution by a regional expert with a sensitivity to
Grenada and the eastern Caribbean. Richard A. Melanson, in
contrast, is a student of U.S. foreign policy since World
War II and has interviewed key Carter and Reagan officials
during the last several years. His essay treats Grenada as
a problem in U.S. foreign relations. It focuses on the
Carter and Reagan administrations' response to the PRG,
their broader Caribbean aims, the justifications offered by
President Reagan for the "rescue mission," the nature of
the domestic support for and opposition to the action, its
implications for Reagan's Central American policies, and
whether the intervention will prove to be the prelude to a
new domestic consensus about the use of U.S. military power
in the Third World.

Thus, because our backgrounds and priorities are
different, we have chosen to write two independent, yet
related, essays, and the reader will quickly see that our
interpretations of events and our evaluations of decisions
are also far from identical. Nevertheless, we believe that
our essays, while distinct in focus and structure, share a
common commitment to coherence and objectivity.

Richard A. Melanson
Kai P. Schoenhals
Gambier, Ohio

Government and Political Leaders

Members of the People's Revolutionary Government

Maurice Bishop, Prime Minister and Minister of Interior and
    National Defense
Bernard Coard, Deputy Prime Minister and Minister of
    Finance, Trade, and Planning
Selwyn Strachan, Minister of National Mobilization
Hudson Austin, Commander of the People's Revolutionary
    Armed Forces and Minister of Labor, Communication, and
    Works
Unison Whiteman, Minister of External Relations
Jacqueline Creft, Minister of Education, Youth, Sports,
    Women, Social Affairs, and Community Development
George Louison, Minister of Agriculture, Rural development,
    and Cooperatives
Chris De Riggs, Minister of Health
Kenrick Radix, Minister of Justice and Minister of
    Industrial Development and Fisheries
Norris Bain, Minister of Housing
Lyden Ramdhanny, Minister of Tourism
Richard Hart, Attorney-General

Members of the Politburo (PB) of the New Jewel Movement
    (NJM)

Maurice Bishop, chairman	George Louison
Hudson Austin	Liam James
Unison Whiteman	Ewart Layne
Selwyn Strachan	Chalkie Ventour

Members of the Central Committee (CC) of the New Jewel Movement (NJM)

Maurice Bishop, chairman
Hudson Austin
Selwyn Strachan
George Louison
Unison Whiteman
Phyllis Coard
Leon Cornwall
Ian St. Bernard

Liam James
Ewart Layne
Christopher de Riggs
Chalkie Ventour
Kamau McBarnette
Tan Bartholomew
Fitzroy Bain

Members of the Revolutionary Military Council (RMC)

Hudson Austin
Liam James
Ewart Layne
Leon Cornwall
Tan Bartholomew
Ian St. Bernard
Chris Stroud
Keither Roberts

Basil Gahagen
Lester Redhead
Hughie Romain
Cecil Prime
Rudolph Ogilvie
Iman Abdullah
Kenrick Fraser
Raeburn Nelson

GRENADA: THE BIRTH AND DEATH OF A REVOLUTION

Kai P. Schoenhals

1
The Historical Background, 1498–1951

Prior to March 13, 1979, few people had ever heard of Grenada, one of the smallest countries of the Western Hemisphere. On that day, however, a group of leftist revolutionaries seized power in the Caribbean nation and from then on, Grenada became part of the worldwide confrontation between the two superpowers and assumed prominence totally out of proportion to its size. As a result of the U.S. military occupation of Grenada in October 1983 and Grenada's subsequent metamorphosis from a Cuban and Soviet ally to a ward of the United States, Grenada is bound to maintain a prominent position among the small Caribbean states.

The nation of Grenada actually consists of three islands: Grenada proper and two smaller islands, Carriacou and Petit Martinique. The latter two form part of a large number of islands known as the Grenadines,[1] which are strung out between Grenada and St. Vincent. About 110,000 Grenadians inhabit these three islands, but there are 300,000 Grenadians who live outside of their country. Their political support is eagerly sought by Grenada's politicians, and the financial remittances of these Grenadians residing abroad constitute an important source of foreign currency earnings for the Grenadian government. Grenada's exports consist of spices (particularly nutmeg and mace) as well as fruits and vegetables. Tourism, too, plays a vital role in the island's economy.

Like all of the other Caribbean islands, Grenada was first settled by Amerindians who came from South America (Venezuela and the Guyanas) and worked their way north across the chain of islands. The Caribs, who gave their name to the entire region, proved to be the most successful and permanent of the Amerindian groups.

1

After the European discovery of Grenada during Columbus' third voyage (1498), an inevitable struggle ensued between the various European powers for mastery of the Caribbean island. After unsuccessful attempts at the colonization of Grenada by England and Spain, a French force from Martinique began to systematically exterminate the Caribs on the island during the seventeenth century. By 1654, the French had pushed the Carib Indians to the northernmost cliff of the island. Rather than surrender, the Caribs--men, women and children--jumped to their death into the ocean below, an event much depicted and commemorated in present-day Grenada.[2] The place where the Caribs committed suicide is now called La Morne des Sauteurs (Leapers' Hill). Instead of building a monument at this spot, some Grenadians constructed a set of rails to the cliff; from there they used to push old car wrecks into the sea!

After exterminating the Caribs, the French controlled Grenada for more than a century and left a permanent imprint upon the island. First, they established their religion, Roman Catholicism, as the official faith of Grenada and in spite of all subsequent British attempts to make the Anglican church supreme, most Grenadians today are still Roman Catholics. Secondly, they gave French names to places and despite centuries of Anglicanization, half of Grenada's towns and villages still bear French names (e.g., Lance-aux-Epines, Sauteurs, La Sagesse, Paraclete, Perdmontemps). Finally, even after decades of British rule, many Grenadians continued (until the 1940's) to speak a patois consisting of French and African words.

After they had vanquished the Caribs, the French settled Grenada with what they regarded as undesirable elements from France, such as religious dissenters, debtors, and criminals. These immigrants became small farmers, who raised indigo, tobacco, and cotton for export. By 1700, sugarcane had been introduced to Grenada, and throughout the eighteenth century, sugar was the most important export of the island.

The introduction of sugar production wrought two important changes on Grenada. (1) The small landholdings of the farmers were rapidly absorbed by the large sugar plantations. Yet the sizes of the Grenadian sugar estates were relatively small in comparison to those on other Caribbean islands (e.g., Barbados) because of the mountainous nature of Grenada's terrain. (2) Because sugar production required huge amounts of cheap labor, a great many African slaves were brought to the island. By 1753, they numbered 12,000.[3]

Today the descendants of these black slaves constitute the overwhelming majority of Grenada's population, and African traditions persist on Grenada. One custom is the "maroon"--voluntary labor contributions for common projects such as the building of a new home or the gathering of crops. On the island of Carriacou, maroons are accompanied by the Big Drum Dances of African antecedents. Many of the rural people on Grenada still believe in obeah (magic and witchcraft).

As on all other West Indian islands, the African slaves on Grenada were treated with great cruelty. As the island was French, the slaves lived under the jurisdiction of the Code Noir (1685), which specified that slaves could be sold or mortgaged; yet they all had to be baptized in the Catholic faith. Barbaric punishment was administered to slaves who tried to run away. After a first attempt at escape the slave's ears were severed and one of the shoulders branded. A second try was punished by cutting off the buttocks and having the other shoulder branded. [4] A third attempt resulted in immediate execution.

The fate of the African slaves worsened when the British acquired Grenada by the Treaty of Paris (1763), which concluded the Seven Years' War. The British decided to work the slaves even harder, and within a decade the workers had doubled the amount of sugar exported from the island, making Grenada Britain's most valuable possession in the West Indies after Jamaica. [5] British rule brought other changes. Many of the French plantation owners were bought out by their British and Scotch counterparts. A number of French names were converted to English nomenclature. Thus the capital's name was changed from Basseterre to St. George's, and Fort Royale, the mighty bastion that the French built in 1705 to guard the excellent harbor of St. George's, was renamed Fort George. [6]

During the American Revolution, the French were able to recapture Grenada along with several other West Indian islands. The reconquest of Grenada, although of short duration (1779-1783), made the British residents deeply resentful toward the French because the French commander ordered the sinking of all English vessels in the harbor of St. George's and the imprisonment of the British governor. [7] He also permitted his soldiers to plunder the island.

When the Treaty of Versailles (1783) restored Grenada to England, the British resumed control with a vengeance. They confiscated the buildings and the land of the Catholic church and declared that all baptisms, marriages, and funerals had to be conducted in the presence of an Anglican

minister. Catholics were barred from all political
activity. These regulations adversely affected both whites
and mulattoes. During the French colonial regime,
Grenadian society had consisted of three main strata: the
white French settlers at the top; the free, property-
holding mullatoes (children of French colonizers and
African slaves) in an intermediate position; and the slaves
at the bottom. (As in the United States, the household
slaves were usually better off than the field hands.) The
discriminatory laws of the British, which were directed
against all three of these groups succeeded in fusing them
into an anti-British alliance.

The final explosion of Grenada was provoked by the
French Revolution of 1789, which proclaimed the liberty,
equality, and fraternity of all human beings. The hopes of
the suppressed blacks of the West Indies, already stirred
by these lofty principles and the successful slave revolt
in Haiti (1791), were further raised by the revolutionary
French government's abolition of slavery in 1794. A
special representative, Victor Hugues, was dispatched by
the French government to Guadeloupe in order to spread the
ideas of the French Revolution throughout the West Indies.

Living under the repressive rule of British Governor
Ninian Home, the white Frenchmen and the mulattoes of
Grenada decided to establish contact with Hugues, who
provided them with arms, ammunition, and propaganda
material and appointed the well-to-do Grenadian mulatto
plantation owner, Julien Fedon, as the representative of
the French Revolution on Grenada. Fedon waited for the
right moment to unleash a revolt against the British
overlords.

The opportunity came on March 1, 1795, when Governor
Home, playing host to British politician Alexander
Campbell, left St. George's for his country estate at
Paraclete in the Parish of St. Andrew. On the following
day, Julien Fedon launched a revolt from his estate at
Belvidere in St. John Parish and captured the towns of
Gouyave and Grenville, which are located on Grenada's west
and east coasts respectively. Home, who was informed of
the rebellion and feared being captured, decided not to
return via the southern route, but to ride north to
Sauteurs where the Caribs had made their last stand. One
of the governor's black slaves named Orinoko found out
about Home's escape plan and reported it to Fedon who was
able to intercept Home and forty-seven members of his
retinue.

Fedon then sent a message to the British at St. George's, asking them to surrender or face the execution of their governor and the other hostages. The British response was to send for reinforcements from all of their West Indian possessions as well as from England and to stage a relentless campaign to defeat the rebellion.[8]

The revolt had begun as an attempt by white Frenchmen and mulattoes to restore French control over Grenada, but as time went on, many of the 24,000 black slaves on the island joined the uprising, burning down sugar and rum factories and killing their owners. Within a few months, Fedon found himself in control of the entire island except for St. George's, which served as a refuge for the remaining British settlers. Enraged by the death of his brother Joseph, who had been killed fighting the British, and upset by the failure of the enemy to reply to his ultimatum, Fedon ordered the execution of Governor Home and the other hostages. A tablet erected in the Anglican church at St. George's commemorates the forty-eight Englishmen.[9]

Aided by French provisions and a tropical fever that decimated the ranks of the British troops, Fedon maintained control of most of the island for fifteen months; but the British were finally able to sever his French supply line. They encircled his forces which had retreated to a mountain top near his Belvidere estate. The British either killed or captured Fedon's remaining troops in June 1796. The fate of Julien Fedon remains a mystery. He is rumored to have drowned while trying to escape to Trinidad. After executing the top thirty-eight French leaders, the British deported most of the prisoners to Honduras. With most of the French whites and mulattoes as well as a quarter of the black slaves either killed or deported, Fedon's defeat spelled the end of French power on Grenada.

Two centuries later in March 1979 Julien Fedon was proclaimed Grenada's greatest national hero by the People's Revolutionary Government (PRG). When Maurice Bishop visited Francois Mitterrand during September 1982, the French president promised to appoint an historian to research, in the French archives, the relations between the French revolutionary government and the famous Grenadian rebel.[10]

While the British were doing everything in their power to maintain the system of slavery of Grenada in the 1790s, a development was taking place back in Great Britain that was to undermine the very system the British were trying to preserve on Grenada. This phenomenon, which was to transform not only the Caribbean Basin but the entire world, was the Industrial Revolution.

As a result of that Revolution, the mercantile system under which sugar imports from the British West Indies to the home country had been protected from foreign competition was destroyed and replaced by the Free Trade Scheme under which the British West Indian sugar interests had to compete openly with the vastly superior sugar plantations of such places as Brazil and Cuba. Actually it is difficult to speak of "competition" because the small, exhausted cane fields on the tiny (often mountainous) British islands in the Caribbean were no serious rivals to the large sugar plantations on the fertile flatlands of Cuba and Brazil. Consequently, disaster struck the sugar plantations of the the British West Indies, and by 1856 forty-seven sugar estates on Grenada alone had been abandoned.[11]

The decline of the sugar plantations lessened the need for black slaves, and by 1838 slavery had been abolished in the British colonies. Although the majority of Grenada's ex-slaves continued to work on the remaining estates as day laborers or sharecroppers, one-third of them decided to strike out on their own by buying, renting, or simply seizing tiny plots of land (between 1 and 2.5 acres) on which they grew crops for their own use and for export to the neighboring islands of Barbados and Trinidad. Thus the post-emancipation period on Grenada witnessed the development of a substantial class of peasants holding small plots of land. This class persists today; its existence has insured the absence of wide-spread undernourishment on Grenada. The exportation of Grenadian vegetables and fruits to neighboring islands, which originated at that time, also continues to the present and is carried out by so-called traffickers in rickety boats, many of which sink during storms between Grenada and Trinidad.

With many of the former slaves preferring to work on their own plots of land rather than continuing to labor on the estates of their former owners, the Grenadian plantocracy decided to tap new sources of cheap labor. The labor was provided first by the British capture of French and Spanish slave ships off the coast of Grenada and the subsequent settlement of the freed slaves on Grenadian soil. Thus in 1849, for example, about 1,000 freed African Yoruba tribesmen were settled on Grenada, where they introduced the Shango religious cult that persists to this day. Other population groups migrated during the

nineteenth century to Grenada as indentured laborers,
because of the depressed economic conditions in their
native lands. Some were inhabitants of the island of Malta
in the Mediterranean Sea, some Portuguese from the island
of Madeira off the coast of Africa, and some natives of
India, who also emigrated at that time in large numbers to
other Caribbean locations such as Guyana and Trinidad.[12]

In the wake of the sugar industry's decline, new
agricultural products were introduced, which soon
constituted the bulk of the island's exports. Cocoa was
brought to Grenada from South America during the eighteenth
century. The mountainous terrain of Grenada was well-
suited for the growing of cocoa, which became the leading
export crop by the 1880s. Grenadian plantation owners, who
had been sent by the British to the East Indies to assist
in the development of sugarcane in their Asian colonies,
returned to their homeland with nutmeg seeds. In 1843
these seeds were first planted by Frank Gurney on his
estate, Belvidere, which had belonged to Julien Fedon.[13] A
disease that ravaged the nutmeg trees in Asia in the 1850s
facilitated Grenada's entry into the nutmeg market. Within
a decade, Grenada was covered with nutmeg trees, and nutmeg
and mace (the fibrous covering of the nut) became the
second most important export item of Grenada's economy.
Today, as the primary export crop, nutmeg has become the
island's symbol and is represented in the national flag.
The growth and sale of other condiments, such as saffron
and cinnamon, have made Grenada the "Spice Island of the
West Indies."

Along with economic and social change came political
transformation. When Great Britain had acquired Grenada in
1763, a legislature was established to assist the British
governor in ruling the island. This legislature was
controlled by the English plantation owners. But the
British government feared that 23,000 slaves (85 percent of
the population) freed after the emancipation of the 1830s
would eventually attain a voice in the legislature and turn
Grenada into "another Haiti."[14] As a result of these
apprehensions, the British government placed the island
under its direct control by making it a crown colony in
1877. The British governor assumed all legislative
control. He was to be assisted by a legislative and
executive council consisting of Grenada's elite. The
members of this council, who were handpicked by the British
Crown, could not overrule the governor. The Grenadian
elite, which did not relish this curtailment of its former
power, nevertheless, put up with it, since it, too, did not

want the bulk of the population to gain any voice in the government.

With the development of commercial life in the urban centers (St. George's, Grenville, and Gouyave) of the island, a small, native bourgeoisie had emerged by the end of the nineteenth century. This incipient Grenadian middle class, made up mostly of mulattoes with a smattering of blacks and whites, objected to the monopoly of power held by the Crown and the plantation owners. Certainly as far as their education was concerned, the teachers, civil servants, lawyers, physicians, and merchants who constituted this new stratum of Grenada's society, could more than hold their own. They saw no reason why they should be excluded from the political life of their country. Many of their ideas and aspirations were reflected in the newspaper, The Federalist and Grenadian People, which was published in the 1890s under the slogan of "A Naked Freeman Is Nobler than a Gilded Slave" by the half-Grenadian, half-Irish editor William Galway Donovan.[15]

However, a young apprentice journalist of Donovan's, named Theophilus Albert Marryshow, became the greatest spokesperson for the rising middle class as well as the most prominent Grenadian citizen during the first half of the twentieth century. T.A. Marryshow was born in 1887 into a poor family. Apprenticed as a young boy to a carpenter, Marryshow switched jobs and became a compositor and a printer. In 1904, when he was seventeen, he began to work for Donovan, who became his mentor.

By 1915, Marryshow and the Grenadian lawyer C.F.P. Renwick had founded a newspaper called The West Indian, which basically espoused many of the same ideas that had been expressed in Donovan's paper. The West Indian, edited by Marryshow for twenty years, bore the slogan, "The West Indies Must Be West Indian," and advocated greater independence from Great Britain as well as the setting up of a West Indian Federation.

On September 19, 1915, a Grenadian troop contingent destined for the battlefields of Europe sailed from St. George's. With Grenada's black soldiers fighting for the British Empire, Marryshow became all the more incensed over a racist speech given during the First World War by South African statesman General Jan Smuts. In a series of articles published in 1917 under the title, Cycles of Civilization, Marryshow condemned Smuts and predicted that just as Europe had been the predominant world influence for the past centuries, it was now Africa's turn to set the course of history, but not before "the scattered sons of

New Ethiopia" would rally to free Africa from "the
murderous highwaymen of Europe who have plundered her,
raped her, and left her naked in the broad light of the
boasted European Civilization."[16]

The legislative councils of the Anglophone Caribbean
islands with the exception of Barbados and Jamaica were all
appointed by the representatives of the British Crown. In
1917 Marryshow, who was determined to change this
situation, founded the Representative Government
Association (RGA), which in 1920 petitioned the British
government for elected legislators. During the following
year, Marryshow journeyed to England at his own expense and
remonstrated with officials at the colonial office about
the lack of representative government on Grenada. As the
direct result of his intercession, the Wood Commission was
dispatched to the Caribbean. It recommended a measure of
representative government not only for Grenada, but also
for the rest of the Windward Islands as well as for the
Leewards and Trinidad. Thus Marryshow, who despised what
he called "parish pump politics" and always thought of the
English-speaking Caribbean as a whole, was able to win
concessions not only for his own island, but also for the
rest of the British West Indies.

The proposals of the Wood Commission resulted in a new
constitution for Grenada in 1925, which provided for five
elected members of a sixteen member legislative council.
(The other eleven members were still to be appointed by the
Crown.) Marryshow, who was elected to the council, held
the seat representing the capital of St. George's for
thirty-three years until his death in 1958.[17]

Just as in the rest of the world, the 1920s was a
period of turmoil for Grenada. The boom produced by the
First World War was followed by an economic slowdown and a
sharp drop in the demand for cocoa and nutmeg, Grenada's
main export items. There was bitterness among some of the
returning Grenadian soldiers who were unable to find jobs.
The ideas of Marcus Garvey, a Jamaican who preached black
separatism and the eventual return of all blacks to Africa,
found support among some Grenadians.[18] In order to halt
the dissemination of Garveyite literature, the British
Crown enacted a Seditious Publications Bill, which was
opposed in vain by Marryshow, who cherished the idea of
freedom of the press.

The depression of 1929 aggravated the economic plight
of Grenada even further, and Marryshow as well as the other
elected members of the legislative council demanded relief
measures such as easy credits for the peasantry, social

services, and an increase in the minimum wage. None of
these demands were accepted by the British Crown, but
Marryshow was able to persuade the government to build some
small houses for workers. The houses could be bought for
$3 a month, payable for twelve years.[19]   Upon his
suggestion, the government also bought up land and
distributed it among poor farmers.   In 1931 when British
Governor Vans Best raised taxes, in spite of the hardships
of the Great Depression, Marryshow organized the first mass
demonstration (more than 10,000 people) on Grenada and
forced the governor to revoke the unpopular ordinance.

Despite these occasional espousals of the interests of
the poor, Marryshow remained basically a representative of
the middle class who was opposed to militant trade unions
and universal suffrage.   Marryshow preached loyalty to the
British Empire and harmony among the social classes.   He
hardly fit alongside Julian Fedon and Tubal Uriah "Buzz"
Butler in the pantheon of Grenadian revolutionary heroes to
which he was elevated by the New Jewel Movement after the
victory of 1979.

The third figure in this trinity of Grenadian
revolutionary heroes was of a different mettle than the
conciliatory Marryshow.   Tubal Uriah "Buzz" Butler[20] was
born in 1897, the son of a poor blacksmith who was also the
sexton at St. George's Anglican church.   Because of his
father's position, young Butler was able to attend St.
George's Anglican school where he maintained a
distinguished record.   Like Marryshow, however, he was not
able to go to secondary school.   After dabbling in a number
of jobs, Butler volunteered at the age of seventeen for
service in World War I with the First Contingent of the
West Indian Regiment.

When Butler returned to Grenada in 1919, he was
appalled by the fact that the momentous events of the war
had changed little on his island.   The political and
economic life of this crown colony continued to be
controlled by the British governor in conjunction with the
white or mulatto plantocracy.   Poor and black, Butler found
his life as circumscribed as when he had left Grenada for
the war.   Determined to change all this, he founded the
Grenada Representative Government Movement, which advocated
universal suffrage and thus the enfranchisement of
Grenada's poor.   He also organized the Returned Soldiers'
Association, which demanded pensions, health benefits,
educational opportunities, and jobs for the island's World
War I veterans.

Unable to obtain a decent job on Grenada, Butler
emigrated in 1921 to Trinidad where he settled at Fyzabad,
a town whose population was 25 percent Grenadian. For the
next eight years he worked in the oil fields as a pipe
fitter until a serious industrial accident forced him to
retire. Always a deeply religious person, he became the
chief pastor of the Butlerite Moravian Baptist Church and
used the pulpit to call for higher wages for black workers
and land for the landless Indian peasants in the
countryside surrounding Fyzabad. Having gained a large
following, he organized hunger marches to Trinidad's
capital, Port-of-Spain. In June 1937, calling for better
wages, greater safety measures, decent housing, and an end
to racism, Butler organized a massive strike of oil field
workers that spread to many other sectors and threatened to
close down the economic life of Trinidad. As a result of
this strike, Butler was incarcerated by the British
government from 1938 until 1945.[21] He emerged from prison
as one of the great trade union leaders and heroes of the
Anglophone Caribbean.

During the 1930s, trade unions were founded elsewhere
in the Caribbean; in fact, many of the politicians who were
to lead their islands to independence in the 1960s and
1970s started out as heads of labor unions during the
decade preceding World War II. The formation of unions was
accompanied by unrest and strife, culminating in riots on
Jamaica in 1938 that persuaded the British government to
appoint the West India Royal Commission (known as the Moyne
Commission) to investigate the situation in the Caribbean.
In 1939 the Moyne Commission visited Grenada, where it
found undernourishment, poor housing, a lack of health
care, and a meager minimum wage amounting to twenty-four
U.S. cents per day for men and twenty U.S. cents for
women.[22]

The economic hardships on Grenada and the rest of the
Caribbean were somewhat alleviated by the Second World War,
which triggered an economic boom. Trinidad, because of
increased oil production and construction of U.S. military
bases, provided employment for many thousands of
Grenadians. But for those who continued to labor on the
estates of the Grenadian plantocracy, there was only a life
of grinding poverty. In spite of the wave of militant
trade unionism that had swept the West Indies in the 1930s
and the legalization of trade unions on Grenada in 1933,
the mass of Grenadian agricultural workers had remained
unrepresented. When two trade unions (the General Workers'

Union and the St. George's Workers' Union) were finally
organized on Grenada in 1946, they turned out to be urban
based. These decades of neglect of Grenada's agricultural
laborers were to come to an end in 1951 when the Grenadian
countryside exploded in revolution.

2
The Decades Under Gairy, 1951-1979

The Consolidation of Power, 1951-1967

The former Grenadian ambassador to Cuba and the Soviet Union, W. Richard Jacobs, once remarked: "If all of the approximately 300,000 Grenadians who reside abroad would suddenly decide to return to their native country, our little island nation would sink into the ocean."[1] The former Rhodes scholar and historian was not exaggerating the numbers. Although about 110,000 Grenadians live in their homeland, there are more than 300,000 abroad. Most of them reside in the United States (in Brooklyn), Canada, and the United Kingdom, but substantial numbers of Grenadians live on neighboring Trinidad and the Dutch ABC (Aruba, Bon Air, and Curacao) islands.

One of these many Grenadians who had gone abroad was a young black[2] named Eric Matthew Gairy, the son of impoverished peasants. He had been born in the countryside outside of Grenville, Grenada's second largest town. Gairy had emigrated to Aruba, where he worked as a primary school teacher and part-time trade union organizer. The latter activity resulted in his expulsion from Aruba in December 1949.

Upon his return to Grenada, he devoted himself to trade union and political activities. In July 1950, he founded the Grenada Manual and Mental Workers Union (GMMWU) and the following year, the Grenada People's Party (GPP), which was later renamed Grenada United Labor Party (GULP).[3] The GMMWU was by far the most radical trade union ever founded on Grenada. It appealed to the most neglected and poorest segment of Grenada's rural society: the largely landless rural workers who labored on the nutmeg, cocoa, and sugar estates. (Their wages in 1950 amounted to

13

eighty-two cents per day for the men and sixty-two cents
per day to the women.)[4]

Neither the plantation owners nor the British colonial
regime recognized Eric Gairy's GMMWU as a legal bargaining
agent for Grenada's rural workers; therefore, on February
19, 1951, Gairy called a strike. It was not only the first
general strike in Grenada's history, it also turned into a
rural insurrection. Many plantation houses were looted and
burned; stocks of nutmegs and cocoa were destroyed; road
blocks were set up all over the island; and the economic
life on Grenada ground to a halt.

On February 21, 1951, Gairy led thousands of
impoverished rural followers in a massive demonstration to
York House, the seat of Grenada's parliament and highest
court at the capital, St. George's. The British governor
declared a state of emergency, sent for British naval units
as well as extra police detachments from the islands of St.
Lucia and Trinidad and deported Gairy to the Grenadian
island of Carriacou. These measures only helped to fan the
flames of discontent on Grenada and provoked protests on
Trinidad and Jamaica. During the following month the
governor was forced to end Gairy's exile on Carriacou
because the governor needed him to calm the continuing
rebellion on Grenada. The twenty-nine-year-old labor
leader, who was by then called "Uncle Gairy" by his adoring
followers, was able to restore peace by his often-quoted
radio address of March 15, 1951, which illustrates Gairy's
folksy and egocentric style:

> Yes, folks, this is your leader, "Uncle Gairy"
> speaking to you. My dear, fellow Grenadians, you know
> that I am deeply concerned over the present state of
> affairs in this our dear little island. . . . As head
> of Grenada's two largest organizations—the Grenada
> People's Party and the Grenada Manual and Mental
> Workers Union, I feel obligated morally and
> spiritually to do something to alleviate, to stop, and
> when I say stop, I mean stop, the burning of buildings
> and fields; interfering with people who are breaking
> your strikes! Stop taking things away from the
> estates that are not belonging to you, particularly
> cocoa and nutmeg. And now we take another matter—the
> going back to work—when I lifted my finger on the
> 19th of February and said "strike" several thousand
> went on strike, that is because you have confidence in
> me and you know very well that "Uncle Gairy" knows his
> whereabouts.[5]

Elections held during October 1951 demonstrated that
Eric Gairy had become the most popular politician on
Grenada. Aided by the fact that universal suffrage had
been instituted a year before, Gairy's GPP-GMMWU obtained
71 percent of the votes cast and six of the seven
legislative council seats.[6] It looked as if he had a
successful political career ahead. Soon after the
elections, however, his weak points became apparent.
Instead of building up a strong trade union and political
party with a long-range program, Gairy essentially
transformed the GPP-GMMWU into a one-man show. Elected as
a champion of the downtrodden agroproletariat, he was eager
to be accepted by the Grenadian establishment and the
British colonial officialdom. While trying to impress his
rural following with his alleged power of obeah
(witchcraft) and knowledge of unidentified flying objects
(UFOs), he simultaneously attempted to win the goodwill of
the Roman Catholic church on Grenada by presiding over
Grand Masses and by erecting a cross (54 by 16 feet and
illuminated by 200 lights) on a hilltop at St. George's.[7]

Gairy had personally selected the six candidates who
ran in October 1951 on the GPP-GMMWU ticket. Four of these
candidates (the other two were Gairy and a peasant)
belonged to the propertied class and had no interest in
helping the rural poor who had voted for Gairy.[8] Of the
110 pieces of legislation that were considered by the
legislative council between 1952 and 1954, only four could
be considered of interest to labor.[9] It is, of course,
true that under the 1951 constitution, the British governor
retained fiscal control and could ignore the legislative
council, but during its six years in office (1951 to 1957)
Gairy's GULP (known as GLP until 1953) made no attempt to
further the cause of the very people who had supported him.
The plight of the poor during this period was made even
worse by Hurricane Janet, which devastated Grenada's
houses, roads, and nutmeg and cocoa plants during 1955 and
killed more than one hundred people.

In 1957, the Grenadian voters expressed their
disappointment with Gairy by bringing to power the Grenada
National Party (GNP), which claimed to represent all strata
of society. The GNP in reality was the party of the
privileged. Had the GNP taken measures to appeal to the
GULP's constituency, Gairy might have faded from the
political scene forever; instead, led by Herbert Blaize, a
proprietor from Carriacou, the GNP espoused the interests
of Grenada's plantocracy and business circles. The GNP
government provided subsidies that enabled the planters to

diversify their crops and sold the telephone and electricity services to private investors. The Blaize government did establish programs in the areas of livestock, fishing, and afforestation, but it did not do anything to aid the rural poor. Between 1957 and 1960, the income of the planters increased by 170 percent; in the same period, the wages of agricultural laborers went up by only 15 percent. By 1960, 42.6 percent of the Grenadian workforce was unemployed.[10]

It was no surprise, therefore, that the GULP was able to win the elections of 1961. The provision in the new constitution of 1960 enabling the chief minister of state to rule through a wholly elected executive council meant a considerable increase of power for Gairy. He used his added clout not only to enrich himself but also to work out corrupt government-business deals with some of his backers.[11] He wanted to utilize these elements to form a group of nouveau riche that would destroy the economic monopoly held by the established elite.

At the urgings of the anti-Gairy people, the British colonial administrator, James M. Lloyd, appointed a special commission to look into the corrupt practices of the GULP government. The commission issued the so-called Squandermania Report (March 1962), which accused Gairy not only of corruption but also of undermining the morale of the civil service by a campaign of intimidation.[12] Suspending the 1960 Grenada constitution, the British dissolved the fifteen-month-old GULP government and placed the island under the direct control of the colonial administrator until elections, scheduled for September 1962.

The September elections were fought not only over the Squandermania scandal, which had damaged Gairy's reputation, but also over the question as to whether Grenada should unite with seven other small British islands to the north (the Little Eight) or merge with the southern oil-rich Trinidad. A West Indian Federation, long championed by Grenada's prominent writer and politician, T.A. Marryshow, had been founded in 1958. Jamaica's decision to quit the federation led to its demise by 1962. Many Grenadians, feeling that their little islands were not viable as an independent economic and political unit, sought alternatives to the moribund West Indian Federation. The position of Gairy and his GULP was unclear with respect to a choice between the Little Eight or Trinidad. Gairy certainly dreaded unification with Trinidad because that island was led by one of the Caribbean's most famous

intellectuals, Eric Williams, who would have totally
eclipsed the eccentric Gairy. A Grenadian calypsonian, who
called himself "The Eight Hater," reflected the mood of the
Grenadian electorate in the following song:

>Come early or come late
>Uncle is for "Little Eight"
>But Uncle knows that Trinidad
>Is what makes Grenada glad
>
>"Little Eight" is Uncle pet
>Because that's where he's sure to get
>Motor car and house and ting
>Plenty cash for him to fling
>
>But now he find the pressure hard
>The people voting Trinidad
>So Uncle said: "You have to see
>Williams will only talk to me"
>
>If we see we put Gairy back
>That will be his same attack
>Make as if for Unitary State
>Then sell us out to Little Eight[13]

The GNP won the 1962 election. The party's support of
union with Trinidad was the decisive issue in its victory.
However, the Trinidadian government of Eric Williams had
never supported this idea; thus the whole campaign for
unification turned out to be an electoral mirage. The
election victory was the GNP's second and last chance to
adopt policies that would broaden its base of support
beyond the plantocracy and the business interests, but the
GNP missed this opportunity to cut into Gairy's following.
Blaize's party granted the plantation owners government
subsidies for fertilizers and insecticides; the GNP helped
Grenada's merchants by lifting taxes on their enterprises.
For the workers, the GNP did not have anything to offer
besides the Essential Services Ordinance of 1966, which
prohibited strikes by workers in the telephone,
electricity, and water services and left it up to the
minister to forbid strikes "in any industry that might be
deemed essential."[14]
Gairy, who after his spectacular actions in the early
1950s had done little for the rural workers, now made new
efforts on their behalf via the GMMWU, which succeeded
between 1962 and 1967 in raising the wages of agricultural

workers by 22.2 percent. A 14.5 percent increase in the
cost of living, and a decrease in social services, however,
reduced the effect of this wage augmentation.[15]

The Grenadian electorate, disillusioned by the
performance of the GNP, enabled Gairy's GULP to make a
strong comeback during the elections of 1967. During the
same year, Great Britain granted Grenada "associate
statehood," which meant total domestic independence and an
even greater strengthening of the premiership.

Gairy's Government, 1967-1979

The new status of associate statehood as well as the
concurrent election of Eric Gairy as prime minister
represented a watershed in modern Grenadian history. The
British dissolution of the GULP government in 1962 over the
Squandermania scandal showed that the colonial
administrators had exercised a restraining influence upon
the corrupt practices of Gairy. Associate statehood meant
that only the external affairs and the defense of Grenada
remained in the hands of Great Britain. As far as domestic
matters were concerned, Gairy was now able to seize
complete control and maintain it for the next twelve years
through vote rigging, gerrymandering, patronage, and
corruption.[16]

During the following decade even the smallest matters
had to await his personal decision. Members of the
Grenadian civil service and the police had to follow all of
his orders or face dismissal. For the right amount of
kickbacks, some of Gairy's supporters were able to obtain
the exclusive right to import certain commodities, a
valuable privilege in a country so dependent--as were the
other Caribbean islands--on imports. One of Gairy's
friends who held the monopoly on sugar imports bought every
200-pound bag of sugar for 53 East Caribbean Dollars (EC $)
and then turned around and sold each bag for EC $113.[17]
Fugitives from justice in the United States or Europe were
given asylum by Gairy. One such individual was a race
horse trainer named Edmund Zeek (alias Clancy) of
Baltimore, Maryland, who had absconded from the United
States with a million dollars and was wanted by both the
authorities and the underworld. Zeek was able to open a
string of business ventures, which included a large
nightclub called Love Boat (the nightclub became government
property after the 1979 revolution), whose raucous
nocturnal music kept St. George's population awake even

during the days of the Bishop regime (1979-1983).[18]

During the 1960s, Grenada's economy, heretofore almost entirely agricultural, became diversified with the establishment of a few manufacturing plants, increased construction and trade, and especially the growth of tourism.[19] Realizing the importance of the rapidly expanding tourism sector, Gairy acquired a string of hotels, restaurants, and nightclubs.[20] Gairy's business interests did not remain confined to the tourism sector. One scheme that aroused his interest was a $500-a-ticket "international lottery." The only problem was that nobody ever got a winning ticket![21]

On the one hand Gairy was diverting government funds to his private ventures, on the other, the public sector of the economy was virtually starved during the last twelve years of his reign. Support for education was at the very bottom of his priorities. The prime minister, who believed in witchcraft, UFOs, and dreams,[22] viewed any kind of education as a potential threat to his corrupt and bizarre rule. He knew that educated Grenadians held him in contempt and that his sway over the rural poor was partly due to the peasants' lack of education.

Education under Gairy was a disaster on all levels. The vast majority of Grenada's eighty-two schools had not been repaired in decades, while twenty-five of them had been rebuilt in 1955 after their total destruction by Hurricane Janet. Only 7 percent of the 400 secondary school teachers could claim professional training. Of the 900 primary school teachers, only 36 percent possessed a professional background. At times, seventy to eighty pupils found themselves packed into a single classroom. During Gairy's regume only 15 percent of Grenada's primary school children went on to secondary schools. Since Grenada does not possess any institutes of higher learning, Grenadians are forced to study abroad. Many of them study at the Barbados, Jamaica, and Trinidad campuses of the University of the West Indies, but because the Gairy GULP government owed that institution more than US $1.5 million, the UWI was reluctant to accept any more students from Grenada. During the last full year of Gairy's rule (1978), only three Grenadians went abroad for university study. (One of them was Gairy's daughter.)[23]

The health system of Grenada was also in a deplorable state. Hospitals lacked basic equipment, medicines, beds, and even linen. Women often had to deliver their babies on concrete floors. The General Hospital at St. George's was referred to derisively as "a branch of La Qua's."[24]

Perhaps it was no coincidence that visitors upon entering the hospital's grounds, noticed first the mortuary. Those who could afford it went for medical treatment to Barbados, Jamaica, or the United States. Dental care was particularly poor: The fact that there was not a single free dental clinic in the whole country meant that most rural people had never been to a dentist in their lives.

In November 1970 about thirty nurses from St. George's General Hospital took to the streets to demonstrate against the miserable conditions at their place of work. Gairy responded by having some of them transferred to remote parts of the country, an action that triggered even larger demonstrations in December. The December protests included nurses, school children, students, trade union officials, and members of the GNP. Gairy's police responded to the peaceful demonstrators with clubs and tear gas, creating a stir not only on Grenada, but also in other parts of the Caribbean. The twenty-two nurses who were arrested were ably defended by two young lawyers, Maurice Bishop and Kenrick Radix, who had formed a partnership after their graduation from law school in England and Ireland respectively.[25]

During the early 1970s a third political force that offered the Grenadian people a choice between the Scylla and Charybdis of Gairy's GULP and Blaize's GNP emerged. This new movement consisted primarily of Grenada's young intelligentsia, the daughters and sons of middle- and lower-middle-class parents, who, during the 1960s had studied at various universities in Canada, the United States, and Europe and were now returning to their homeland.

Whereas the older generation of Grenadians had by and large accepted and even imitated the ways of the British masters, these young rebels, many of whom had experienced racial prejudices during their sojourns abroad, had shed any veneration for British traditions. Instead, they were attracted to the Black Power movement, which had become significant in the United States as well as the Caribbean in the 1960s. They were emboldened by the writings of Walter Rodney, a black Guyanese historian who, as lecturer on African history at the Mona Campus of the University of the West Indies in Jamaica, had castigated the cultural influence of white hegemony upon blacks throughout the world. Another writer that influenced this group was the black doctor Frantz Fanon from Martinique who had served as a psychiatrist with the Algerians in their War of Independence (1954-1962). Fanon's book, <u>The Wretched of</u>

the Earth, is respected throughout the Third World. The
writings of the Ghanian statesman, Kwame Nkrumah, the U.S.
civil rights leader, Martin Luther King, Jr., and
especially the speeches of Malcolm X (whose mother was a
Grenadian) also influenced Grenada's young
intelligentsia.[26]

There were certain political events that left their
imprint upon these Grenadian iconoclasts. In 1966, Great
Britain attempted to form an associated state consisting of
three of her Lesser Antilles islands: St. Kitts, Nevis,
and Anguilla. The first two were willing to associate
since they were separated by only a small channel, but the
population of Anguilla, a tiny, eellike island off the
coast of Dutch- and French-controlled St. Martin, saw no
reason for joining St. Kitts and Nevis, two islands located
seventy miles to the south of Anguilla. When Great Britain
attempted to force the issue, Anguilla declared its
secession from the association on February 27, 1967. In
1969, British paratroopers descended upon the coral island
to reestablish British control. Four years earlier, the
much more important Rhodesia had declared independence from
Britain; and yet no British troops were dispatched to
Africa to reassert control over the region now known as
Zimbabwe. To the young Grenadians the reason for the
difference in British conduct towards these two
dependencies seemed obvious: Rhodesia was ruled by fellow
whites against whom it was felt improper to use troops.
Anguilla, in contrast, was inhabited by blacks against whom
it was acceptable to use force.[27]

Whereas the events on Anguilla filled them with rage,
these young Grenadians found inspiration and hope in
Castro's revolution in Cuba. Here on an island at the very
doorstep of the United States, was a government that was
carrying out a social revolution in defiance of its great
northern neighbor and at the same time encouraging other
revolutions in Latin America and the Caribbean. It seemed
to these young intellectuals that just as Fidel Castro had
been able to overthrow the corrupt Fulgencio Batista after
years of political and armed struggle, they too might one
day succeed in getting rid of Gairy. As a visual symbol of
their admiration for Castro, the male adherents of this
movement began to sprout Castro-like beards. Besides
Castro, they revered Che Guevara and mourned his death in
Bolivia in 1967.[28]

Typical of this new breed of young radicals that
emerged in the early seventies was a highly intelligent,
well-educated, and charismatic lawyer, Maurice Bishop, who

became their leader from 1973 until his murder on October 19, 1983. Maurice Bishop's father, Rupert, who had eked out a living as a plumber for the Public Works Department in St. George's, had tried to improve his lot by working abroad. Rupert Bishop moved to the island of Aruba, which had become prosperous because of the oil refineries located on the Dutch ABC islands. Soon after settling there in the late 1930s, Rupert sent for his wife Alimenta. They had two daughters and one son, Maurice, who was born on May 29, 1944. By the time Maurice left Aruba in 1950 with his parents for Grenada, he spoke not only English but also Dutch and Papiamento, the ABC islands' native language, a mixture of Dutch, English, and Spanish.

When Rupert Bishop returned to Grenada he had saved up enough money to purchase a small business, which proved to be quite successful. The former plumber became a respected and well-liked member of Grenada's small urban middle class. His son Maurice attended a Roman Catholic primary school and in 1956 won a scholarship to Grenada's Catholic secondary school for boys, Presentation College. During his six years at this school he developed his love for history and politics and displayed the qualities that would propel him into a position of leadership in the 1970s. While at Presentation College, he served as president of the student council, editor of the school newspaper and president of the Historical and Debating societies.

There had long existed an intense rivalry between the Catholic Presentation College and the Anglican Grenada Boys Secondary School (GBSS). Maurice Bishop considered the rivalry between the two schools childish and harmful, a feeling shared by a bright student at GBSS named Bernard Coard. Upon graduating from their respective schools in 1962, Bishop and Coard formed the Grenada Assembly of Youth After Truth, an organization designed to bridge the confessional differences between the two secondary schools and to enable the students of both institutions to address the important questions of the day. Every second Friday the organization held meetings on the Central Market Place of St. George's to discuss with the general population some issues of concern to all Grenadians. The activities ended within nine months because Maurice Bishop left for Great Britain to study law, and Bernard Coard went to Brandeis University in the United States to study economics. The two friends frequently corresponded with each other during their six years abroad.

A very disciplined and methodical person, Bishop decided at the beginning of his stay in London not to return home for a vacation because he felt that he could not restrain himself from becoming embroiled in the Grenadian political scene--an action that might put a permanent end to his study of jurisprudence. He intended to use his legal knowledge to study the constitutional development of Grenada as well as to help the victims of the Gairy regime.

While in Great Britain, he worked hard for the unity of all Caribbean students in that country and became the president of the West Indian Students' Union as well as the director of the Standing Conference of West Indian Organizations. He also became the cofounder of a legal aid clinic in the Notting Hill Gate ghetto of London where racial clashes had been a frequent occurrence in the 1950s. Bishop received his law degree in 1969.

In London he did not neglect his primary love: the study of history. He scoured the English libraries for books on Grenadian history and discovered three books on the life of Julien Fedon, who had led the 1795 Uprising against the British school masters of Grenada. Convinced that no old books on Fedon existed on Grenada, Bishop and his future wife Angela painstakingly copied one of these books by hand, only to discover upon their return to Grenada that a replica of this book existed in their homeland.[29]

As Maurice Bishop was returning to Grenada during the early part of 1970, he passed through Trinidad where he witnessed large Black Power demonstrations in which the many Grenadians who participated were arrested. Although he had extended his vow not to become involved in Grenadian politics for two additional years in order to establish his law practice in St. George's, the plight of his countrymen in Trinidad and at home led him to help in organizing a Black Power demonstration in Grenada's capital. It was this demonstration of about 200 persons on May 10, 1970, that convinced Gairy that he was facing a new and powerful threat by a group that appealed to the very constituency (black rural and urban poor) that constituted the rank and file of his Grenada United Labor Party. It was obvious to him that this new opposition called for tougher countermeasures than those used against Blaize's GNP, which represented the small elite of businessmen and plantation owners.

Although he belittled his new opposition as "hot and sweaty youth," he unveiled a secret police force--the "Mongoose Gang"--that he had been building up since 1967. Today Gairy describes his thugs as "just some unruly fellows from my union who were always fighting in the rum shops,"[30] they were, in fact, hardened criminals such as Norrel Belfon, alias "Tallboy," convicted thirty-four times between 1955 and 1970 for crimes such as assault, damage to public property, and illegal possession of firearms, and Crafton Fraser, alias "Tantie Gomez," convicted thirty-two times for such crimes as robbery, physical aggression, burglary, and assault.[31]

In a special radio address on May 23, 1970, in which he referred to neighboring Trinidad as "a house on fire," Eric Gairy informed the Grenadian people that he had already brought them Black Power in 1951 and that he would, therefore, not tolerate on Grenada any Black Power outbursts such as were transpiring on Trinidad:

> It is said that when your neighbor's house is on fire, keep on wetting your own house. We are now doubling the strength of our Police Force, we are getting in almost unlimited supplies of new and modern equipment . . . The opposition referred to my recruiting criminals in a reserve force. To this I shall not say yes or nay. Does it not take steel to cut steel? I am proud of the ready response to my call on Grenadians regardless of their record to come and join in the defense of my government and in the maintenance of law and order in their country. Indeed, hundreds have come and some of the toughest and roughest roughnecks have been recruited.[32]

Two days before his radio address, Gairy had decreed the Emergency Powers Act, which allowed the police to search without a warrant the premises of Grenadians for subversive literature, guns, and ammunition; restrict the right of assembly and movement of citizens; and ration essential resources and commodities.[33] This act was followed by the Public Order Amendment Act, which imposed a fine of EC $500 or six months in prison for anyone promulgating abusive language and slogans against any particular race or class of people.

In November 1970 came the nurses' strike, followed in December by supportive demonstrations, which were broken up by Gairy's police with clubs and tear gas. After these disturbances, Gairy once again went on the air and announced that in addition to the Mongoose Gang, the army (called "Green Beasts" by the populace) and the police, he was now forming two new outfits, a "Night Ambush Squad" and a "Special Secret Police Force."[34]

General elections were held in early 1972, and several young progressives (among them Unison Whiteman and Selwyn Strachan), hoping to radicalize the party from within, decided to run on the GNP ticket. Their hopes were vain, however, because Gairy was able to win a huge electoral victory through a combination of vote rigging, gerrymandering, the use of patronage and genuine support among the rural poor who were still identifying more with "Uncle Gairy" than with the elitist GNP.

It became apparent to the young progressives that they must form their own organizations if they wanted to influence political life on Grenada. Shortly after the elections of 1972, two populist organizations were formed: the urban-centered Movement for Assemblies of the People (MAP), headed by Maurice Bishop and Kenrick Radix and the rural-based Joint Endeavor for Welfare, Education and Liberation (JEWEL), led by a young economist, Unison Whiteman, who had obtained an M.A. in 1969 from Howard University in Washington, D.C.

Soon after its founding, the JEWEL group received an appeal from some Parish of St. David residents who had been denied the use of a popular beach located near the La Sagesse estate, which had recently been acquired by a Lord Brownlow. The access road to the beach happened to run through the estate. Lord Brownlow had a fence erected across the road in order to keep hoi polloi out of his property.

When an appeal to Gairy did not lead anywhere, Brownlow's opponents turned towards the newly founded JEWEL group, which held a People's Trial with several older Grenadians testifying that the access road had been used for generations by the surrounding population to reach the beach. The People's Court found the absent Lord Brownlow "guilty of obstructing the people's rights" and after the verdict was rendered, a large crowd demolished the fence that blockaded the road. More than twenty people were arrested for invading Lord Brownlow's property; during the subsequent trial, the popular lawyers Bishop and Radix defended once again the interests of the average citizens just as they had done during the nurses' trial a year before.[35]

The La Sagesse affair had brought the MAP and JEWEL groups closer together and at a conference held on March 11, 1973, it was decided to merge the two organizations into the New Jewel Movement (NJM). Maurice Bishop and Unison Whiteman became its joint coordinating secretaries. In a special manifesto, the NJM called for the forming of grassroot organizations that would fight for greater social justice, reduce unemployment (which hovered around 50 percent during most of Gairy's last decade of rule), and develop a program "to improve housing, apparel, education, public health, food and recreation for the people."[36]

During the elections of 1972, Gairy announced that if reelected, he would push hard for complete independence from Great Britain. After his victory he did begin a campaign to attain independence as soon as possible. Gairy's efforts were unpopular with the political opposition. The West Indian Federation had been short-lived, and the union with Trinidad had proved to be chimerical. The GNP and NJM espoused eventual independence, but not at the price of having Gairy acquire even more power. Their demand for a referendum on the issue was rebuffed by Gairy. Although critical of Gairy's independence moves, nevertheless, the GNP's leader Blaize joined the Grenadian premier in May 1973 on a trip to London to work out the final details of the independence constitution.

The NJM, for its part, arranged for a "People's Conference on Independence," which was attended by thousands of people. A month earlier a young NJM member, Jeremiah Richardson, had been killed by Gairy's secret police while distributing the NJM's newspaper, The New Jewel. Large demonstrations, which closed down Pearls Airport for three days, followed this murder and Jeremiah Richardson became the first martyr of the NJM.[37]

The opposition to Gairy during 1973 culminated in a People's Congress, convoked by the NJM at Seamoon in the Parish of St. Andrew on November 4. With more than 10,000 people in attendance, the congress passed a resolution accusing Gairy of twenty-seven crimes including corruption, incompetence, and murder. The premier was called upon to resign within two weeks or face a general strike. Gairy's response was to harass many of the people who had participated at the congress. In a minatory radio address he stated: "We will bring the NJM to their senses and wake them up from their dreams in a very short time for 54 reasons, including treason and sedition."[38]

These were no idle threats. Gairy had been made aware of his waning support when he had called his own followers to make a counterdemonstration on the central square in Grenville in response to the NJM congress at Seamoon. In contrast to the 10,000 people at the NJM rally, only 2,000 Gairy supporters appeared at Grenville. Gairy decided to prevent the upcoming general strike by terrorizing the NJM leadership into submission.

In the evening of November 17, 1973, Gairy asked his superintendent of police, Innocent Belmar (known as the "Sheriff"), to appear at Gairy's official residence at Mount Royal in St. George's. Belmar was instructed to block a meeting scheduled at 3 P.M. on the following day at Grenville's Deluxe Cinema. There the leadership of the NJM planned to work out the final details of the general strike with a group of businessmen led by a Grenadian merchant of Indian descent, R.M. Bhola.

The following day, as six of the top leaders of the NJM (Maurice Bishop, Unison Whiteman, Kenrick Radix, Selwyn Strachan, Hudson Austin, and Simon Daniel) left St. George's in two cars for Grenville, they observed that they were being followed by the police. Upon reaching Grenville, they noticed that the Deluxe Cinema had been cordoned off by the police and the Mongoose Gang. Hopelessly outnumbered, they decided to repair to Bhola's living quarters, which were located above his supermarket at a busy intersection in downtown Grenville.

When they arrived at the Bhola residence, they were set upon by a squad personally led by Belmar who shouted at his men: "Get them, dogs!" Austin, Radix, and Daniel were able to race up the stairs to Bhola's apartment, but Bishop, Whiteman, and Strachan had to take cover behind a wall near the house. They were subjected to a hail of bullets, all of which missed their mark because of the bad marksmanship of Belmar's "dogs." These ruffians then closed in on their victims whom they beat mercilessly with clubs, axe handles, and pistol butts. The three NJM leaders, bleeding profusely (Bishop had a broken jaw) and semiconscious, were then dragged off to the local jail and thrown into a small cell that was already inhabited by three common criminals.

Belmar then returned to the Bhola house and told the remaining NJM leaders to surrender or face an assault. Austin, Radix, and Daniel, who wanted no harm done to their hosts, gave themselves up. They were promptly transported to the jail (however, without a beating) and thrown into the same cell as their comrades and the three criminals. During the night, Belmar made frequent visits to this cell. He had the NJM leaders stand at attention (a procedure particularly painful for Bishop, Whiteman, and Strachan because of their injuries) while asking them mockingly, "Do you still want to seize power, gentlemen?" He also ordered their heads shaved with broken glass shards and threatened

to make them eat the mixture of blood and hair--the result
of this particular torture. On the following day, the six
political prisoners were denied bail, medical attention,
legal aid, as well as visits by their families or even the
clergy.[39]

When Belmar and his men were working over Bishop,
Whiteman, and Strachan, the "Sheriff" had exclaimed:
"Listen, this is Grenville and not St. George's." By this
statement, Belmar meant that he and his men could get away
with mistreating the NJM leaders in Grenville, whereas in
the capital everybody would have known about it and
protested. But news travels fast in Grenada. When the
public heard about the situation of the NJM leaders there
was an unprecedented outpouring of sympathy from all strata
of society.

A committee of twenty-two groups was formed to
organize a general strike. Included in this coalition were
all of the labor unions (except Gairy's GMMWU), the Taxi
Drivers and Owners Association, the Lions and Rotary clubs
as well as the Jaycees, the Chamber of Commerce, the
Grenada Hotel Association, the Civil Service Organization,
and the Roman Catholic, Anglican, Methodist and
Presbyterian churches. The Committee of 22 demanded the
arrest and punishment of those responsible for Bloody
Sunday, the dismantling of Gairy's Mongoose Gang, an end to
arbitrary arrests and searches and the release of the six
NJM leaders. It also called for the setting up of a
special Commission of Inquiry to look into the events of
Bloody Sunday.[40] Frightened by this outburst of
indignation, Gairy released his six political prisoners and
agreed to all demands. Thereupon, the Committee of 22
called off its strike that had lasted for a week.

As soon as the crisis seemed to have blown over, Gairy
reneged on all of his promises, except for the Commission
of Inquiry, which was established under the direction of a
renowned Jamaican jurist, Sir Hubert Duffus. The resultant
Report of the Duffus Commission to Grenada denounced the
brutality of the Gairy government during the events of
Bloody Sunday, called for the complete reorganization of
the police force and the abolition of the secret police and
declared Innocent Belmar unfit for holding public office.[41]
Gairy ignored these recommendations and made Belmar special
adviser to the premier and later on even a government
minister. The Mongoose Gang became yet more brutal during
the years following Bloody Sunday.

The protests, demonstrations, and strikes that had
shaken the Gairy regime during 1973 carried over into the

new year when it became apparent that Gairy would not
fulfill most of the promises which he had made after Bloody
Sunday. On January 21, 1974, a peaceful anti-Gairy
assembly along St. George's waterfront (known as the
Carenage) erupted into bedlam when Gairy's Mongoose Gang
commandeered a soft-drink truck and pelted the rally with
hundreds of bottles. The panicky crowd, which contained
many women and children, fled into adjacent buildings, such
as the Otway House, where Maurice Bishop's father, mother,
and sister had also taken refuge. Fearing that the
Mongoose Gang would invade the building, Rupert Bishop
stepped out of the Otway House in order to plead with the
secret police to let the women and children leave safely
for their homes. The response of Gairy's agents was to
kill him at the entrance of the building. This gentle man,
who initially had disapproved of his son's involvement in
demonstrations and radical politics, thus became another
martyr of the struggle against Gairy, and the day of his[42]
death was commemorated as Bloody Monday.

Complete independence for Grenada was slated for
February 7, 1974, but by late January it seemed that Gairy
would not be able to cling to power until that day. Fuel
and food supplies were running dangerously low, and the
Grenadian premier did not even have the money to pay his
secret police, not to speak of his civil service. At this
point several forces both outside and within Grenada
decided to come to Gairy's rescue because they preferred
him with all of his shortcomings to anarchy and revolution.
An independence gift from Great Britain of 100,000 pounds
enabled him finally to pay all government personnel—who
had been threatening to strike. The United Kingdom and
Canada also sent three armed vessels to St. George's to
shore up the Gairy government; Trinidad and Tobago as well
as Jamaica and Guyana made loans of US $2 million to
Grenada. The most important break for Gairy, however, came
when the Seamen and Waterfront Workers Union (SWWU) under
Eric Pierre ended its strike and allowed food and fuel once[43]
again to be imported into Grenada.

The achievement of complete independence on
February 7, 1974, meant that Gairy was henceforth the prime
minister of Grenada. He was able to use international
organizations such as the United Nations and the
Organization of American States (OAS) as platforms for his
bizarre ideas. In an address to the General Assembly of
the United Nations on October 7, 1977, he called upon that
body to set up an Agency for Psychic Research into[44]
Unidentified Flying Objects and the Bermuda Triangle.

Gairy's enhanced position scarcely impressed the other Caribbean heads of state, who held the Grenadian leader in contempt. Trinidad and Tobago's prime minister, Eric Williams, gave orders that he did not want to be seen in public with Gairy and the prime minister of Barbados at that time, Errol Barrow, dismissed Gairy as a "political bandit."[45] But Gairy was able to find at least one supporter in Chilean dictator Augusto Pinochet whom he visited in 1976. A year later, Gairy openly defended Pinochet and accused the governments that denounced the brutal events in Chile as being "under the influence of emotional intoxication." Pinochet, in turn, not only trained members of Gairy's army and the Mongoose Gang in "counterinsurgency," but also shipped arms and ammunition into Grenada under the guise of "medical supplies."[46]

In Grenada itself, Gairy showed every intention of remaining in power indefinitely. Alarmed by the fact that the NJM's newspaper, The New Jewel (circulation: 10,000), was outselling all other Grenadian publications, he issued a new law in 1975 requiring a deposit of EC $20,000 for the right to publish a newspaper. In order to restrict the influence of rival labor unions and political parties, he put through a regulation that denied the use of loudspeakers to all oppositional elements. During the elections of 1976 he displayed the full range of his repressive measures. On the one hand, the names of hundreds of members of the opposition were stricken from the voting rolls, and on the other, many of Gairy's followers were permitted to register twice, and the names of deceased persons were added to the voters' lists. The police and army were used to break up anti-Gairy political rallies; the only radio station—controlled by Gairy— informed the population that all men over forty were to be slain and the churches turned into discotheques if the opposition should win.[47] On election day (December 7, 1976) all polling inspectors turned out to be Gairy's agents.

In spite of all of these illegal moves on the part of Gairy, the opposition showed surprising strength. The People's Alliance, consisting of the NJM, the GNP and the United People's Party (UPP)—a conservative group that had split off from the GNP, garnered 48.5 percent of the vote, gaining six of the fifteen legislative seats. Of the six seats, the NJM obtained three, the GNP two, and the UPP one. Maurice Bishop became the chief spokesperson for the parliamentary opposition. Gairy's GULP, with its nine seats, retained control of the government. During the

thirty-eight months of its existence, the Grenadian
parliament met only nineteen times for a total of seventy
days.[48]
     On June 19, 1977, Gairy played host to the Annual
Meeting of the Organization of American States. With St.
George's crowded with many foreign delegates and
journalists, the NJM used this opportunity to stage a large
rally to protest the living conditions and violations of
human rights on the island. Gairy's police fired on the
demonstration, killing seventee-year-old Alister Strachan,
who became another martyr for the NJM. Gairy had expected
to reap beneficial publicity from the OAS meeting; instead,
his reputation suffered from this display of police
brutality. A year later, in May 1978, the Commonwealth
Parliamentary Association meetings were being held on
Jamaica and Trinidad. It was customary under the
Westminster System for each country to include at least one
member of the political opposition in the delegation.
Gairy, however, absolutely refused to invite any member of
the People's Alliance to join the Grenadian delegation. By
1978 also five opponents of Gairy's had "disappeared"
forever, showing that Gairy's police were learning
Pinochet's favorite method of eliminating political
enemies.[49]
     Gairy's relationship with the civil servants and
teachers degenerated considerably during the final phase of
his regime. The civil servants had not obtained wage
increases since 1970 even though the cost of living had
risen more than 200 percent between 1970 and 1976. When
Gairy and the Civil Service Association could not agree on
a wage settlement, the Grenadian head of state decided to
create a Salaries Review Commission, stating that he was
"prepared to accept in principle the findings of a salaries
commission."[50] When the commission, however, recommended a
salary increase, he refused to accept its judgment. The
civil servants, thereupon, called for a strike, but Gairy
threatened to fire them or to withhold their salaries if
they were to go through with it. In June 1978, when the
secondary school teachers called in sick as a protest
against their low salaries, Gairy denounced them as "part-
time strikers who are selling insurance, distributing
Communist literature and preaching indiscipline and
disrespect to pupils."[51]
     While Gairy thus was losing the support of many
segments of Grenada's population, the NJM was
simultaneously growing in strength among all the strata of
the island's society. Having already forged a

parliamentary alliance with the middle class, it began to
win over urban workers by founding the Bank and General
Workers Union (BGWU), which was led by Vincent Noel, one of
the top leaders of the NJM.[52]   The movement paid particular
attention to the setting up of youth and women's groups,
which became the nuclei of the future National Youth
Organization (NYO) and National Women Organization (NWO).
The NJM even organized a secret insurrectionary detachment
that proved to be of great value. The army and police were
infiltrated by the NJM, and soldiers and policemen who were
sympathizers of the movement provided it with important
information. Thus when Eric Gairy allegedly gave the order
to have the directorate of the NJM eliminated during his
planned absence from the island, this intelligence was
promptly relayed to the NJM leaders, who decided to get rid
of Gairy's government before it had the chance to liquidate
them.

The Seizure of Power, March 1979

On March 12, 1979, Gairy left Grenada for the United
States and on that same day, shortly before midnight,
Maurice Bishop, Bernard Coard, Hudson Austin, Unison
Whiteman, Selwyn Strachan, George Louison, and Kenrick
Radix[53] met with about forty young members of the NJM at a
chicken farm near Grand Anse Beach outside of St. George's
in order to plan a nocturnal assault on Gairy's army of
about 230 men, who were in their barracks in the valley of
True Blue. Among the core of young NJM members who had
been selected to attack the True Blue barracks were Leon
"Bogo" Cornwall (later the head of the National Youth
Organization and the last PRG ambassador to Cuba) and
Einstein Louison, who was to become the chief of staff of
the People's Revolutionary Army (PRA). The whole operation
was led by Hudson Austin, the future general and commander-
in-chief of the PRA, who ordered the assault for 4 A.M. on
March 13.
At the appointed hour, the forty-six NJM fighters
discovered to their delight that all of Gairy's "Green
Beasts" (including the sentries) were fast asleep. Since
only eighteen of the combatants were armed at all (their
armament consisted of eight M-1 rifles, two 303s, two
hunting weapons, a few pistols, dozens of Molotov cocktails
and a few homemade bombs), the first task of the NJM
members was to seize the army's arsenal, which they found
unguarded. Most of the weapons they found were in poor

shape except for the new Chilean SLR rifles that Pinochet had dispatched to his friend Gairy. After the capture of the arsenal, they assaulted the three barracks with Molotov cocktails, setting the buildings aflame. The attack on the True Blue army camp, which Cuban Premier Fidel Castro was to label "a successful Moncada,"[54] went without a hitch.

The next task was the capture of the Radio Grenada broadcasting station, which was normally heavily guarded. When the sentries there, however, observed that the True Blue barracks were burning, they fled, enabling Bishop and his followers to seize Radio Grenada at 4:30 A.M. The seizure of this radio station, which was turned into the revolution's headquarters, was the decisive event of that night. From there, Bishop was able to inform the Grenadian people of the startling events of the past few hours and appeal for support for the "Revo." The response was overwhelming, with people pouring into the streets in support of the NJM. Members of Gairy's Mongoose Gang were rounded up, police stations were seized and the identifying symbol of the NJM revolution appeared everywhere: a white flag containing a red disc. By 4:30 P.M. on March 13, 1979, Grenada, Carriacou, and Petit Martinique were firmly in the hands of the revolutionaries. The entire operation had cost the lives of only three people.[55]

The passing of the Gairy regime was not mourned by anyone except for Gairy's closest cronies and the Mongoose Gang. The man who had emerged as a genuine popular hero in the early 1950s had become partially discredited by the 1970s because of his repressive methods, his personal corruption, his ties with foreign dictators, and his bizarre ideas, which made him the laughingstock of the Caribbean.

Enemies of the Grenadian revolution of 1979 have claimed that this revolution was merely a coup d'etat, lacking popular support. Such a view, however, ignores the fact that the military action was preceded by decades of political struggle and that Gairy's repression and vote rigging really left the NJM little choice but to overthrow him by armed force.

Bishop's promise that "this Revolution is for work, for food, for decent housing and health services, and for a bright future for our children and great-grandchildren,"[56] met with the overwhelming approval of the Grenadian people. If elections had been held during summer 1979, Bishop and the NJM would have won a landslide victory.

Who could have foretold then that only four-and-a-half years later, this very same NJM leadership that had been

welded together by Gairy's persecution would tear itself
apart and bury their young revolution? But on March 13,
1979, the jubilant people of Grenada were not disturbed by
any ominous forebodings as they danced in the streets in a
typical Caribbean "jump-up" and shouted:

> "Freedom come, Gairy go
> Gairy gone with U.F.O."

3
The People's Revolutionary Government, 1979-1983

Initial Reaction to the Grenadian Revolution

With the people joyfully dancing in the streets and all segments of Grenadian society, including the civil service, the Chamber of Commerce and Governor-General Sir Paul Scoon pledging loyalty,[1] the People's Revolutionary Government (PRG) knew that it had the support of the country. Of greater concern to the PRG was the question of how the international community, particularly the United States and the neighboring Caribbean states, would react to the changes on Grenada. It was assumed at St. George's that Washington was aware of New Jewel Movement statements sharply critical of U.S. foreign policy. There was, for instance, the 1973 manifesto of the New Jewel Movement, which read in part: "We condemn in the strongest possible terms the intervention of the USA in the internal affairs of the South East Asian countries and the genocidal practices being committed on their peoples. We support in particular the heroic struggle of the people of Viet Nam and Cambodia."[2]

The first signals sent out by the PRG were conciliatory. The new government pledged not to take any reprisals against members of the Gairy administration and vowed to establish a mixed economy, consisting of state and free enterprise sectors. All foreigners were urged to maintain their residence on the island.

The initial response of the Carter administration was mixed. A plea by Gairy for U.S. aid in restoring him to power was turned down as were requests by Maurice Bishop (April 6 and 8) for arms to repel a possible invasion by mercenaries on behalf of the deposed prime minister. The National Security Council is said to have rejected a request by the Pentagon to clamp a naval blockade on

Grenada.[3] After a Cuban delegation visited Grenada on
April 7, the State Department rushed the U.S. ambassador to
the Eastern Caribbean, Frank Ortiz,[4] to St. George's on
April 10 for a meeting with Bishop that was to have far-
reaching consequences.

The interpretations of this visit have varied widely.
Publications friendly towards the Grenadian revolution have
blamed the Ortiz mission for driving the PRG into the arms
of the Cubans.[5] Ambassador Ortiz has described the visit
as a friendly mission during which he offered $5,000 in aid
for a variety of projects on Grenada.[6] The PRG apparently
did not realize that U.S. ambassadors must have special
authorization to offer anything beyond $5,000 from their
discretionary fund for aid projects in countries within
their jurisdiction. In any case, the offer of $5,000 by
Ortiz was interpreted as a deliberate insult by Bishop and
the other cabinet ministers who participated at this
meeting. There is no doubt, however, that Ortiz bluntly
warned the new government not to develop closer ties with
Cuba if it wanted to get along with the United States. His
comment that the PRG's talk about "mercenary invasions by
phantom armies" would cut down the flow of tourists to
Grenada was seen as an additional threat. Even the
moderate landowner and businessman, Lyden Ramdhanny, who
was a PRG cabinet member at the time, remembers that "Ortiz
attempted to call the shots" and "we said we'd like to have
relations with everybody, left-leaning and right-leaning;
he said he saw difficulty in that."[7]

Nevertheless, if it was Ortiz's mission to prevent the
establishment of Cuban–Grenadian relations, it must be
considered a failure because on April 11 Cuba and Grenada
decided to open embassies in each other's countries and on
April 13 Maurice Bishop went on the radio and gave a
stinging rebuke to the United States:

> From Day One of the revolution we have always striven
> to have and develop the closest and friendliest
> relations with the United States, as well as Canada,
> Britain, and all our Caribbean neighbors. . . .
> But no one must misunderstand our friendliness as
> an excuse for rudeness and meddling in our affairs,
> and no one, no matter how mighty and powerful they
> are, will be permitted to dictate to the government
> and people of Grenada who we can have friendly
> relations with and what kind of relations we must have
> with other countries. We are not in anybody's
> backyard.[8]

The Cuban government had already sent (on April 6) a
shipment of arms and cement that arrived on Grenada on
April 14.[9] This initial assistance was followed during the
next four-and-a-half years by a constant flow of Cuban aid,
which was manifested in diverse ways. Besides the much-
publicized arms shipments and the training that the Cubans
provided for Grenada's People's Revolutionary Army (PRA)
and the militia, there were Cuban dentists who set up
dental clinics in regions of Grenada and Carriacou whose
populace had never received dental care before. Twelve
Cuban physicians provided free medical care in Grenada
which until then had only seven Grenadian doctors. A
donation of Cuban fishing trawlers enabled Grenada to set
up its own fishing industry. Thousands of Grenadians were
able to study at Cuban universities and technical schools
on Cuban scholarships. The Cuban-built Sandino Complex, a
factory for cement blocks to be used in constructing
inexpensive housing on Grenada, was completed in March
1983. But above all Cuba's offer to be of major assistance
in the realization of the PRG'S dream—building a jet
airport on Grenada—became the symbol of Cuban-Grenadian
friendship. Three hundred Cuban construction workers and
engineers, using trucks and heavy equipment brought from
their homeland, worked in twenty-four-hour shifts, six days
a week, to build the new airport at Point Salines. In
connection with the airport, the Cubans also constructed an
asphalt factory as well as the Quintana Stone Crushing
Plant. All in all, the initial Cuban contribution to the
airport came to EC $30 million. The Cuban ambassador to
Grenada, Julien Rizzo, who, along with his wife, Gail Reed,
a U.S. citizen,[10] was to reside on Grenada from 1979 until
1983, became the doyen of the miniscule diplomatic corps at
St. Georges, which by 1983 consisted merely of the
diplomatic representatives of Cuba, Great Britain, the
USSR, Libya, and Venezuela.

The close ties that developed between Cuba and the PRG
from the very start were not the result of the Ortiz
mission. They were, in a way, preordained by the long-
standing admiration felt by Maurice Bishop and the NJM
leadership for Fidel Castro and the Cuban Revolution. The
relationship was reinforced by the close personal
friendship that developed between Bishop and Castro, a
friendship that has been described by Bishop's mother,
Alimenta, as almost a father-son relationship.[11]

Actually, there was no reason why these close ties to
Cuba should have prevented normal relations between Grenada
and the United States. The PRG, despite its closeness to

Castro, was able to develop perfectly normal relations with
such nonrevolutionary governments of those of Canada,
France, and Venezuela. But it must be remembered that
under successive U.S. administrations since 1959, U.S.-
Cuban relations have not been normal. As long as Cuba is
depicted in Washington as simply a Soviet surrogate
attempting to set up Communist centers of subversion
throughout Latin America and the Caribbean, there is no
chance of a real breakthrough in relations between Havana
and Washington. Because Grenada was viewed by the U.S.
government as a new Cuban center of subversion and the
first Communist bridgehead in the Anglophone Caribbean,
U.S.-Grenadian relations were doomed from the start.

The vacillating Carter administration, torn between
the rivalry of its secretary of state and its national
security adviser, could hardly be expected to change its
policy toward Cuba. President Carter did lift the travel
ban to Cuba, but by 1980, with the U.S. presidential
elections approaching and the Republicans blaming the
Democrats for the "loss" of Iran, Grenada and Nicaragua,
the hard-liners within the Carter administration were
winning. With the sudden discovery of a Soviet Training
Brigade on Cuba and the setting up of a Caribbean
contingency Joint Task Force at Key West, Florida, as part
of a Rapid Deployment Force, U.S.-Cuban relations took a
new turn for the worse.

Since relations between the United states and Grenada
were so heavily predicated upon U.S.-Cuban interchanges,
the scenario of the dealings between St. George's and
Washington was a response to the atmosphere between the
United States and Cuba. However, in spite of the warnings
issued by Ortiz about the ramifications of close Cuban-
Grenadian links, the U.S. ambassador to the Eastern
Caribbean did offer Grenada economic aid and the PRG was
recognized by the United states. When the Grenadian
government asked for the extradition of Eric Gairy from San
Diego, California on the grounds that he was responsible
for the murder of Bishop's father, Rupert, on January 21,
1974, the United States replied that such an extradition
could not be carried out if it were based on this
assassination since the statute of limitations (five years)
had expired. The U.S. Department of State, however, sent a
legal expert to Grenada to assist the PRG in finding
sufficient legal evidence of Gairy's other wrongdoings to
be able to extradite the former prime minister.[12] The PRG,
allegedly, never cooperated with this official.

The 1980 chill in U.S.–Cuban relations further cooled
U.S.–Grenadian contacts. The U.S. State Department refused
to accept the credentials of Dessima Williams, who had been
designated by the PRG as ambassador to the United States.[13]
The new U.S. ambassador to the Eastern Caribbean, Sally
Shelton (1979–1981), after an initial meeting with Maurice
Bishop, was told by her superiors not to visit Grenada in
the future. When a storm hit Grenada in early 1980, the
United States allegedly tried to prevent the dispatch of
emergency aid from the Organization of American States, and
when Hurricane Allen destroyed 50% of Grenada's bananas, as
well as the banana crops of neighboring islands, the Carter
administration offered help to WINBAN (Windward Islands
Banana Growers Association), provided that none of this aid
would go to Grenada.[14]

During the last phase of the Carter administration,
the "domino theory, which had justified U.S. actions in
Southeast Asia, was applied to the Caribbean. After the
successful NJM takeover of Grenada, influential officials
in Washington feared other Anglophone islands would fall to
armed Marxist groups.[15]

There existed and there exist today two fundamental
obstacles to Marxist takeovers in Anglophone Caribbean. In
the first place, almost all people on these islands are
deeply religious and, therefore, reject the atheistic
component of Marxist ideology. Secondly, after centuries
of British rule, the Westminster model of parliamentary
democracy is deeply imbedded in the political consciousness
of the population. Grenada had been an exception. In
contrast to most of the other Caribbean island states
(e.g., Barbados, Jamaica, St. Vincent, St. Lucia) Grenada
had experienced decades of government by a corrupt and
repressive leader under whom the parliamentary government
had become a sham. Any Anglophone Caribbean island that
maintains a genuine parliamentary democracy (which includes
a vigorous opposition party and a free press) has nothing
to fear from radical political movements. There are only
two East Caribbean islands with significant revolutionary
movements similar to the NJM: Antigua, with its ACLM
(Antigua Caribbean Liberation Movement) under Tim Hector,
and Dominica, with its DLM (Dominican Liberation Movement)
under Bill Riviere. Antigua has been ruled for more than a
decade by a corrupt family dynasty (Vere Bird, Sr., and his
sons); on Dominica, Prime Minister Eugenia Charles' ruling
Dominica Freedom party controls the only newspaper and
radio station on the island. The opposition Labour party
has been rendered inoperable by tripartite fragmentation

and its erstwhile leader, Dominica's first prime minister, Patrick John, has been jailed and allegedly tortured.[16]

The reactions of the other Caribbean governments to the NJM's victory were varied. Although all of them welcomed the termination of Gairy's bizarre rule, which had become an embarrassment to the entire Caribbean area, some of the Caribbean governments did not like the alternative either. Prime Minister Tom Adams of Barbados, although recognizing the PRG within ten days of its coming to power, attempted to persuade the United States, Canada, Great Britain, and France to withhold recognition from the new government. He also tried unsuccessfully to block Grenada's admission to the Socialist International. Prime Minister John Compton of St. Lucia went as far as to ask Great Britain to send troops to Grenada to put an end to the Bishop regime. The prime minister of Trinidad and Tobago, Eric Williams, distanced himself as much from Maurice Bishop as he had from Eric Gairy and refused to send any economic aid to Grenada. (After Williams's death, the new prime minister, George Chambers, took a much more positive attitude towards the new Grenada and was probably most responsible for blocking Tom Adams and Edward Seaga's efforts at the Third CARICOM Summit Conference, held in November 1982 at Ocho Rios, Jamaica, to expel Grenada from the Caribbean Common Market.[17]) The reverse situation occurred in Jamaican-Grenadian relations. The Social Democratic prime minister of Jamaica, Michael Manley, immediately rushed to the aid of the Grenadian revolution and attended the celebration of the first anniversary of the Grenadian revolution (1980) along with the Nicaraguan Sandinista leader, Daniel Ortega. Manley was replaced by Edward Seaga, who assumed a bitterly hostile attitude towards the PRG. Grenada, however, still profited in a way from the change of government at Kingston because hundreds of the Manley government's economic and technical experts who had been purged by Seaga came to Grenada to work for the PRG. A Jamaican lawyer, Richard Hart, even became attorney-general of Grenada in June 1983.

Another large contingent of foreign experts was made up of Guyanese nationals, whose prime minister, Forbes Burnham, had provided a shipment of rice and guns for Grenada immediately after the March 13 revolution.[18] It was a Guyanese, Christopher Ram, who developed for the first time a social security system for Grenada (enacted in April 1983) known as the National Insurance Scheme (NIS), which covered all working people between sixteen and sixty and provided for sickness, maternity, invalidity, and

survivors' benefits as well as old age pensions.[19]
Guyanese Shehiba Strong became the Grenadian Foreign
Ministry's chief of protocol.

PRG Suppression of the Press

The People's Revolutionary Government thus had its
supporters and detractors, but it supplied ammunition to
its enemies on October 13, 1979, when it closed down
permanently the Torchlight, the island's only opposition
newspaper, which in the past had exposed the corruption and
repression of the Gairy regime. This newspaper had aroused
the ire of the PRG during the summer of 1979 by revealing
the location of a new People's Revolutionary Army camp
(which was probably known anyway since nothing remains a
secret on tiny Grenada) and by reprinting an article from
the West German mass-circulation magazine Die Bunte that
erroneously claimed that Cuba and the Soviet Union were
constructing missile and submarine bases on Grenada. What
constituted the final straw, however, was an article
entitled "Rastas to Protest," which appeared in the
Torchlight on October 10. According to this article,
Grenada's Rastafarians were complaining because the PRG was [20]
supposedly interfering with their religious practices.
In order to understand the wrath of the PRG concerning
this article, one has to understand that the Rastafarians,
who had been persecuted by Gairy and defended by lawyers
Bishop and Radix, constituted some of the most loyal
supporters of the Grenadian revolution and that many
Rastafarians were serving in the PRA. There had been no
difficulties between the Rastafarians and the PRG except on
the issue of marijuana, the use of which is part of the
Rastafarian cult. The PRG did not object to the
Rastafarians' smoking marijuana in private, but those
selling marijuana to the general public were prosecuted.[21]
The Bishop regime viewed the Torchlight article as a
deliberate attempt by counterrevolutionary elements to
create dissension between the PRG and the Rastafarians.
After closing the Torchlight, the PRG declared that no
newspaper (except for the government-controlled Free West
Indian) would be allowed to appear before a new media code
had been decreed.[22]
In 1981, when about a year had passed without the
appearance of any media code, a group of twenty-six
prominent members of Grenada's elite, including some of the
same people who had been shareholders and directors of the

extinct Torchlight, with the aid of Grenada's most
prominent journalist, Alister Hughes, decided to publish a
new opposition paper, called the Grenadian Voice. After
only one stenciled issue had appeared, the PRG cracked down
hard. Maurice Bishop labeled the twenty-six men behind the
Grenadian Voice "political Judases, parasites, pimps,
prostitutes, CIA agents and foot soldiers of imperialism"
and Alister Hughes "a man who has sunk lower and lower over
the years."[23]

This time the PRG did not limit itself to rhetoric. A
number of the shareholders of the Grenadian Voice, among
them the businessman Leslie Pierre and the PRG's first
attorney-general, Lloyd Noel, were sent to Richmond Hill
Prison, which looms forbiddingly over the town of St.
George's. They were held there without trial until their
liberation by U.S. forces on October 26, 1983. Alister
Hughes was too prominent a journalist to be arrested in
1981, but the PRG kept a wary eye on him and at times
prevented him from leaving the island. For example, right
after the Grenadian Voice episode he was barred from
boarding a LIAT plane at Pearls Airport to fly to Trinidad
where he was to attend a meeting of the Caribbean Press
Council (CPC), of which he was the executive secretary.[24]
Finally, Hughes too was sent to Richmond Hill Prison for a
few days during General Hudson Austin's Revolutionary
Military Council's (RMC) ephemeral reign between October 19
and 25, 1983. After being freed, Alister Hughes stated:
"I want to be clear about one thing: I think that the PRG
did some very good things in Grenada. But nothing can
excuse the detention of political opponents."[25] Even
Rickey Singh, one of the very few Caribbean newspaper
editors sympathetic to the PRG, was critical of these
actions which he described as "an overkill."[26]

The banning of all nongovernment newspapers[27] was
paradoxical because the PRG permitted the unrestricted sale
of Newsweek and Time throughout the four-and-a-half years
of its existence even though these two U.S. newsmagazines
contained much material (including articles on
revolutionary Grenada) that the PRG found objectionable.
The official Free West Indian was of such poor quality and
appeared so infrequently (once a week if the printing press
did not break down, which happened often) that many
Grenadians turned to the foreign press or to foreign
broadcasts to find out what was going on in the world.
Equally deplorable were the only two St. George's
bookstores which sold mostly cheap novels and religious
tracts. In a speech to the First Conference On Culture And

Sovereignty In the Caribbean in St. George's in November 1982, Belize's minister of health Assad Shoman, complained to the assembled delegates that he was appalled that the bookstores on Grenada did not carry a single book by the famous Barbadian novelist, George Lamming, one of the chief organizers of the conference and a great friend of revolutionary Grenada.

Antiparliamentary Sentiment and Grass Roots Organizations

Another matter that proved to be disturbing to the governments of the United States, the United Kingdom, and the surrounding Caribbean nations was the failure of the People's Revolutionary Government during its entire rule to permit opposition parties and free elections, in spite of Maurice Bishop's promise in telephone conversations with Ambassador Ortiz right after the revolution that there would be "the prompt and free election of a legally constituted government."[28] Foreign friends of revolutionary Grenada have often wondered why Bishop did not simply go ahead and hold elections; he could have won by a landslide.

What these sympathizers do not realize is that the NJM never had any intention of setting up a parliamentary democracy along the British Westminster model, which had been imitated throughout the Anglophone Caribbean both during and after British colonial rule. The NJM leaders, in defending their decision not to hold elections and allow a parliament on Grenada, stated that the Westminster model had been totally discredited by Gairy, who had maintained formally all of the British institutions, while, in reality, running a quasi dictatorship.[29] It seems hardly logical, however, for a government to discard a time-honored system of government that has worked so well in the English-speaking part of the world, simply because it was manipulated and distorted by a corrupt statesman on a tiny island in the Caribbean.

The real reasons for the Grenadian leaders' rejection of the Westminster model of parliamentary government must be sought elsewhere. In the first place, these young revolutionaries had a strong streak of nationalism and resentment toward their former colonial masters. The revolutionaries were eager to get rid of a system that was so closely identified with Great Britain. Secondly, they had boundless admiration for their idol, Fidel Castro, and they were determined to use the Cuban revolution and, to a

lesser extent, the institutions of the Soviet Union as the
model for their rule.

Thus there was the emergence of a Politburo and a
Central Committee and the creation of Mass Organizations
such as the National Women's Organization, the National
Youth Organization for youth between the ages of fourteen
and twenty-two, and the NJM Young Pioneers for the five- to
fourteen-year olds. The parish and zonal councils, which
were designed to form the most vital link between the
Grenadian masses and the leadership recalled not only New
England town meetings, but also the workers' and peasants'
councils (Soviets) of the Bolsheviks. Just as in the
Communist countries, different years were given special
appellations. Thus 1981 turned out to be "The year of
Agriculture and Agro-Industries"; 1982, "The Year of
Economic Construction"; and 1983, "The Year of Political
and Academic Education." There were plans to designate
1984 as "The Year of the International Air Port."

The PRG sincerely believed that all of these grass
roots organizations, reflecting "People's Power," were much
more democratic than the previous infrequent sessions of
the Grenadian parliament and the periodic elections. In
order to make sure that there was a constant interaction
between the government and the population, parish and zonal
council[30] meetings were to be held at least once a month
and a member of the NJM's Politburo had to be present at
each meeting. Such gatherings usually consisted of a
cultural presentation (musical performance, dance, poetry
reading), and address by the Politburo member, who often
explained how the PRG had responded to grievances voiced at
the previous month's meeting, and finally comments by the
audience. Most complaints dealt with water shortages,
power blackouts, the insufficient telephone system,
abominable roads (except for Dominica, Grenada has the
worst roads in the Caribbean), and deficiencies in the
transportation system. The head of Grenada's Water
Department and the managers of Grenlec (Grenada Electric
Company) and Grentel (Grenada Telephone Company) were often
subjected to heavy criticism at such gatherings.[31]

Many of the popular programs, institutions, and laws
of the PRG had their origins in the debates of the parish
and zonal councils as well as in the mass organizations.
Frequent complaints about the expense and irregularity of
the existing transportation system, which did not even
reach all parts of the island, resulted in the government's
decision to use an unrestricted grant of US $1 million from
the Organization of Petroleum Exporting Countries (OPEC) to

set up a National Transportation System (NTS), beginning
with the purchase of twenty-six Japanese minibuses. Not
only did the NTS provide cheap and improved transportation,
but it also created more than seventy additional jobs (bus
drivers, conductors, administrators, clerks)--important in
a country that had more than 50 percent unemployment at the
time of Gairy's overthrow.[32]

Concerned about the remonstrances expressed at parish
and zonal council meetings about the poor housing
conditions in the Grenadian countryside, the PRG used
another OPEC loan to organize a housing repair program
through which poor families could get a loan of EC $1,000
per household to purchase building materials to repair
their homes. This loan was repayable at $17 a month over a
period of ten years. For those with an income of less than
EC $150 a month, less than two-thirds of the loan had to be
repaid over a ten-year period at $5 a month.

Pressure from women through the NWO led to the passage
in October 1980 of a maternity leave law which for the
first time in Grenadian history guaranteed maternity leave
of three months including two months with pay if the woman
had worked at least eighteen months at her place of
employment prior to the leave) to all women workers,
including domestic servants--a large and poorly paid
segment of Grenada's female workers.[33]

One of the most persistent demands that could be heard
at the parish and zonal council meetings from their very
beginning was a call to cut down on imports and use more
Grenadian products. When the PRG decided to let the entire
Grenadian population participate in the drawing up of a
people's budget, beginning with the national budget for
1982, the same demand was voiced all over the country.[34]
It seemed senseless to many Grenadians that their food
markets should be replete with U.S. and European-made jams,
jellies, and juices when their own land possessed an
abundance of tropical fruits. Nor did it make any sense
that Grenada, an island surrounded by the sea, should be
dependent on the importation of Canadian, Japanese, and
Norwegian fish.

In order to remedy this situation, the PRG constructed
its own agroindustrial plant (at True Blue), which used
Grenadian mangoes, soursops, papayas, tamerinds, guavas,
and bananas to produce a line of jams, jellies, juices, and
chutneys under the label of Spice Island Products which
were sold not only on Grenada, but also in many other
countries, particularly in Great Britain and Trinidad. A
coffee processing plant, a spice grinding plant and a

Grenada sugar factory constituted other government enterprises as did the National Fisheries Industry. But the industrial sector (both state and private) on Grenada remained small. By 1982 only 10 percent of the work force was employed by industry.[35]

Agriculture Under the PRG

During the PRG's reign, the mainstay of Grenada's economy remained agriculture, in which more than 10,000 people were employed. The revolutionary government knew from the start that its attempt to create a thriving economy hinged largely upon success in building up the agricultural sector, which Gairy, along with everything else, had left in shambles. In spite of the fact that the former prime minister had used the bitter grievances of the agricultural workers to construct his political machine, agricultural workers remained the poorest stratum of Grenadian society, and despite a 50 percent unemployment rate, young Grenadians under Gairy avoided agricultural work because of the low wages and the social stigma attached to it. As a result, one-third of all agricultural land lay fallow, and (in March 1979) the average age of the Grenadian peasant was sixty-two years.

In order to reduce food imports, provide enough produce for the developing agro-industry, increase foreign exchange earnings, relieve unemployment, and raise the standard of living of the agricultural sector--the bulk of Grenada's population--the Bishop government did everything possible to make farming an attractive occupation for young people. Under the slogan of "Idle Hands + Idle Lands = End To Unemployment," the PRG established a National Cooperative Development Agency (NACDA), which encouraged unemployed youths to set up agricultural cooperatives by supplying them with loans, access to land, and training in farming, bookkeeping, and marketing. NACDA's loans, designed for the purchase of fertilizers, seeds, farm implements, and means of transportation, averaged EC $25,000. If the cooperative were successful, it could apply for a second loan after nine months. By the end of 1981 there were twelve agricultural cooperatives with 160 young people farming 146 acres on Grenada.[36]

There were basically three types of landholdings on Grenada during the PRG years. First of all, there existed the typical small and medium-sized landholdings (five acres or less) that constitute 95 percent of Grenada's cultivated

land, on which the peasants grew the three main crops of
nutmeg, cocoa, and bananas along with squash, yams,
breadfruit, cabbage, eggplants, and callaloo. Secondly,
there were the twenty-three state farms (established in
1980 under the name, Grenada Farms Corporation), which were
supposed to increase the output of traditional export
crops, grow and sell new crops for export, and develop
livestock production. The third category consisted of
about forty private estates; it was on these landholdings
that almost all of the fallow land could be found. In
September 1981, the PRG passed a Land Utilization Act,
which allowed the government to take out a compulsory lease
for ten years on any estate of more than one hundred acres,
if the land were idle or underutilized unless the owners
could provide a plan for the agricultural development of
the land.

In order to secure assured markets for the farmers
and, at the same time, reduce the price for the general
public by eliminating the middleman, the PRG created the
Marketing and National Importing Board (MNIB), which saw to
it that the prices of such items as cement, fertilizers,
sugar, milk, and vegetables were much lower on Grenada than
on other Caribbean islands. The Mirabeau Farm School,
which had been closed by Gairy, was opened again by the
PRG, which also founded four new rapid-training
agricultural schools at Bocage, Boulogne, La Sagesse, and
Six Roads on Carriacou.[37]   One of the most successful and
impressive innovations of the revolution was the creation
of the Grenada National Institute of Handicraft (GNIH),
which encouraged the production of beautiful wood carvings,
furniture, wall hangings, and other handicraft items that
were marketed through Grencraft both at home and abroad and
provided added employment for Grenada's rural population.

In spite of all these improvements, Grenada's
agriculture still had many problems during the PRG period.
The worldwide recession caused a sharp drop in the demand
for Grenada's main agricultural export items. At the same
time, the prices paid for these products tumbled, and the
prices of imported fertilizers and farm machinery rose
steadily. One example of the world recession's effects was
that Poland, because of its severe economic crisis, totally
eliminated its purchase of Grenadian nutmegs by 1980 and
thereafter. Previously, Poland had bought 20 percent of
the nutmeg crop for its meat and sausage manufacture.[38]

According to Deputy Prime Minister and Minister of
Planning, Finance and Trade Bernard Coard, the long-range
answers to Grenada's agricultural difficulties were to be

found in the introduction of modern machinery and scientific methods of agriculture. This in turn required the education of Grenada's agricultural workers:

> We are still scratching the soil with the cutlass and the fork as in the days of Job. This kind of technology is all well and good for our backyard gardening. It is all well and good for the Caribs and Arawaks, who knew no better than living from hand to mouth. But for large-scale agricultural production which aims at feeding a nation properly and making money to raise the general living standards of that nation, agriculture has to use modern technology.
> . . . Many agricultural workers, foremen and managers, are comrades who have not been able to gain much education. Long ago we used to think that you didn't need education if you were going to work with your hands. . . . But today when we are trying to bring our country into the twentieth century, it is becoming clear to us that education is necessary not only for "office work" but for every kind of work. A worker can do better work if he/she is educated: better carpentry, better road-building, better cultivation. Modern methods of agriculture demand educated workers.[39]

Education Under the PRG

It was indeed in the field of education that the PRG registered some of its great accomplishments. But just as in the case of selecting its form of government, the leadership chose an educational policy designed to constitute a radical break with the traditions implanted by the British. At the first international conference in solidarity with Grenada (November 1981), the Grenadian minister of education, Jacqueline Creft, who had been a former secondary-school teacher, described the prerevolutionary shortcomings:

> Comrades, ever since our party was founded in March 1973, high upon our list of priorities has been the transformation of this twisted education system that we inherited from colonialism and from Gairy. We were determined to change a system which so powerfully excluded the interests of the mass of our people, and which also wove webs of fear, alienation and irrelevance around our children's minds. . . . whether

it was Little Miss Muffet, the Cow That Jumped Over the
Moon, William the Conqueror, Wordsworth's Daffodils, or
the so-called "Discoveries" by Christopher Columbus of
the "New World."
    The lucky few of us who went to secondary school,
learned about Cromwell's Revolt but not about that of
Fedon. We learned about the reforms of Wilberforce yet
nothing of Marryshow. They made us read Shakespeare
and Jane Austen, but kept silence about George Lamming.
Right from the beginning of our struggle we called for
an education system which not only serviced all our
people, secondary schools which would freely open the
doors to all our people without the constraint of fees,
but also a curriculum which would eliminate absurdity
from our classrooms and focus our children's minds upon
their own island, their own wealth, soil and crops,
their own solution to the problems that surround them.
For too long we had been brainwashed to think that only
Europe and America held the answer.[40]

The leader of the Grenadian revolution, Maurice Bishop,
expressed similar thoughts: "The history we did, apart from
Columbus and his voyages, was about English adventurers:
Drake, Hawkins, Raleigh, Morgan the Pirate. We were told
nothing about the Negroes--ourselves. Singing consisted
mainly of old English, Scottish and Irish ballads. If we
were overheard singing calypsoes, we were ordered to go and
wash out our mouths because those were 'devil songs'!"[41]
    It was in an address to the executive board of UNESCO
on September 18, 1982, in Paris, that Bishop explained the
PRG's educational strategy, which, according to him,
consisted of five Main Pillars: Continuous Education,
Education for All, New Content in Curriculum, a Work-Study
Approach, and the Integration of School and Community.[42]
Under the rubric of Continuous Education a massive literacy
campaign was launched through the newly founded Centres for
Popular Education (CPE). The CPE's first task was to reduce
total illiteracy on Grenada, the condition of 7 to 10
percent of the island's population,[43] especially the
agricultural workers. Under the slogans of "Each One, Teach
One!" and "If You Know, Teach! If You Don't, Learn!"
thousands of volunteers of all ages went to seek out the
illiterates. By the beginning of 1983, illiteracy had been
reduced to less than 3 percent. The campaign had taught
reading and writing to 881 illiterates and 287
semiliterates, 58 percent of whom were women and 42 percent,
men.[44]

Already during this campaign against illiteracy, the Ministry of Education was determined to use a literacy primer that would be relevant to Grenadian life. Under the guidance of the famous Brazilian educator, Paulo Freire, who visited Grenada in 1980, a reader entitled Let Us Learn Together was produced by the Centre for Popular Education. It emphasized some of the major themes of the Grenadian revolution.

In Caribbean island nations that consist of one major island surrounded by one or more smaller ones, the junior partners feel neglected by the principal island and often threaten secession. This has been the attitude of Tobago toward Trinidad, Aruba toward Curacao, and (under Gairy) of Carriacou and Petit Martinique toward Grenada. The PRG made great efforts to achieve equality between Grenada and the other, hitherto neglected, islands.[45]

In order to emphasize this point, the CPE placed a map showing the three islands constituting Grenada in Let Us Learn Together, accompanied by the following text: "Grenada, Carriacou and Petit Martinique are one people. Grenada, Carriacou and Petit Martinique are one nation. We are a proud people."[46]

Although the PRG cultivated a spirit of Grenadian patriotism, it simultaneously stressed the necessity of unity among the various Caribbean counties, thought unity was vital, given the efforts of the Reagan administration to ostracize Grenada and Cuba. The CPE's reader underlined the principle of Caribbean unity by presenting a map of the entire region followed by the passage:

One Caribbean
I am from Grenada, Carriacou and Petit Martinique.
You are from Martinique.
He is from Cuba.
She is from Aruba.
We are from the Caribbean.[47]

Other passages in the reader deal with the construction of the new international airport, the free distribution of milk by the PRG for mothers and babies, the dispensing of free medical care, the creation of the state-owned National Commercial Bank, the importance of growing more food on Grenada in order to cut down on imports, and the necessity of vigiliance on the part of the population against a possible counterrevolution.

Another part of the First Pillar (Continuous Education) consisted of the National In-Service Teacher Education

Program (NISTEP). This was a program designed to further
the education of the approximately six hundred Grenadian
primary school teachers, most of whom had completed only
primary school, or at the most secondary school. To train
all of these teachers at colleges abroad would have cost EC[48]
$17.5 million and would have taken too many years.
Meanwhile, the island would have been stripped of its
teachers. Thus it was decided to organize instead a
compulsory, three-year, in-service program at three centers
located at St. George's, Grenville, and the island of[49]
Carriacou.

The teachers were to attend NISTEP courses one day a
week during the school year and for several weeks during
their vacations. The first two years of the program focused
on language arts, mathematics, and education methods.
During the third year of the program (1983), the teachers
studied science, social studies, agricultural science, and
health education. Teachers enrolled in the NISTEP program
were supervised by special NISTEP tutors as well as fellow
teachers (called teacher partners) who had already passed
through some NISTEP training. After completing NISTEP,
teachers received an increase in salary. The PRG hoped that
teachers who had gone through NISTEP would have a greater
sense of professionalism and would decide to make teaching
their permanent career instead of using it merely as a
stepping-stone to more lucrative jobs in other fields.

Within the framework of the campaign for Continuous
Education, the teacher-pupil ratio was reduced from 1:51 to
1:30, a worker-education program was started for government
employees and increasingly also for those in the private
sector. A number of skills-training institutes and programs
were initiated for workers in agriculture, fisheries,[50]
tourism, and public service.

The Second Pillar of revolutionary Grenada's
educational strategy was labeled Education for All. As the
second phase of the CPE program, its goal was to enroll
10,000-12,000 Grenadians in adult education courses in
mathematics, English, and basic sciences during the coming
years.

The PRG also introduced free secondary education for
all students who passed a rigorous common entrance
examination. Forty percent of all Grenadian students in
1983 attended secondary schools compared to 11 percent prior
to the 1979 revolution. In 1980, the Bernadette Bailey
secondary school was opened in Happy Hill. It became the
second government secondary school in Grenada's history. As
the minister of education, Jacqueline Creft proudly stated:

"Four hundred years of colonialism gave us one, the second
year of the Revolution gave us our second!" The number of
Grenadian students who received a free university education
abroad had increased considerably. To quote Jacqueline
Creft once more: "The one yearly Island Scholar, that
ornament to colonial elitism, has grown to 300 university
scholarships last year, to countries stretching as far as
the world stretches. Look for us in Hungary, in Australia,
in India, the Soviet Union, in Venezuela, Canada,
Czechoslovakia, Tanzania, Zambia, Nigeria, Cuba, Bulgaria,
France and Mexico--you will see young Grenadians studying
hard preparing to return to serve our people."[51]

The Third Pillar of the Grenadian education strategy,
New Content in Curriculum, has already been discussed in
connection with the anti-illiteracy campaign and its basic
reader, Let Us Learn Together. Until the latter part of
1982, however, there were still no common texts for primary
school pupils on Grenada. They were being taught how to
read from antiquated British and Canadian primers that
contained illustrations of white children and their
environment and bore no resemblance to Grenadian life.
In October 1982, a Cuban ship docked at St. George's,
bringing over 10,000 copies of new readers (named after the
national hero, T.A. Marryshow) that had been printed in
Havana, but written and illustrated by Grenadian teachers
and artists. These had been produced over a period of
fourteen months under the direction of the Curriculum
Development Unit of NISTEP.[52]
Since most of the Grenadian people are involved in
agriculture and fishing, the Marryshow Readers show life in
a rural setting. Marryshow Reader Infant I-a, called All of
Us, shows the interior of a house that definitely belongs to
a poor member of the population--the living room contains no
furniture except for an old wooden crate marked "fragile."
The only decoration on the wall is a small shelf with a vase
containing flowers.[53]
The Marryshow Readers try to avoid stereotypes. A
father is shown sitting on the staircase of his home,
holding a baby, and feeding it with a bottle. Even when his
wife and grandmother join him, he does not hand the baby
over to them. The former coordinator of NISTEP, Chris
Searle, stated: "The picture of a man holding a child in
the book All of Us is unique and heroic because no other
readers in the English world have used such pictures."[54] In
the Marryshow Reader entitled We Work and Play Together a
group of girls is shown playing together. Four boys

approach and try to bully them, but the girls are able to
chase away the boys, questioning thereby the stereotype that
boys must always be stronger than girls.[55]

Emphasizing the great importance of creating an
educated population, the PRG was eager to involve
intellectuals in the process of production so that they
would be able to contribute to the building of their nation.
The alienation that exists in many societies between the
ivory tower of scholarly learning and the real world
outside, was to be avoided. Thus the Fourth Pillar of the
Grenadian education strategy, named the Work-Study Approach,
was described by Prime Minister Maurice Bishop:

> We can no longer tolerate a situation in which our
> youths leave school clinging to certificates which make
> them feel that the only job possible for them is behind
> some desk. We can no longer tolerate an educational
> system where, as had been said so often before, a child
> can pass from kindergarten to university and never see
> a cocoa tree, or a banana or a nutmeg. Rather, our
> educational system must produce the skills that can be
> absorbed in our economy—we must produce the
> agriculturists, the mechanics, the engineers, the
> hoteliers, the boat captains, etc. . . . That we need
> to man our agriculture, our agro-industries, our
> fisheries, and our tourism.[56]

The Fifth Pillar of the PRG's educational policy
consisted of the Integration of School and Community, which
was carried out by the Community Educational Councils
(CECs), which were in charge of school curricula, the
supervision and maintenance of schools, and the transition
of students from school to life in society. The CECs
contributed substantially to the repair of Grenada's school
buildings. During January 1980, for example, the CECs fixed
up sixty-six primary schools within two weeks, thereby
saving the PRG almost EC $2 million.

As has been pointed out earlier, all primary school
teachers had to attend NISTEP once a week. Somebody had to
take care of the pupils when the teachers were absent, and
it was decided to bring in talented people from the local
community to instruct the children on that day. The PRG's
minister of education, Jacqueline Creft, described the
Community School Day Program (CSDP):

> The Community School Day Program has started the
> process of returning our schools to the community and

the community to the schools. We encouraged anyone in the community who had a valuable popular skill to come into the school--no longer the colonial fortress--and teach it to the children on the day when their teachers were studying at the NISTEP centers. We asked for and got farmers, singers, drummers, artists, carpenters, masons, accordionists, patois teachers, storytellers, boat builders, basket makers, seamstresses, medical workers and others. All these brothers and sisters are making the schools their own on this day.[57]

Much was accomplished by the PRG in the field of education, but much remained to be done. During the next ten years, the Ministry of Education as well as the Ministry for Women's Affairs planned extensive improvement and expansion of preprimary schooling on Grenada. Such an effort was considered necessary for two reasons: First of all, the improvement of preprimary schools meant a better preparation of Grenada's children for their primary school years. Secondly, a greater number of preprimary schools were needed because more of Grenada's mothers were entering the country's work force. In September 1982, NISTEP started a one-year training program for preprimary teachers.

In the area of primary education, heavy emphasis was placed upon repairing the existing primary schools over the next three to four years. Plans were to be drawn up for the construction of new primary schools and for a more rational zoning of these schools. The three Marryshow Readers that were issued in October 1982 took care of only the first grade. New standard textbooks were to be developed for the other six grades of primary school.

On the secondary level, there were plans to build more government secondary schools and to transform all junior secondary schools into secondary schools. The goal was eventually to have every primary school student continue on to secondary school.[58]

As far as Grenadian education was concerned, the PRG seemed indeed to live up to its favorite slogan: "Forward Ever, Backward Never!" It remains to be seen whether subsequent Grenadian governments will be able to continue the rapid pace of educational improvements that was set by the Bishop regime during its four-and-a-half-year reign.

The New Airport at Point Salines

The educational reforms of the PRG probably constituted its most impressive accomplishment, but it was the construction of the new international airport (begun in January 1980) that was its most spectacular undertaking. The Grenadian public, supporting it enthustiastically, formed local airport development committees and bought a great many airport bonds. As the president of the Grenadian Chamber of Commerce, Richard Menezes, put it: "One project that's had unanimous support is the airport. Not many people outside Grenada know the extent to which Grenadians have put their money and sweat into it."[59]

Feasibility studies undertaken by the British as early as 1954 and during the Gairy regime in the 1970s, clearly emphasized the need for a new Grenadian airport, whose logical location would be at the southwestern coast at Point Salines, only a ten–minute drive from St. George's.[60] The old airport at Pearls, with its 5,300–foot runway, could serve only small propeller-driven planes. Situated near high mountains along the eastern coast and exposed to dangerous crosswinds, Pearls possessed no landing lights and had to be shut down each evening. This meant that travelers to Grenada were forced to stay overnight at Barbados or Trinidad, where most hotels are expensive. In addition, the PRG claimed that its own officials as well as foreign dignitaries traveling through Barbados to Grenada were frequently harassed by Barbadian authorities at the Grantley Adams International Airport. The weary traveler arriving at Pearls faced a forty–five–minute taxi ride to St. George's on one of the worst roads anywhere in the Caribbean.

The PRG expected tourist arrivals to increase from 32,000 (in 1979) to 40,000 during the first year of the new airport's operation. According to projections, the new air field would dramatically increase the ability of Grenada to export its agricultural products all over the world. However, it was feared that the future demise of Pearls Airport would further complicate the already critical situation in St. Andrew's (Grenada's largest parish where Pearls is located). According to a NJM Central Committee report of July 1983 this parish was characterized by "The proliferation of petty rumors, the continued inflow of marijuana and a stepped–up growth in some areas and evidence of hoarding of money by some elements of the rural bourgeoisie."[61]

The largest contribution to the building of the new airport was made by Cuba, which sent US $60 million in the form of materials, designs, and labor, equal to US $500 for every inhabitant of Grenada. Substantial aid for this project also came from such non-Communist countries and organizations as Venezuela, Algeria, Syria, Iraq, Libya, Nigeria, and the European Economic Community (EEC).[62]

Companies from western countries made successful bids to obtain their share in the construction of the new airport. A Miami-based firm, Layne Dredging, won the contract to dredge Hardy Bay over which the runway passes and sent thirty U.S. workers to Grenada.[63] A Finnish company named METEX was awarded the job of supplying and installing the lighting equipment for the runway, parking apron, car park, and access road. The supply and installation of air traffic control, navigational, communications, ground-traffic handling and electronic equipment for the terminal building was handled by the English firm, Plessey Airport Ltd.[64] After the U.S. intervention on Grenada, Plessey issued a statement refuting the Reagan administration's claim that a Cuban-Soviet-Grenadian air force base was being built at Point Salines. According to Plessey, the new airport lacked eleven facilities essential for a military base, including radar and underground fuel tanks.[65]

If the PRG really intended Point Salines to be an air force base, it seems strange that the security arrangements around the construction site were so lax. Grenadian and foreign visitors were allowed to wander all over the new airport grounds, taking as many photographs as they desired. Foreign correspondents (including U.S. television crews) frequently interviewed the Cuban construction workers, who lived in barracks right at their place of work. One of the two campuses[66] of the U.S. institution, St. George's University School of Medicine, was located only a few yards from the airport site and medical students could be seen jogging along, or even upon, the 9,000-foot runway.

The Reagan administration, however, had made up its mind that the new international airport, which Grenada needed so desperately, was really a Cuban-Soviet air force base in the making and was going to threaten the vital sea-lanes of the United States. In a speech to the National Association of Manufacturers on March 10, 1983, President Reagan referred to "the so-called expert"[67] who "had argued that we shouldn't worry about Castroite control over the island of Grenada. Their only important product is nutmeg. Grenada is building a new naval base, storage bases and barracks for troops and training grounds. And, of course, one can believe that they are all there to export nutmegs.

It is not nutmeg that is at stake in the Caribbean and
Central America. It is the United States' national
security."[68]

Continuing the verbal onslaught against Grenada during
a nationwide radio and television address on March 23, 1983,
President Reagan held up a picture taken by an U.S.
reconnaissance plane and exclaimed: "And on the small
island of Grenada, at the southern end of the Caribbean
chain, the Cubans, with Soviet financing and backing, are in
the process of building an airfield with a 10,000 foot [!]
runway. Grenada does not even have an air force. Who is it
intended for?"[69]

Reagan's two March 1983 attacks, citing the allegedly
sinister purpose behind Grenada's projected new airport,
represented only the climax to an invariably hostile
attitude towards Grenada that the adminsitration had assumed
since Reagan took office. In April 1981 the Reagan
administration had launched a diplomatic offensive at an ECC
conference at Brussels to prevent Grenada from obtaining US
$30 million for its new airport; the administration had
succeeded in blocking US $30 million in International
Development Agency (IDA) concessional funds to Grenada; it
tried to prevent an International Monetary Fund (IMF) loan
to the island; and the administration offered a US $4
million gift to the Caribbean Development Bank (CDB) for
basic human needs, provided that Grenada would not obtain
any of this money.[70] The Reagan administration did not
confine itself to economic pressure, but held a series of
huge military maneuvers (Ocean Venture '81, Ocean Venture
'82, and Readex '83) in the Caribbean that were perceived by
the PRG as massive threats. During Ocean Venture '81, which
involved more than 120,000 troops, 250 ships, and 1,000
aircraft from 14 nations, U.S. troops staged a mock invasion
off the coast of Puerto Rico on Vieques Island--
approximately the same size as Grenada. Vieques during
these maneuvers became "Amber and the Amberines--our enemy
in the Eastern Caribbean,"[71] which had seized U.S. hostages
who had to be liberated by U.S. airborne troops, marines,
special forces, and navy underwater demolition teams, all of
which were employed during the actual invasion in October
1983. After landing at "Blue Beach," securing "a nearby air
field" and rescuing the "hostages," the U.S. troops,
according to the maneuver's script, were to remain on Amber
in order to establish a government "favorable to our way of
life."[72]

The PRG had planned to celebrate the fourth anniversary
of the Grenadian revolution (March 13, 1983) in a very

low-key manner by holding a series of minirallies around
the country. This decision was made by minister of national
mobilization, Selwyn Strachan, anticipating that the fifth
anniversary in 1984 would constitute a major event. It was
going to coincide with the opening of the new international
airport at which Fidel Castro, who had not yet visited
Grenada, was sure to be present.[73] Reagan's speech of
March 10, in which the U.S. president had implied that
Grenada represented a threat to the national security of the
United States, led to a change in these plans. The PRG
decided in the last minute on a display of military
strength.

During the previous year, during the evening of
August 26, 1982, the electricity had been shut off on the
entire island while heavy military equipment was being
unloaded from a Cuban ship in St. George's harbor. There
had been endless speculation among Grenadians as to the true
nature of this newly arrived military hardware. The
Grenadian people were finally able to view all of these new
weapons when the PRG decided to send a military convoy,
consisting of six new Soviet armored personnel carriers,
seven Soviet field guns, mobile search lights, trucks,
jeeps, and ambulances on a trip around the entire island on
March 13, 1983. Maurice Bishop, who had returned only the
previous day from the seventh summit meeting of the
Non-Aligned Countries at New Delhi, India, participated in
the convoy in one of the leading vehicles. In a speech
concluding the motorcade the Prime Minister warned that an
invasion by mercenaries or U.S. troops could come at any
time and he urged the Grenadian people to watch the sky for
enemy planes and the beaches for invading vessels. Bishop
appealed for more volunteers for the People's Militia and
the return to that organization of former members who had
dropped out.[94]

In view of the threatening situation, the PRG ordered
the Jeremiah Richardson Defense of the Homeland Maneuvres,
which were to run from April 21 to April 24. Members of the
leadership were to direct the mobilization of the various
parts of the island: Maurice Bishop, Bernard Coard, and
Hudson Austin in charge of the Parish of St. George; Kenrick
Radix and Unison Whiteman, the Parish of St. David; and
Selwyn Strachan and Chris de Riggs, the West Coast.
Bishop's friend, Colonel Desi Bouterse of Suriname, sent
fourteen officers to observe the maneuvres.[75] Shortly after
these Grenadian exercises, President Reagan, in an address
to a joint session of Congress on April 27, once again
mentioned the Point Salines Airport. This time, Reagan

claimed that in case of a major conflict, the Soviet Union
would make use of this new airfield to intercept U.S.
reinforcements to Europe and the Middle East, making the
airport thus a threat not only to the Caribbean, but also to
NATO and all other U.S. commitments in the world.

4
The Downfall of the PRG
and the Aftermath

The external crisis situation of March and April was
followed by an internal malaise, which increased during the
summer and culminated in the self-immolation of the
Grenadian revolution in October 1983. The almost unanimous
outpouring of support that had greeted the NJM takeover on
March 13, 1979, had long since dissipated.

Internal Problems in 1983

The major part of the bourgeoisie had turned against
the revolution when it became apparent that the Bishop
regime had no intention of holding free elections and
replacing the quasidictatorship of Gairy with a genuine
parliamentary system. The closing of the <u>Torchlight</u>, the
government's control of the mass media, the arrest and
imprisonment without trial of prominent members of the
business community, and the PRG's close ties to Cuba and
the Soviet Union all served to alienate this influential
segment of Grenada's society. It is true that the PRG had
not seized a single private enterprise (except for Gairy's
large holdings) and that it vowed to maintain the private
sector, which by October 1983 still controlled two-thirds
of Grenada's economy. The business community, however,
felt instinctively that the PRG had not nationalized the
economy and collectivized agriculture only because it did
not feel strong enough yet to do so. Grenada's business
and professional elite, meeting at the St. George's Club
(restricted to members) in order to play billiards, sip
drinks, read the <u>Financial Times</u> and discuss business and
politics under the faded pictures of Queen Elizabeth and
the Duke of Edinburgh, did not approve of the course the

revolution had taken. Nor did the churches in St. George's.

As on most Caribbean islands, the churches on Grenada exercise a profound influence upon a deeply religious population. The predominant faith is Roman Catholicism; Anglicanism is second. Many other churches and religious groups are present on Grenada, such as the Methodists, Presbyterians, Baptists, Pentecostals, Seventh Day Adventists, Rastafarians, and Bahai. Like the bourgeoisie, the churches were opposed to the brutalities of the Gairy regime. As a matter of fact, the Roman Catholic bishop, Patrick Webster, a native Grenadian, became so involved in political protests against Gairy that the Catholic hierarchy pulled him out of the island and replaced him with the more conservative Trinidadian, Bishop Sidney Charles. The churches approved of Gairy's demise but, at the same time, expressed apprehension of the Socialist bent of the New Jewel Movement. Although approving the PRG's educational reforms, the construction of the international airport, and the program to shift unemployed Grenadians to the agricultural sector, the churches criticized the lack of a free press, the failure to hold free elections, and the detention of political opponents without a trial. The churches did not encourage their parishioners to attend meetings of the parish councils and the "mass organization" (e.g., NYO and NWO), which often coincided with church services.[1] By the summer of 1983, the churches were definitely no longer supportive of the revolution and were, in turn, viewed by the PRG as inimical to its aims. A Central Committee meeting of the NJM during July expressed alarm over "the growing influence of the Church and religion among students" and ordered as a countermeasure that "religious classes be optional in state schools and the period of time of this subject on the time table be lessened."[2]

That the bourgeoisie and the churches would turn against the revolution as it proceeded was to be expected. A much more alarming development was the disillusionment of the general populace (the "masses" in NJM parlance) with the PRG. As the minutes of an emergency meeting of the NJM Central Committee on August 26, 1983, stated: "At present the Revolution is facing its worst crisis ever and the most serious danger in 4 1/2 years. The mood of the masses is characterized at worst by open dissatisfaction and cynicism, and at best by serious demoralisation. Overall the mood is 1-2 on a scale of 5."[3]

This pessimistic mood was produced by a variety of factors. With the memories of the corruption and brutality of the Gairy era fading, dissatisfaction with the current Bishop regime was becoming more pronounced. As one of the top commanders of the PRA, Leon "Bogo" Cornwall, put it: "The honeymoon period of the Revolution is over. In the past 4 1/2 years, progress was seen in many areas and the masses were on a high. Now the work is becoming much more difficult and complex."[4] Prime Minister Maurice Bishop himself admitted that "our propaganda has fed Economism. We have failed to point out to the masses that this period requires a number of sacrifices and if we are not prepared to build the economy through hard work, we will not make it."[5]

The many educational and social reforms, such as free medical and dental care and free milk for mothers, which had initially been received with great enthusiasm, were being taken for granted. The public expected as a matter of course a steadily rising standard of living as well as a continual decline of the rate of unemployment. But during the summer of 1983, the Grenadian Ministry of Economy experienced extreme difficulties in mobilizing new foreign aid and obtaining already promised financial help. In a desperate effort, two special missions, one headed by minister of tourism, Lyden Ramdhanny, the other by Nelson Louison of the Ministry of National Mobilization, were dispatched to Libya to pry extra money out of Col. Muamar Qaddafi.[6]

A serious cash flow problem threatened to halt key capital investment projects such as the agro-industries, the fisheries, the farm machinery pools and even the airport project. For the first time since 1979, there were layoffs of workers. A second conference on culture and sovereignty in the Caribbean, which was scheduled to take place during summer 1983 was abruptly canceled. The only newspaper of the island, the weekly Free West India, appeared only once in May because of a printing press breakdown. Maurice Bishop informed the Soviet ambassador in late May that Television Free Grenada (TFG) was about to go off the air since its transmitter could no longer be repaired and there was no money to buy a new one.[7] The shortage of cash affected Grenada's diplomatic missions abroad. In Cuba, where the Grenadian government had been unable to pay its bills, the telephones, telex machines, and electricity had been cut off, not only at the embassy[8] but even at the Grenadian ambassador's private residence.

As always during tense situations, Grenada abounded
with wild rumors, which, according to the PRG, had been
deliberately planted by local "counters." One widely
circulating rumor had it that Maurice Bishop had placed
Bernard and Phyllis Coard under house arrest because they
had secretly siphoned off Grenadian government funds to
build themselves a luxurious home on Jamaica.[9] Grenada,
since the revolutionary takeover in 1979, had been a very
safe place to reside, in spite of the claims of many travel
guides. By the spring of 1983, however, there were some
ominous occurrences (never reported in the press), that
indicated that counterrevolutionary elements were resorting
to acts of terrorism to destabilize the country. In order
to poison the friendly relations between Grenada and
Venezuela,[10] a sharpshooter using a Belgian-made FAL rifle
(which was not used by the armed forces of revolutionary
Grenada) attempted to kill the Venezuelan ambassador,
Romulo Nucete Hubner, in front of his house. The bullet
missed the diplomat but hit his young daughter in the leg.
Prime Minister Maurice Bishop immediately visited Romulo
Nucete Hubner to express his regrets and outrage, but the
terrorist was never caught.[11] One night shortly
thereafter, another terrorist entered the home of General
Hudson Austin's girlfriend and injured her severely with a
burst of gunfire. The PRG was convinced that the bullets
were really meant for Austin, the commander-in-chief of the
PRA. He usually spent his nights at his girlfriend's home
but had not been there the night of the assassination
attempt.[12]

It was exactly during times like these that the role of
the People's Revolutionary Army and the militia (the Eyes
and Ears of the Revolution, according to the PRG) took on
added importance. Yet in summer 1983 the vitally important
PRA and militia had themselves become part of the
disintegration process. At the same time that the PRG,
alarmed over Ronald Reagan's speeches and the incursions
into Nicaragua, was expecting a mercenary assault on
Grenada, the village militia units were decreasing both
quantitatively and qualitatively. There was even an
incident where militia members formed a protective ring
around a church in which an anti-PRG sermon was being
preached.[13] The mood in the PRA was no better, with many
soldiers complaining about the poor conditions in the
military camps while leading party and government members
were being supplied with new automobiles. The average
monthly pay in the 2,000-man PRA was the pitiful sum of EC
$200, and many soldiers were leaving for Trinidad. General

Hudson Austin remarked that many members of the PRA were saying that at the end of their five-year enlistment they were no better off than before their entry into the army. Given the critical situation, he asked to be relieved of his position as minister of labor, communication and works, in order to devote all of his time to the armed forces.[14]

In view of all these problems, the Central Committee of the NJM decided to hold its "First Wholistic [sic!] Plenary,"[15] which lasted for six-and-a-half days between July 13 and July 19, 1983. After fifty-four hours of deliberations, the Central Committee produced a twenty-page document (the so-called July Resolutions), which seemed to be strangely divorced from the urgency of the situation. Although critical of almost all aspects of government and party work, the Central Committee exercised little self-criticism and maintained that its "line of march" was essentially correct.

The Crisis of August and September

The crisis in the country intensified, and the government and party were still adrift in spite of the July plenum. Then some members of the Central Committee demanded an emergency meeting, which took place on August 26, 1983. Even though this meeting lasted only two hours (8:00-10:00 A.M.), it was of great significance. A strong group within the Central Committee emerged and began a veiled attack upon Maurice Bishop, which foreshadowed the all-out assault on the prime minister's alleged lack of leadership at the decisive Extraordinary Meeting of the Central Committee between September 14 and 16, 1983.

Before going into these two important meetings of August and September, it is perhaps best to analyse the composition of the Central Committee of the New Jewel Movement as it was constituted at the time. The Central Committee consisted of fifteen members, six of whom were full ministers in the PRG: Prime Minister Maurice Bishop, who was also the chairman of the Central Committee, the minister of construction and commander-in-chief of the PRA, Hudson Austin, the minister of national mobilization, Selwyn Strachan, the minister of agriculture, George Louison, the foreign minister, Unison Whiteman, and the minister of health, Chris de Riggs. Two Central Committee members were leaders of mass organizations: Phyllis Coard, president of the NWO, and Tan Bartholomew, director of the NYO. The trade unions were represented by John "Chalky"

Ventour, general secretary of the Grenada Trades Union
Council (GTUC) and Fitzroy Bain, president of the
Agricultural and General Workers' Union. The Grenadian
police force was represented by its commissioner, Ian St.
Bernard, and the NJM, by Kamau McBarnette. Finally, there
was the military group consisting of Lt. Col. and Deputy
Minister of the Interior Liam James, Lt. Col. Ewart Layne
(who at the time of the August 26 emergency meeting was
still studying military science in the USSR), Major Leon
"Bogo" Cornwall (who had succeeded W. Richard Jacobs as
ambassador to Cuba),[16] and, of course, Hudson Austin, whose
personal life style and lack of military education, did
not augur well for the long-range prospects of his military
career. It was this military group (minus Hudson Austin),
that was to spearhead the attack on Maurice Bishop at the
Extraordinary Meeting of the Central Committee in
September. Only three members of the Central Committee
were eventually to side with Bishop and two of these—Uni
(Whiteman) and Fitzy (Bain), as they were called by their
party comrades—were to pay with their lives for this
support of the prime minister.

At the Emergency Meeting of the NJM Central Committee
on August 26, 1983, Liam James pointed out that little had
been done to implement the Central Committee resolutions of
the July plenum and that the situation had deteriorated
further because the party itself was now beginning to
disintegrate. Selwyn Strachan presented the alarming news
that sections of the NJM had begun to rebel against the
higher organs of the party and that this silent rebellion
could easily turn into an open revolt unless proper
measures were undertaken. At the heart of the problem,
according to Strachan, stood the fact that the Central
Committee in July had not really criticized itself. Some
Central Committee (CC) members remarked that the general
membership of the party did not dare to express their
criticisms of the CC openly because of their feeling that
certain committee members were hostile to criticism. It
was decided to convoke a full Central Committee meeting in
mid-September and for this three-day gathering to bring
back to Grenada all members of the committee who were
working abroad. In concluding the August Emergency
Meeting, Bishop agreed that the party was in danger of
disintegration and that many party members were afraid to
speak up. In preparation for the September meeting, he
urged all Central Committee members "to rap with party
members, leading mass organizations, activists, leading
militia types, consistent participants in Zonal Councils,

and party support groups" and to study the history of the
Communist party of the Soviet Union.[17]

Of all of the many Central Committee meetings that took
place between July and October 1983, none was as decisive
as the Extraordinary Meeting convoked between September 14
and 16, 1983. It was at this gathering that the comrade
leader himself came under attack for not providing any
guidance or leadership at this critical moment in the
country's history. What is most interesting is the fact
that even those Central Committee members (George Louison,
Unison Whiteman, and Fitzroy Bain) who were to form the
minority, pro-Bishop faction within the CC by October, all
joined in the criticism of the prime minister. Bishop
himself, during this gathering, as well as all previous and
future meetings, had astonishingly little to say in his
defense and almost always agreed with his critics. The
most important speech given during the Extraordinary
Meeting was delivered by the deputy minister of the
interior, Lt. Col. Liam James, who called for "an honest,
cold-blooded, objective and scientific approach" to save
the party. While admitting Bishop's "ability to inspire
and instill confidence in the people, to unite the masses
and hold high the banner of the Revolution regionally and
internationally," he also observed that "Comrade Bishop
lacks the precise qualities and strengths that are
particularly required to carry the process forward in these
most difficult times." These qualities and strengths,
according to Liam James, were all possessed by Deputy Prime
Minister Bernard Coard. He therefore suggested that the
party should "marry the strengths of comrades Maurice and
Bernard in the form of a Joint Leadership." Bishop,
according to this scheme, was to mobilize the masses and
the militia and perform his usual regional and
international work. He would also remain the chairman of
the Central Committee. Bernard Coard would be in charge of
party organization, ideological development, cadre
formation and strategy and tactics. He would once again
become a member of the Central Committee and the Politburo
and chair all Politburo meetings. The Central Committee
and the political bureau were to discuss and ratify any
major proposals and decisions sought by either of the two
leaders of the NJM in order to guarantee "the Leninist
principle of collective leadership." The July resolutions
of the Central Committee were to be rescinded.[18]

Bishop's response to the joint leadership proposal is
fascinating, given the later turn of events. The prime
minister emphasized that he had never had any problem with

sharing power and that he had worked very well with Comrade
Coard over the years. Ever since their school days,
according to Bishop, they had shared many policy decisions
as well as the authorship of the NJM manifesto and the
People's Congresses' indictments of Gairy. He also
reminded the Central Committee that in 1977, when Coard was
accused of aggressiveness and power grabbing, he had
defended him. Bishop stated that Coard's intelligence and
skills certainly entitled him to return to the political
bureau. The prime minister, however, expressed his concern
over the manner in which the joint leadership proposal
would be articulated to the masses, who might think that
this development heralded a power struggle and the imminent
collapse of the revolution.[19]

Both George Louison and Unison Whiteman expressed their
approval of Bernard Coard's return to the Central Committee
and the Politburo, but they also stated their opposition to
the formation of a joint leadership. George Louison's
particular adamance in opposing the elevation of Coard to
an equal position in the party led Liam James to exclaim,
"Comrade Louison is seeking to disturb the proceedings of
the meeting for opportunist reasons."[20] When Lt. Col.
Ewart Layne observed that "the concrete situation we face
is the unfolding of the dialectics in the combining of the
two qualities to strengthen the leadership in a Leninist
way for the building of Socialism in Grenada," George
Louison could only comment that "I regard Comrade Layne's
comments as 'Shit.'"[21]

When a vote was taken on the joint leadership proposal,
it became clear that the majority of the Central Committee
members were in favor of its enactment. Nine committee
members voted in favor, one (George Louison) was opposed,
and three (Maurice Bishop, Unison Whiteman, and Hudson
Austin) abstained. Some of the members who had voted in
favor of joint leadership proposed that Bernard Coard be
invited to the extraordinary meeting in order to explain
his position vis-a-vis the new form of leadership, but
Maurice Bishop opposed this suggestion, stating that he
needed more time to reflect on the whole issue because "it
was difficult for him to understand the question of Joint
Leadership and his own role and function in this model".[22]
He proposed instead that a meeting of the Central Committee
and Bernard Coard be held during his trip to
St. Kitts-Nevis for the upcoming independence celebration.
The committee agreed with this request but, at the same
time, made it clear that the vote just taken on joint
leadership was binding and not to be reversed.

The final question to be debated at this meeting was the manner in which the decision was to be relayed to the general membership of the NJM as well as to the Grenadian people. Those who had voted for joint leadership demanded that the complete minutes of the Extraordinary Meeting be submitted to the party membership (the NJM had about three hundred members), a suggestion that Bishop called "idealistic and divorced from reality." Stating that the lack of frankness had brought the party to near collapse, Lt. Col. Layne, on the other hand, felt that the Central Committee had much more to lose by holding back the minutes. The vote was ten to one (with two abstentions) in favor of submitting the minutes to the general membership. In spite of the constant exhortations of the NJM and PRG that the masses—the Grenadian people—must participate in all decisions and that nothing ought to be hidden from them, the Central Committee members agreed that the masses must not be informed (the vote on whether the masses should be informed was nine against and three abstentions).[23]

In retrospect, such a decision was a fatal error for everybody concerned. As has been pointed out before, on an island as small as Grenada, nothing remains secret for long. Even if the vote had favored confining the minutes of the meeting to the committee, the details of the Extraordinary Meeting would have undoubtedly seeped out to the public. But once the decision had been made to reveal the minutes to the general membership, the news of the intraparty struggle was bound to spread among the populace. How much more advantageous, it could have been to inform the public by a communique emanating from the party than to have the news leak out in the form of a myriad of rumors. Hudson Austin was to admit this error during his radio address on October 16: "We have tried to keep the problem away from the masses in order to maintain the unity of the party and the prestige of the Grenada Revolution. The Central Committee took a decision of maintaining the unity of the party at all costs and as it turns out, this position has been incorrect, because it has allowed the problem to get worse."[24]

On the day following the conclusion of the Extraordinary Meeting, the Central Committee met again, but this time without the presence of Maurice Bishop and his supporters. The prime minister, along with Unison Whiteman and George Louison, had left for St. Kitts. The only pro-Bishop committee member remaining in the country, Fitzroy Bain, was ill and could not attend the meeting of September 17. The gathering had been convoked to listen to

Bernard Coard's response to the joint leadership decision.

Coard drew a gloomy picture of the situation. He stated that he had originally estimated that the PRG would collapse within a year, but "the amount of disgust and the disintegration of the party masses" had now persuaded him "that the loss of state power was only a few months away." The United States was stepping up its attacks all over the area and getting ready to intervene in Central America at a time when the militia was dissolving, the PRA was demoralized, the Grenadian revolution defenseless, and the NJM discredited in the eyes of the masses. Only a fundamental package of reform measures could save the revolution.

Coard then explained why he had resigned from both the Politburo and the Central Committee in October 1982. He recalled that he had been depended upon for everything, especially in the field of economics, and that "he was sick and tired of being the hatchet man who had to push through all of the hard decisions such as Torchlight, the 'Gang of 26,'[25] Comrade Layne over Einstein"[26] while the comrade leader, vacillating between the Marxist-Leninist and petit-bourgeois trends in the party, was making only the easy decisions. Coard emphasized that, had he been an ordinary committee member, he would have disciplined Bishop much earlier. In his position as deputy prime minister, however, he was afraid to do so because his comrades would have felt that he was trying to grab the leadership himself. He repeated again and again that he was perfectly happy in his present position as minister of the economy and that he did not want to resume his membership on either the Politburo or the Central Committee unless he was ordered to do so by the party. He promised to do everything in his power to help in reorganizing the NJM and PRG, but not as a member of the CC and PB. In the past, according to Coard, the Politburo had hidden matters from the Central Committee and the Central Committee from the general membership. What was needed now was a genuine collective leadership, working in an atmosphere of frankness and bluntness.[27]

Following its initial meeting with Coard on September 17, the Central Committee met day after day with the deputy prime minister in order to devise the means to strengthen the party and the government. Not once during these meetings was there any more criticism of Bishop, who had returned from St. Kitts on September 22 and was expected to express his conclusive ideas on the joint leadership on September 23. Yet when the Central Committee

met on that day, the prime minister did not appear, citing
as an excuse the fact that he had not yet had enough time
for self-reflection.

Bishop was also missing at the opening of the
Extraordinary General Meeting of Full Members of the NJM,
which took place on September 25. Given Bishop's intention
not to attend this meeting with the full membership, Coard
also decided not to appear, although he let it be known
that he would put in an appearance if the meeting requested
him to do so. Bishop and Coard's absence left the
leadership of the gathering in the hands of that powerful
and unbending military triumvirate of Liam James, Ewart
Layne, and Leon "Bogo" Cornwall, who once more proceeded to
castigate Bishop for his alleged "petit bourgeois,
opportunist conduct" and "contempt for Democratic
Centralism." The general membership of the party made it
very plain that it was unhappy about the absence of both
the prime minister and the deputy prime minister and it was
decided by a vote of forty-six to one (with one abstention)
to send a delegation to Bishop's residence to demand his
appearance at the meeting. He finally agreed.

Once it became apparent that Bishop would come, Coard
too, made up his mind to join. After a great deal of
discussion and several workshops, the general membership
unanimously endorsed the Central Committee's joint
leadership scheme, whereupon Maurice Bishop embraced
Bernard Coard and announced that he too now fully accepted
this decision. Bishop expressed his desire to use the
criticism that had been directed at him in a positive
manner and to march along with the entire NJM to build a
Marxist-Leninist party that would lead the Grenadian people
to socialism and communism. He stated that he had never
experienced difficulties in working together with Coard and
that the joint leadership plan would push the party and the
revolution forward. At the end of the prime minister's
remarks, the whole audience joined in singing the
"Internationale" and then all participants of the meeting
filed past Bishop and Coard in order to embrace the two
leaders. There was an immense feeling of euphoria. It
seemed that the severe crisis had been overcome and that
the entire NJM would now pull together to save the
revolution and the nation.[28]

Further Deterioration in October

But that was not to be. As a matter of fact, beginning with Bishop's trip to Hungary and Czechoslovakia on September 28, the situation grew steadily worse. As soon as the prime minister had put some distance between himself and his native island, he once again began to have doubts about the feasibility of sharing power with Coard. For four-and-a-half years he had basked in the fame and prestige of being the sole leader of his country. To descend to a position of equality with Bernard Coard who, in spite of his brilliant management of the Grenadian economy, was not too popular with the population, was simply too much of a change for Bishop psychologically. His renewed vacillation was reinforced by his two supporters, Unison Whiteman and George Louison, who had accompanied him on the journey and told him that Coard ought to be able to carry out all of the tasks that the Central Committee had assigned to him from his position as deputy prime minister. In Budapest, Bishop told his loyal security guard, Cletus St. Paul, that the whole crisis was really a "power struggle" because "no state had joint leadership." George Louison held a meeting with Grenadian students in Hungary and informed them that neither he, Bishop, nor Whiteman had accepted the idea of a joint leadership.[29] News of George Louison's meeting traveled back to Grenada where it infuriated many Central Committee members, who were to accuse George Louison of "violating the rules of the CC" and "manipulating as well as poisoning the mind of Maurice Bishop."[30] Upon his return to Grenada, George Louison was expelled from the Central Committee and the Politburo and incarcerated along with Bishop's former law partner, minister of legal affairs, agro-industries and fisheries, Kenrick Radix.

On its way back home, the Grenadian delegation made a thirty-six-hour stopover in Cuba. (It arrived in Havana during the night of October 6 and left in the morning of October 8.) On October 7, Fidel Castro invited Maurice Bishop to join him in inspecting new construction sites at Cienfuegos. There the two leaders discussed Bishop's visit to Eastern Europe and other international matters. As far as Grenada's internal situation was concerned, Bishop stated only that he had not paid enough attention to the problems of the armed forces and the mass organizations in his country. At no time during his brief sojourn in Cuba did he even hint at the serious intraparty struggle that had been going on for months. Whether the Grenadian prime

minister withheld this information because of his "great
dignity and respect for his party and for Cuba" as the
Havana government was to put it later, or whether he failed
to divulge his difficulties in order to maintain his status
vis-a-vis Castro, will never be known. What is apparent,
however, is the fact that it was not until October 12 that
both Bishop and his opponents informed the Cuban ambassador
at St. George's of their problems. The news came as a
total surprise to Fidel Castro, who in a message to the NJM
Central Committee on October 15 warned of the dire
consequences of this schism and expressed his hope "that
the difficulties could be overcome with the greatest
wisdom, calmness, loyalty to principles and generosity."[31]

Unfortunately for the Grenadian revolution, neither
wisdom nor calmness and certainly no generosity was to
prevail on either side when Bishop returned to Grenada on
October 8. The pro-Coard majority on the Central
Committee, already perturbed by the report on George
Louison's activities in Budapest, became highly alarmed
over a phone call that Bishop's security guard, Cletus St.
Paul, had made from Cuba to a NJM party member on Grenada.
During this telephone conversation St. Paul not only
confirmed that Bishop was no longer abiding by the joint
leadership decision, but the security guard also warned
that "blood would flow." Bernard and Phyllis Coard
interpreted St. Paul's ominous remark as an indication that
Bishop was getting ready to kill them. Since they were
next-door neighbors of the prime minister, they decided to
hide out at the home of a Guyanese friend.[32] Maurice
Bishop, on the other hand, was deeply shocked when he
arrived at Pearls Airport and found there only one Central
Committee member, who greeted him in a most frigid manner.
Gone were the days when the entire leadership would turn up
at the airport to welcome him home and an honor guard would
present arms while a military band would strike up the
Grenadian national anthem. He had at least expected that
Bernard Coard would greet him, but the Coards had gone into
hiding. During the following days, nobody appeared at his
residence to present the daily briefings. Only Hudson
Austin and the minister of education, Jacqueline Creft,[33]
came to visit him. Having been the center of attention for
so many years, he found himself "marginalized," as he put
it at the meeting of the Central Committee and Politburo on
October 12.

Having lost control over the Central Committee, the
Politburo, the NJM party, and the People's Revolutionary
Army, Bishop tried to break out of his isolated position by

stirring up the masses. He ordered one of his main security guards, Errol George, to report to him with pencil and paper in order to jot down the "names of important opinion makers" at St. George's, who were to be contacted and told that Bernard and Phyllis Coard were out to kill the comrade leader. Errol George did contact two of the people on the list, which consisted of middle- and upper-middle-class businessmen and hotel owners. He then decided to turn himself in to the security forces in order to reveal this entire matter.[34] Bishop's attempt to mobilize the general public with the assistance of the bourgeoisie seemed to constitute the final proof to his opponents that the prime minister was turning into a counterrevolutionary. As far as the majority of the Central Committee members were concerned, Bishop's move was an incredible act of betrayal. Here was a man who, as recently as two weeks ago, had been adamantly opposed to revealing the intraparty struggle even to the general membership of the party and yet was now perfectly willing to incite the uninformed masses in order to cling to power. At the same time that Errol George was making his confession to the security forces, it also became known that Fitzroy Bain, one of the few pro-Bishop Central Committee members, was threatening to mobilize Grenada's agricultural workers for the prime minister.

At the subsequent meeting of the CC and PB on October 12, Maurice Bishop, George Louison, and Fitzroy Bain were to experience the full fury of the pro-Coard majority. Bishop was accused of "one manism," "cultism," "Gairyism with a Bishop face," and "spreading rumors as a pre-condition for murdering the CC and chasing the party off the streets." He was told that he did not even qualify as an applicant for membership in the NJM and that he should go to South Africa if he wanted to rule with a minority. There were demands for his expulsion from the party, the only questions being "whether he be allowed to operate as a private citizen or be arrested and courtmartialled for stirring up the counters against the revolution." Fitzroy Bain, who during the meeting expressed his desire to resign from the party "in order to join the poor people as a simple citizen," was told that he was an unruly peasant, was behaving like Gairy, and ought to be jailed. George Louison was removed from the Central Committee and threatened with expulsion from the party.[35]

Towards the close of the meeting, Liam James announced that the security forces had adopted a number of measures "to secure the lives of the Central Committee and Party comrades." These measures consisted of confining Maurice Bishop indefinitely, cutting off his telephones, disarming him "to guarantee his own safety" and suspending as well as confining the PRA's chief of staff, Major Einstein Louison, who had opposed a People's Revolutionary Armed Forces (PRAF)[36] resolution condemning the pro-Bishop faction of the CC. Liam James demanded "Bolshevik staunchness" and stated that "Communists without belly better hop the next plane."

What was amazing once again was the meek nature of Bishop's response. The prime minister remarked that he was willing to accept the blame for his petit bourgeois weaknesses as exemplified by his attitude towards the CC decision on joint leadership. He also declared that he was willing to accept his confinement, but not on the basis of rumormongering, which he strongly denied.[37] On the following day, during yet another meeting of the CC Bishop once more admitted his errors while also repeating his denial of originating the rumor that the Coards were out to kill him. Errol George then stepped in front of the assembled CC and related how the prime minister had sent him to St. George's with a list of names in order to disseminate the very same rumor. Bishop was then called upon to deny Errol George's testimony, but he refused to do so, which persuaded the audience that he was indeed guilty of the accusation.

After the meeting on October 13, which ended with Bishop being placed under house arrest, life on Grenada moved rapidly toward disintegration and anarchy. On the following day, Selwyn Strachan appeared during the morning in front of the Free West Indian office in downtown St. George's, near the Central Market Square. There the minister of national mobilization proclaimed to a hostile crowd of about three hundred people that Bishop had been replaced by Coard as prime minister, a piece of news that was officially broadcast by Radio Free Grenada (RFG) at 3:30 P.M. on the same day. Only half an hour later, RFG broadcast the startling news that Bernard and Phyllis Coard had both resigned from the PRG in order to quash the "vicious rumor" that they were trying to kill Bishop. At the same time, it was announced that Victor Nazim Burke, an economist in his early twenties, had replaced Coard as minister of finance. The RFG also told all PRA reservists to report for duty at Fort Rupert. On the morning of October 15, the minister of legal affairs, Kenrick Radix, urged a crowd at the Central Market Square to free Bishop from house arrest and ended his exhortation by shouting:

"No Bishop, no work. No Bishop, no play. No Bishop, no
school. No Bishop, no revolution."[38]

The opposition's answer to Radix's speech came in the
afternoon of the same day, when Major Leon Cornwall spoke
on RFG and accused Bishop of having been directly involved
in spreading rumors about a political upheaval on Grenada.
Cornwall warned that the PRA would not tolerate any
disruption of peace and calm on the island. The prime
minister's sixty-eight-year-old mother, Alimenta Bishop,
who was suffering from cancer and heart disease, was
allowed to visit her son under guard. She declared after
her visit that "It is time for him to be given the
opportunity to be free to tell the Grenadian people who
love him what is really the problem. I feel they should
quickly settle their differences for the sake of the
people."[39]

On the following day (October 16) both Kenrick Radix
and George Louison were arrested, but Louison was
periodically allowed to leave his confinement in order to
try to reach a modus vivendi between Bishop and Coard.[40]
An attempt to mediate between the two factions was also
undertaken by Michael Als, the leader of the small Trinidad
and Tobago People's Popular Movement. The atmosphere,
however, had become so poisoned by then that any compromise
solution was illusory. Also on October 16 Hudson Austin
spoke for half an hour over RFG, giving the Grenadian
people for the first time an official account of the
struggle between the two CC factions. One of the fiercest
tropical rain storms to hit Grenada in years occurred on
Monday, October 17, and practically everybody stayed
indoors. Even though the rain, albeit less torrential,
continued on Tuesday, there were pro-Bishop demonstrations
on October 18, in Gouyave, Sauteurs, and Grenville, where
students staged a sit-down strike at Pearls that
temporarily closed the airport. On the same day, four pro-
Bishop ministers of the PRG (Jacqueline Creft, Lyden
Ramdhanny, Unison Whiteman, and Norris Bain) turned in
their resignations.[41]

By the momentous "Bloody Wednesday," October 19, the
rains had vanished and a hot tropical sun was blazing down
on St. George's, where more than 10,000 Grenadians (10
percent of the country's population) had gathered at the
Central Market Square to protest the arrest of Maurice
Bishop. All schools, offices, stores, and restaurants were
closed and more and more people were pouring in from the
countryside. Chants of "We want Maurice!" "We want we
Leader!" and "C for Corruption, C for Coard!" could be

heard. There were signs reading "America, we love you!" and "Give us Maurice, or the masses will blast!"[42]

The immense crowd was addressed by Unison Whiteman, who urged the demonstrators to take action and free the prime minister. Eventually about 3,000 persons, for the most part uniformed schoolchildren, broke away from the mass of people and marched uphill from the market to Maurice Bishop's house. About one hundred PRA soldiers, who fired warning shots into the air, surrounded the house but did not dare to shoot into the thousands of Grenadians who were approaching. The crowd simply pushed past the soldiers and liberated the prime minister, who was extremely weak because he had not eaten for days out of fear that his captors might try to poison him. A dazed Bishop, with tears streaming down his face and muttering: "The masses, the masses," was placed in a truck and driven downhill with hundreds of people running alongside the vehicle, and shouting: "We got we Leader back!" At the Central Market Square, a public address system had been set up and everybody expected the prime minister to speak. But Bishop apparently planned first to seize the PRA headquarters at Fort Rupert and capture the arsenal there so that he could arm his followers. He also wanted to free the prisoners who were being held there. His press secretary, Don Rojas, who assumed that the comrade leader would give a speech at the market, later quoted Bishop as telling him: "No, I can't speak to the people now. Those criminals upon the hill (Fort Rupert) are heavily armed and they are going to turn their guns on the people. The people must disarm them."[43] It is also believed that Bishop wanted to obtain medical assistance at the General Hospital, which is located near Fort Rupert.

Bishop, accompanied by Jacqueline Creft, Unison Whiteman, Housing Minister Norris Bain, and the union leaders, Vincent Noel and Fitzroy Bain, as well as hundreds of ordinary followers broke into Fort Rupert and freed the PRA's former chief of staff, Major Einstein Louison, who was being held prisoner at the PRA headquarters. The prime minister then announced that Einstein Louison had replaced Hudson Austin as commanding general of the PRA. "Stein," as he was known among his friends, as well as Vincent Noel then went to the arsenal and began to arm the crowd with Soviet AK-47 rifles. When Stein, however, noticed that persons who had always spoken ill of the revolution were eagerly arming themselves, he decided to leave the scene because he expected imminent trouble.

In the meantime, the pro-Coard majority of the Central Committee, which had been watching Bishop's seizure of Fort Rupert from Coard's house across the bay, met with high-ranking PRA officers at Fort Frederick, which is located on a mountain near Coard's residence. It was decided to dispatch an unarmed negotiating team led by Major Chris Stroud and Captain Lester Redhead to Fort Rupert in order to attempt a last-minute settlement with the pro-Bishop elements. But Whiteman and Noel, buoyed by the massive demonstrations of popular support, shouted: "No compromise, no negotiations." When the pro-Coard team returned empty handed to Fort Frederick, the Central Committee allegedly decided to dispatch to Fort Rupert three Soviet-built personnel carriers, which were commanded by Lt. Col. Ewart Layne and Major Leon Cornwall. The three armored vehicles, rolling up the steep road past the St. James Hotel and the Presbyterian church, then blocked the entrance to Fort Rupert—still occupied by Bishop and hundreds of his followers. Who fired the first shot will probably never be known, but there are neutral (Michael Als from Trinidad) and even pro-Bishop (Einstein Louison) eyewitnesses who later testified that the first shots were fired from the pro-Bishop crowd at the fort. Some writers have suggested that the firing was started by provocateurs who were eager to bring about an armed clash between the two factions. Be that as it may, there were casualties on both sides during the ensuing melee. Vincent Noel, with both of his legs severed, died. Many panicky Bishop followers fell fifty to ninety feet to their deaths by jumping from the walls of the ancient fort to escape the shells and machine-gun fire from the three armored cars. A number of PRA soldiers were killed or injured by AK-47 fire from the fort and were later to be hailed by the Revolutionary Military Council (RMC) as heroes "who had further manured [!] the struggle of our Grenadian people."[44]

The Execution of Bishop and Its Repercussions

It soon became clear that the pro-Coard force with its three armored personnel carriers possessed an obvious advantage. Maurice Bishop, who at the beginning of the fight exclaimed, "My God, they are firing at the people," decided to surrender in order to avoid further bloodshed. After ordering all ordinary people to evacuate the fort, Lt. Col. Layne told Bishop and his entourage that they were under arrest. At 1 P.M. an execution squad consisting of two officers (Captain Lester Redhead and First Lieutenant Iman Abdullah) and two enlisted men lined up Maurice Bishop, Jacqueline Creft, Unison Whiteman, and Norris and Fitzroy Bain and executed them. When Jacqueline Creft, just prior to being executed, screamed: "Comrades, you mean you are going to shoot us? To kill us?" Redhead supposedly replied: "You f---king bitch, who are you calling comrades? You are one of those who was going to let in the imperialists!"[45]

Two hours after this massacre, Hudson Austin described over Radio Free Grenada the events of the morning, including the rally at the Central Market Square, the freeing of Bishop, the subsequent seizure of Fort Rupert and the arming of the crowd. He then asserted that "when a unit of the PRA arrived to re-take the Fort, they were fired upon by Bishop and his group. In the gun battle that followed, the following people were killed: Maurice Bishop, Unison Whiteman, Jacqueline Creft, Vincent Noel, Norris Bain, and Fitzroy Bain, among others."[46] After announcing the formation of a Revolutionary Military Council (RMC), which would rule Grenada until normalcy had been restored, Austin proclaimed an all-day and all-night curfew that would last for four days until Monday, October 24. During this period, all schools and all workplaces were to remain closed. The General warned that "anyone who seeks to demonstrate or disturb the peace will be shot."[47]

At about the same time that Austin was speaking over RFG, the PRAF released a bulletin to its soldiers asserting that "the leadership of the counterrevolutionary elements headed by Maurice Bishop, Unison Whiteman and Vincent Noel," although using the people as a shield, "had only businessmen, nuns, nurses and lumpen elements in the operations center" from where they were directing their activities at the Fort. The bulletin went on to state that "the timely move of our Motorised Unit dealt a devastating blow to these criminals, those opportunist elements who did not want to see Socialism built in our country." It claimed that the outcome of the day's events represented "a victory for progress and Socialism."[48]

Within a twenty-four-hour period, however, it became clear to the sixteen-man RMC (including Lester Redhead and Iman Abdullah) that their victory had been of a rather Pyrrhic nature. The military government found itself totally isolated, not only within its own country, but also abroad. The murder of Bishop and his closest associates had produced a profound revulsion even among the closest

supporters of the Grenadian revolution. The former prime
minister of Jamaica, Michael Manley, released the following
statement:

> The brutal killing of Maurice Bishop and many of his
> cabinet and union colleagues by the Grenadian Army
> represents a squalid betrayal of the hopes of the
> ordinary people of our region. The thousands who
> demonstrated for Bishop during the day, were
> expressing their faith in a leader who has given them
> a new sense of hope and pride as a people. History
> will pass a terrible judgement on those who are
> responsible for this murder.[49]

Even more alarming was the unexpected response of Fidel
Castro, who ordered three days of official mourning for
Maurice Bishop. Starting at 6 A.M. on October 21, the flag
was to be flown at half-mast at all public buildings and
military establishments in Cuba for the duration of the
mourning. In a bitter rebuke to the RMC, the Communist
party and government of Cuba declared that: "No doctrine,
no principle or proclaimed revolutionary position and no
internal division can justify atrocious acts such as the
physical elimination of Bishop and the prominent group of
honest and worthy leaders who died yesterday. . . . The
death of Bishop and his comrades must be cleared up. If
they were executed in cold blood, the guilty should receive
exemplary punishment."[50]
    At an emergency meeting on October 21, the
Revolutionary Military Council attributed the "vicious"
statement of the Cuban leadership to its lack of knowledge
"of the dishonesty and lying of MB [Maurice Bishop] as well
as the wickedness that he and his group did at Fort Rupert
including brutality and stripping of female soldiers."[51]
According to the memorandum drawn up at this meeting, the
RMC felt that the personal friendship between Fidel and
Maurice "had caused the Cuban leadership to take a personal
and not a class approach to the developments in Grenada."
While claiming that the Cuban statement "created an
atmosphere for speedy imperialist intervention," the RMC
defiantly noted "that we must be even firmer and determined
to smash any imperialist intervention even if we have to do
so ourselves." The RMC, however, decided to continue in
its efforts "to clarify the situation in the country by
giving the Cubans the facts" and hoped to maintain the best
relations with Cuba "on the principle of Proletarian
Internationalism."[52]

In spite of its tough rhetoric, the military government was really very frightened and attempted to erase the traces of the massacre. It made use of the curfew to remove the corpses of Bishop and his slain companions from Fort Rupert and cremated them at the army base, Calivigny. The many ordinary dead were also hauled away from the Fort Rupert area and dumped into the sea at Point Salines.[53] The thousands of weapons that Hudson Austin had already collected when he disarmed the People's Militia before Bishop's execution were taken during the curfew in a military convoy to the airport construction site and stored there. These were later regarded erroneously as Cuban weapons by the invading U.S. forces.[54] Fearing the already aroused world opinion, the RMC refrained from any further executions during its six-day reign. It arrested, however, a number of people, among them Alister Hughes, Einstein Louison, and the talented U.S. black artist and poet, Michele Gibbs. She survived the RMC confinement only to be expelled from Grenada by the U.S. military because of her well-known sympathy for the revolution.[55]

The greatest fear of the RMC was a possible U.S. intervention. In order to forestall any attempt on the part of the Reagan administration to use the presence of St. George's University School of Medicine as an excuse to invade Grenada, Hudson Austin visited the school's Vice Chancellor Geoffrey Bourne, on October 20, and presented him with a pass and a police escort, which allowed Bourne to travel anywhere on Grenada in spite of the curfew. Throughout the curfew, Austin and other members of the RMC asked about the welfare of the students from the United States and promised their safety, while at the same time, assuring the students that they were free to leave Grenada any time they wanted to. The RMC inquired whether the medical school had enough food and water and when it was told that the True Blue campus had only enough water for twenty-four hours, water trucks were sent to supply enough water for the four-day curfew. In spite of the suspension of all flights in and out of Grenada, the RMC allowed Kenneth Kurze and Linda Flohr, two diplomats from the U.S. embassy in Barbados, to fly into Grenada on October 22, in order to consult with the medical students. At that time only 15 percent wanted to leave the island. Later on, two more U.S. diplomats were allowed to enter Grenada, one of whom was James Budeit, who had directed the evacuation of U.S. civilians from Beirut.[56]

Since the U.S. diplomats had strict instructions not to talk to Hudson Austin, all of their dealings were with

Major Leon Cornwall, who offered to allow the evacuation of all medical students (if they so desired) either by airlift from Pearls Airport or by Cunard cruise ship from the port of St. George's. Cornwall assured the diplomats that the RMC would be replaced by a civilian cabinet within two weeks, and he even asked them to suggest the names of Grenadians who might serve in such a government.[57]

At the end of one meeting, Cornwall invited Budeit to accompany him to the Sugar Mill, formerly a sugar factory, but converted into a fancy discotheque that was frequented by Grenada's social elite and the U.S. medical students. How ironic that Cornwall, who together with his fellow officer Layne, had led the verbal assault on Bishop at various Central Committee meetings and the armed attack on the prime minister at Fort Rupert, should have invited a representative of "imperialism" to go dancing with him at a night spot of the "upper bourgeoisie"! But then the history of the Grenadian revolution--that is, the period from 1979 to 1983--is filled with paradoxes and ironic twists. It is sad that this miniscule, remote East Caribbean island has been wrenched out of its natural setting and hurled into the maelstrom of the super powers' confrontation.

The RMC's ingratiating moves towards the United States proved to be all in vain. The Reagan administration could not pass up this favorable opportunity to put an end to a revolution that it had viewed with undisguised hostility all along. At 5:00 A.M. on October 25, the United States and its Caribbean allies began their armed intervention on Grenada. But what they found were the pitiful remains of a revolution that had all but destroyed itself at Fort Rupert on October 19.

Aftermath of the Revolution

The self-immolation of the Grenadian revolution occurred only one year before this essay was written, but already many myths had begun to be woven around it, in spite of the fact that there is still much confusion as to what really transpired during those final months of the PRG's rule. One myth had it that Maurice Bishop was really a popular democrat who grew out of the Black Power movement and that Bernard Coard was the real Marxist-Leninist (or even Stalinist) who had his roots in Jamaican communism. Yet the records show that Maurice Bishop believed as much as Coard in democratic centralism and the eventual

evolution of Grenada into a Communist state. It was after
all Bishop who named one of his sons Vladimir in honor of
Lenin and who, at the critical Extraordinary Meeting of the
Central Committee of the NJM during mid-September 1983,
urged his comrades, among other suggestions, to study the
history of the Communist party of the Soviet Union in order
to solve the crisis facing the New Jewel Movement. Given
the nonexistence of an urban working class, the power of
the churches, and the deeply ingrained British traditions
on Grenada, both Bishop and Coard had moved very cautiously
along the road to Marxism, but there can be no doubt as to
their planned final destination.

Another myth had it that Bernard Coard and his wife
Phyllis were plotting for over a year to seize power and
were eventually able to draw into their conspiracy a large
part of the Central Committee and the armed forces. This
myth is so powerful because it is supported by the Reagan
administration, most of the world's press, Fidel Castro
(who has labeled Coard the "Pol Pot" of Grenada) and the
survivors of the pro-Bishop faction within the NJM (George
Louison, Kenrick Radix, Dessima Williams, and others). The
documents that the United States captured on Grenada,
however, clearly indicate that there was a general
dissatisfaction with Bishop's way of running the government
and the party by the summer of 1983, a dissatisfaction
shared by the very people (Unison Whiteman, George Louison,
and Fitzroy Bain) who were to back him during the final
showdown. Given the general unhappiness within the party
with Bishop's lack of organization and leadership, the idea
of "marrying the talents" of the two top ministers in a
joint leadership seemed like a logical solution. Bernard
Coard, rather than being eager to grab power, emphasized at
meetings (during which he had no need for subterfuge
because they were attended solely by his adherents) that he
was most reluctant to become a member of the Central
Committee and Politburo once again and that he was quite
happy just running the economy.

Once it became clear that Bishop did not really want
to go along with the joint leadership plan and in view of
his great popularity both abroad and at home, it was a
grave error of Coard and the majority of the Central
Committee to insist upon this plan in the midst of a severe
crisis. But it was also a serious mistake on the part of
Bishop to accept the joint leadership idea and then change
his mind and spread the rumor that the Coards were out to
kill him, which was bound to inflame the situation. Both
Bishop and Coard must share the responsibility for

destroying the revolution. The greatest blame for its
destruction, however, ought to be fixed upon the military
triumvirate of Liam James, Ewart Layne, and Leon Cornwall.
These three, spouting Marxist jargon, aggravated the
tension within the party by their uncompromising attitude.
Prior to the crisis Cornwall and Layne had spent a long
time abroad (Major Cornwall as Grenadian ambassador in Cuba
and Lt. Col. Layne as deputy defense minister in the USSR)
and seemed to have become divorced from the realities of
Grenadian life. It was also Cornwall and Layne who,
leading the armed assault on Fort Rupert, probably gave the
order for the barbaric execution of Bishop and his closest
companions after their surrender, a brutal act that cannot
be excused on any grounds. It is not clear yet whether
Bernard and Phyllis Coard were involved in this execution
which could have been an on-the-spot decision. Their
trial, scheduled for the summer of 1985, along with
seventeen other defendants (among them Cornwall and Layne),
will probably shed much light on that question.

Finally, there is the myth that the Soviet Union,
being aware of a Coard-Austin conspiracy, backed the ouster
of Bishop because he was too moderate. The same tale, but
involving Cuba, was reported by most of the press at the
time of the U.S. intervention until the official
declarations by the Cuban government condemning Bishop's
murder made these claims untenable. The Soviet Union, a
relative newcomer to the Grenadian scene, closely
coordinated its strategy with its Cuban ally, which had
been involved on Grenada from the very beginning of the
Grenadian revolution. There is no evidence whatsoever that
the USSR knew of the intraparty struggle or condoned the
elimination of Bishop.

In viewing the situation on Grenada it seems, at least
superficially, that the clock has been turned all the way
back to the period before March 13, 1979. Sir Eric Gairy
with his Grenada United Labor Party (GULP) is back on the
political scene, claiming that he was divinely chosen to
lead the people of Grenada once again. Former prime
minister, Herbert Blaize, and his Grenada National Party
(GNP) have also formed a coalition with three other
moderate parties to prevent this from happening and Blaize
is once again Grenada's head of state. Even a remnant of
the New Jewel Movement arose from the ashes when the
survivors of the pro-Bishop faction formed the Maurice
Bishop Patriotic Movement (MBPM). Reports from Grenada
indicate that the programs and institutions of the PRG have
all been thoroughly dismantled and hundreds of NJM members

and sympathizers purged from the government services. Unemployment is back up to 35 percent or more.

Yet as time goes on, it will become apparent that there can be no turning back to the past. The four-and-a-half years of the Grenadian revolution have changed that island forever. Thousands of young Grenadians have studied for years in various Socialist countries and they will hardly support the abolition of such PRG programs as free medical care, agricultural cooperatives, free schooling, and state nurseries for working mothers. Along with unpopular acts like the abolition of all political opposition and jailing of some of its critics, the PRG initiated many measures that were quite popular with the Grenadian people. Maurice Bishop, whether correctly or not, continues to be identified by a large segment of the island's population with everything that was positive about the revolution.

Grenada is a very small country; everybody seems to know each other and it is important to prevent profound and lasting schisms. Unfortunately, many such deep divisions that do not portend well for Grenada's future exist today. There is the gulf between those that supported and those that opposed the revolution. The opponents of the revolution are themselves split into moderate and conservatives, Gairyites and anti-Gairyites. The survivors of the New Jewel Movement, too, are today bitterly divided between the pro-Bishop and Pro-Coard factions who accuse each other of destroying the revolution.

Only by a spirit of compromise, generosity, and reconciliation among all of these factions can there be any hope that the Grenadian people can put behind then the traumatic experiences of October 1983. Then they might be able to establish a stable government on an island convulsed by political turmoil since 1951.

5
The United States as a Caribbean Power

At 5:00 A.M. (EDT) on October 25, 1983, 1,900 U.S.
Marines and Army airborne troops, supported by 300 men from
a handful of Caribbean countries, began landing on the tiny
eastern Caribbean island of Grenada. Four hours later
President Ronald Reagan, accompanied by Prime Minister
Eugenia Charles of Dominica, told a Washington news
conference the reasons for this action.[1] First, the
"personal safety" of between 800 and 1,000 U.S. citizens on
Grenada, including many medical students and senior
citizens, was at stake because "a brutal gang of leftist
thugs" had "violently seized power" there. Second, the
president had acted "to forestall further chaos." Finally,
he wished "to assist in the restoration of conditions of
law and order and of governmental institutions" to Grenada.
President Reagan also revealed that the U.S. actions
had been taken in response to "an urgent, formal request
from the five member-nations of the Organization of Eastern
Caribbean States (OECS)" plus Barbados and Jamaica "to
assist in a joint effort to restore order and democracy" on
Grenada. "This collective action," he emphasized, "has
been forced on us by events that have no precedent in the
eastern Caribbean and no place in any civilized society."
The president concluded by restating U.S. objectives: "to
protect our own citizens, to facilitate the evacuation of
those who want to leave, and to help in the restoration of
democratic institutions in Grenada."
Until that morning few North Americans had ever heard
of Grenada except, perhaps, for those who remembered the
reconnaissance photographs of a large airport under
construction there. President Reagan had told a nationwide
audience several months before that this airport proved
Cuban machinations in the eastern Caribbean. But Reagan

did not mention the airport as a reason for the October 25 landing. Even fewer people had heard of the OECS. Was the United States a member? When had it been formed? What about the Organization of American States?

But several broader questions as well were raised by the Grenada landing. Did it represent another chapter in the history of the Monroe Doctrine? How did it relate to the Reagan administration's Caribbean Basin policy? To what extend was the action to be seen in the context of East-West competition? Did Reagan's decision signify the end of the "Vietnam syndrome"? Was it intended to "send a message" to Nicaragua? How did a host of historical analogies—from Cuba to Iran—figure in the administration's thinking? Was the action justifiable in international law? Did it constitute a "Reagan Doctrine" that articulated new U.S. foreign policy principles? What did the action say about a new phenomenon in international politics—a formally independent island microstate lacking some of the traditional elements of statehood?

The Historical Background

To begin to answer these questions we need to recount briefly the historical background of the United States in the Caribbean. Although the United States formally became a Caribbean power with the acquisition of Puerto Rico after the Spanish-American War, its interest in the region was apparent at a much earlier date. Since the end of the seventeenth century, the Caribbean had been the scene of imperial conflict involving, ultimately, Spain, Great Britain, France, Holland, Denmark, and Sweden. Several of the islands exchanged overlords numerous times, and a few of them prospered, raising and trading sugar, tobacco, and slaves. But as these plantation economies begin to decline in the early nineteenth century, European interest in them waned. Yet as the wars of independence engulfed Spanish America after the Napoleonic Wars, it seemed likely that European powers might seek to impose their own imperia on these territories.

The United States responded to this crisis (and to the alleged threat of Russia to the U.S. Northwest) with the Monroe Doctrine—a set of pragmatic and visionary principles that staked out (in 1823) U.S. moral and security claims on the Western Hemisphere. President James Monroe noted that because the political institutions of Europe were fundamentally different from those of the

United States, "we would consider any attempt on their part
to extend their system to any portion of this hemisphere as
dangerous to our peace and safety." Monroe renounced any
desire to interfere with "the existing colonies or
dependencies of any European power," but he warned that any
attempt to interpose "for the purpose of oppressing"
governments "who have declared their independence and
maintained it" or of "controlling in any other manner their
destiny" would be viewed "as the manifestation of any
unfriendly disposition toward the United States."[2] At the
core of the Monroe Doctrine lay a remarkable claim: The
health of the U.S. domestic institutions was significantly
and necessarily affected by the kinds of institutions
maintained by other states in the Western Hemisphere. By a
neat amalgamation of geopolitical and ideological
considerations Monroe had, in effect, proclaimed the New
World a "moral sphere of influence" for the United States.
Furthermore, Monroe had articulated an early version of
what much later became known as "containment" by roping off
part of the world to penetration from alien institutions,
accepting the legitimacy of the status quo within this
region but declaring that no further inroads would be
tolerated.

Although the United States lacked the means to enforce
the Monroe Doctrine--it was viewed by Europeans as an
impertinence--the British navy and the other powers' more
pressing priorities combined to preserve the political
independence of Latin America for most of the rest of the
nineteenth century. Unfortunately, many people in the
United States interpreted these circumstances as evidence
of the Monroe Doctrine's universal acceptance and of their
country's moral superiority.[3] Occasionally, of course,
U.S. fears of European intervention were renewed,
particularly during the U.S. Civil War when France
attempted to subvert Mexico and Spain tried to reconquer
Santo Domingo. But U.S. interest in the Caribbean remained
sporadic until after the Spanish-American War when the
United States assumed responsibility for the political
status of Puerto Rico and Cuba and when some people began
to ponder the strategic questions posed by the decision to
build an isthmian canal. Suddenly the chronic instability
and financial difficulties of the Caribbean and Central
American states that had increasingly provided pretexts for
European intervention appeared more threatening to U.S.
security.

President Theodore Roosevelt responded with his
infamous 1904 "corollary" to the Monroe Doctrine, which
declared that any Latin American nation

> whose people conduct themselves well can count upon
> our hearty friendship. If a nation shows that it
> knows how to act with reasonable efficiency and
> decency in social and political matters, if it keeps
> order and pays its obligations, it need fear no
> interference from the United States. Chronic
> wrongdoing, or an impotence which results in a general
> loosening of the ties of civilized society, may in
> America, or elsewhere, ultimately require intervention
> by some civilized nations, and in the Western
> Hemisphere the adherence of the United States to the
> Monroe Doctrine may force the United States, however
> reluctantly, in flagrant cases of such wrongdoing or
> impotence, to the exercise of an international police
> power.[4]

Now, however, the United States possessed the naval power
to compel obedience—a power made even more impressive
after the withdrawal of the British navy from the
Caribbean—and during the next twenty-five years the United
States intervened some sixty times in Latin America. These
actions were successful in that no permanent European
outposts in the region were established, but the
long-lasting bitterness engendered by these frequent swings
of "the big stick" was a tragic legacy of the Roosevelt
Corollary. Furthermore, while U.S. interventions often
forestalled revolutions that allegedly created anarchic
conditions, they were much less successful in bringing
democracy to Central America and the Caribbean. Indeed,
the relatively efficient police forces that the United
States trained in Haiti, the Dominican Republic, and
Nicaragua became the backbones of repressive rule after
U.S. troops were withdrawn.

In 1928, however, the Clark Memorandum (named after
Under Secretary of State J. Reuben Clark) narrowed the
meaning of the Monroe Doctrine to rule out future U.S.
interventions undertaken solely to preserve or restore
internal order, though military actions for "self-defense"
would still be legitimate. President Franklin D.
Roosevelt's Good Neighbor Policy substituted a conference
system of multilateral diplomacy for unilateral
intervention as the last U.S. troops in Cuba were recalled
in 1934. By the late 1930s, with the onset of an apparent

Nazi threat to Mexico and parts of South America, Roosevelt
moved to "multilateralize" the Monroe Doctrine by making
the American republics jointly responsible for hemispheric
security.

At the San Francisco conference in 1945 the United
States insisted that Article 51 be included in the United
Nations Charter to enable regional organizations to
exercise collective security. Two years later the U.S.
Senate ratified the Rio Treaty, which specified that "an
armed attack by any State against an American State shall
be considered as an attack against all the American States
(Article 3, Section 1). In 1948 the Organization of
American States (OAS) was created.

Before long the United States attempted to use the Rio
Treaty and the OAS to isolate the democratically elected
but allegedly pro-Communist Jacobo Arbenz Guzman government
in Guatemala. At the Caracas Conference in March 1954
Secretary of State John Foster Dulles urged on the OAS a
resolution that condemned international communism as an
alien ideology incompatible with the political institutions
of the Western Hemisphere. By this time, however, a Central
Intelligence Agency (CIA) undercover operation to depose
Arbenz was well under way, and in June a coup was
successfully carried out.[5] When Fidel Castro's domestic
and international behavior incurred the wrath of the United
States administration six years later, the methods that had
worked so well against Guatemala were incorporated into a
CIA plan (Operation ZAPATA) against Cuba. This time,
however, the Bay of Pigs was the disastrous result.

"Avoiding another Cuba"--i.e., preventing the creation
of additional pro-Soviet regimes in the Western
Hemisphere--now became a unifying slogan that accounted for
every major U.S. initiative in Latin America until the
first year of the Carter administration. That goal
certainly lay at the center of the Alliance for Progress,
for the Kennedy administration believed that democratic
reforms and economic growth in Latin America would prevent
Fidelismo from taking root. And it obviously explains
Lyndon Johnson's decision to send 20,000 U.S. troops to the
Dominican Republic in 1965.

The Dominican Intervention

The Dominican intervention constituted a crucial
episode in post-war U.S. foreign policy. On May 30, 1961,
the assassination of Dominican dictator Rafael Trujillo

ended his family's thirty-year bloody reign, and in late 1962 a left-of-center intellectual, Juan Bosch, was elected president. But Bosch, whom former Venezuelan President Romulo Betancourt called "the best short-story writer and worst politician in the hemisphere," was toppled in a military coup on September 25, 1963, and went into exile. President John F. Kennedy condemned this action and recalled the U.S. ambassador, but the administration gradually grew resigned to the situation and in late 1963 formally recognized the nominally civilian government of Donald Reid y Cabral.

Then on April 24, 1965, a circle of pro-Bosch military officers overthrew the Reid government but seemed unable to consolidate power. Civil war threatened, and on April 27 the U.S. embassy in Santo Domingo ordered the evacuation of all U.S. nationals from the country. But soon some embassy officials grew fearful that the evacuation could not be safely undertaken. Ambassador W. Tapley Bennett told Washington that public order was disintegrating and warned that Communists and Communist sympathizers were attempting to seize control. The next day, April 28, another faction of the Dominican armed forces formed a new junta and asked for U.S. troops to end the chaos. At the same time, the head of the national police told Bennett that he could not guarantee the safety of U.S. citizens and other foreigners fleeing the country. That evening President Johnson announced, "because American lives are in danger, [I have] ordered the Secretary of Defense to put the necessary . . . troops ashore in order to give protection to hundreds of Americans who are still in the Dominican Republic and to escort them safely back to this country."[6]

But what had apparently begun as a rescue mission quickly escalated, and on April 30 Johnson informed the nation that "there are signs that people trained outside the Dominican Republic are seeking to gain control." Because of this threat to "the principles of the inter-American system" a representative[7] of the OAS was to undertake a fact-finding mission there. Two days later Johnson declared that what "began as a popular democratic revolution, committeed to democracy and social justice" had taken "a tragic turn. Communist leaders, many of them trained in Cuba, seeing a chance to increase disorder, to gain a foothold, joined the revolution. The American nations," he intoned, "cannot, must not and will not permit the establishment of another Communist government in the Western Hemisphere." And while "the form and nature of a free Dominican government . . . is solely a matter for the

Dominican people, . . . we hope to see a government freely
chosen by the will of all the people. We hope to see a
government dedicated to social justice for every single
citizen. We hope to see a government . . . whose only
concern is the progress and the elevation and the welfare
of all the people." President Johnson concluded with a
veiled reference to Vietnam: "We will defend our soldiers
against attackers. We will honor our treaties. We will
keep our commitments. We will defend our Nation against
all those who seek to destroy not only the United States
but every free country of this hemisphere. We do not want
to bury anyone. . . . But we do not intend to be buried."[8]
U.S. troops proceeded to evacuate about 4,000 people and
restore order to the island. On May 23 the OAS, under
great pressure from Washington, created an Inter-American
Peace Force, which gradually replaced U.S. forces. The
following June closely supervised elections were
held--Joaquin Balaguer was elected president--and on
September 22, 1966, the last foreign troops were withdrawn.

Several elements about the Dominican intervention and
President Johnson's defense of it deserve emphasis. First,
the failure of Eisenhower and Kennedy to unseat Castro
provided a powerful incentive for Johnson to act
decisively, even though the situation in the Dominican
Republic was ambiguous. Notwithstanding the subsequent
finding by an OAS investigating team that a Communist
takeover had been averted only by the arrival of U.S.
Marines, many commentators have since expressed skepticism
about that possibility. But given the Cuban precedent,
President Johnson was under strong pressure to decide
quickly to intervene.

Second, although Johnson, in principle, could have
defended his actions with explicit reference to the Monroe
Doctrine--and even the Roosevelt Corollary--he was careful
to justify his decision within the context of "the
inter-American system," whose values would allegedly be
subverted by a Communist Dominican Republic. But much to
his embarrassment, many OAS members criticized the U.S.
intervention and only after much U.S. arm-twisting did this
organization finally create a multinational peacekeeping
force. In fact, the intervention represented a defense of
the Monroe Doctrine in all but name, but Johnson realized
that its invocation would enrage the United States' "sister
Republics." At the same time his sweeping promise that
"the American nations cannot, must not, and will not permit
the establishment of another Communist government in the
Western Hemisphere" opened the door wide for future

unilateral interventions undertaken in the name of hemispheric unity.

Third, Johnson's actions must be also seen in the context of Vietnam. His declaration of May 2 that the United States would defend its soldiers from attack, honor its treaties, and keep its commitments had as much to do with Pleiku, the Southeast Asia Treaty Organization, and Saigon as it did with the OAS and the Dominican Republic. Three months after the U.S. bombing of North Vietnam had begun and two months before he announced a massive troop buildup in South Vietnam, Johnson saw the Dominican crisis, in part, as a litmus test of U.S. resolve. To do nothing in the Caribbean—the American Mediterranean—would send the wrong signals to Hanoi and Saigon.

Finally, although the House of Representatives later endorsed the president's action by a vote of 312 to 52 and although 85 percent of the U.S. public had supported the intervention, some prominent U.S. liberals were deeply troubled by the episode and by Johnson's grandiose claims in defense of it. People like J. William Fulbright, Robert F. Kennedy, Walter Lippmann, Archibald MacLeish, and Lewis Mumford protested, and according to one analyst, "adverse public reaction to the administration's Caribbean diplomacy largely destroyed any national policy consensus the Johnson White House enjoyed on foreign policy issues."[9] In short, what had begun as a simple rescue mission had been transformed for some people into an arrogant exercise of power.

But, in retrospect, the Dominican intervention also marked the end of a period of intense U.S. activity in the Caribbean that had begun with Castro's victory in Cuba in 1959. The Johnson administration's growing preoccupation with Vietnam, Richard Nixon and Henry Kissinger's emphasis on detente with the Soviet Union, and Castro's shift away from his foco theory of revolution in Latin America after several setbacks in favor of military actions in Angola and Ethiopia combined to remove the Caribbean from the center stage of U.S. foreign policy. A posture of low-intensity containment replaced active subversion of Cuba, and United States improvised responses toward the rest of the Caribbean when U.S. interests appeared threatened—as in Trinidad in 1970 by a Black Power movement or in Jamaica by the socialist government of Michael Manley a few years later.

U.S. Interests in the Caribbean

What is the nature of U.S. interest in the Caribbean?
U.S. policy has traditionally focused on issues of security
and economics. As we have seen, security has meant keeping
hostile political and military influences away from the
"third border" of the United States, even though this aim
has occasionally justified military intervention. The
Caribbean, of course, provides access to the Panama Canal,
and U.S. military installations from Puerto Rico to Panama
testify to the perceived importance of these sea-lanes,
which carry 50 percent of the oil imported to the United
States. In addition, about half of all U.S. imports of
bauxite and alumina come from the Caribbean (particularly
from Jamaica and Suriname), and imports of nickel,
especially from the Dominican Republic, are substantial.
On the other hand, although the Panama Canal retains
enormous symbolic significance for many people in the
United States, a diminishing portion of U.S. trade passes
through it, and most U.S. aircraft carriers are too large
to navigate it.
The relative importance of the Caribbean for U.S.
trade and investment has also declined. Excluding Cuba,
Puerto Rico, and the U.S. Virgin Islands, Caribbean states
accounted for more than 11 percent of all U.S. direct
foreign investment and an even higher share of its foreign
trade in 1960, but the figure fell to 2.5 percent
investment and 1.7 percent trade in 1979, and more than 40
percent of the investment constituted "paper assets" in the
Bahamas. In 1960 these countries had supplied the United
States with 3.8 percent of its imports, but by 1979 that
figure had fallen to 3.2 percent.
But if U.S. security and economic interests have
become less compelling, objectively at least, two other
interests have grown in significance. First, the
proliferation of newly independent states since the mid-
1960s, particularly the microstates of the eastern
Caribbean, has presented Washington with a new policy
dimension. For some observers, the British withdrawal from
the area has created a power vacuum reminiscent of earlier
British withdrawals from the eastern Mediterranean and the
Arabian/Persian Gulf. At the very least, these new states
constitute an impressive voting bloc in the UN and other
international forums, which the United States needs to take
seriously. On the other hand, as we will see shortly, by
the late 1970s, some U.S. policymakers had concluded that
for a variety of reasons, these Commonwealth countries

(CARICOM) provided Cuba and its Soviet master with "tempting targets of opportunity."

Second, because of large-scale population movements, the Caribbean has become of great demographic importance to the United States. Whereas during the 1950s Caribbean residents made up less than 5 percent of the total legal immigration to the United States, that share increased to 15.6 percent in the following decade and to 17.5 percent between 1970 and 1978. And illegal Caribbean migrations, especially from Haiti and Cuba, have helped to fuel a serious debate in the United States over immigration policy. Since World War II about 4.5 million people from the Caribbean have settled in the United States. One out of every six Barbadians, one out of every five Jamaicans, and about one-tenth of all Cubans now live on the U.S. mainland. In comparative terms legal immigration from the Caribbean since the 1960s has been three times greater than immigration from all of South America. According to one observer, "These migrations are not unrelated events" but "reflect a fundamental, continuous, and probably irreversible response to regional overpopulation and the magnetic attraction that any stronger economy exerts on a weaker one."[10] These Caribbean populations have become growing political forces in states like Florida, New York, and New Jersey, while many of the region's leaders such as Boston-born and Harvard-educated Edward Seaga of Jamaica have been heavily influenced by their exposure to the United States.

The international economic crisis sparked by the 400 percent increase in petroleum prices set by OPEC during 1973 and 1974 hit the Caribbean particularly hard. Save for Trinidad and Tobago the area is made up of net oil importers, and its fragile economies were confronted with enormously inflated energy bills that the countries were unable to pay with their foreign exchange earnings. Balance of payments worsened, currency reserves were depleted, budgetary problems grew, and falling commodity prices triggered even higher unemployment. Although political adjustments varied from state to state, a broad leftward trend, especially in Jamaica and Guyana, had emerged by the end of the Ford administration. Furthermore, several Caribbean governments began to show sympathy for the agenda known as the New International Economic Order.

6
Carter, the Caribbean, and Grenada

A New Approach to Foreign Policy

By the mid-1970s disaffection by prominent members of the U.S. foreign policy establishment with both the Vietnam War and an allegedly overmilitarized diplomacy was gradually gaining coherence around a set of values, priorities, and prescriptions increasingly referred to as "world order politics."[1] Many well-known academics helped to articulate this approach, but perhaps the most influential proponent was Stanley Hoffmann at Harvard University, who elaborated his vision fully in Primacy or World Order: American Foreign Policy Since the Cold War.[2]

Hoffmann recommended a U.S. "world order policy" based on "moderation plus" to manage the problems of global interdependence. Such a policy was aimed at an international environment that Hoffmann found full of ambiguity and complexity. He argued that U.S. leaders since at least 1947 had felt responsible for the achievement of world order, but their main action had been to construct a dam against communism.[3] Containment was imbued with an unfortunate blend of paranoia and moral arrogance, yet, for Hoffmann, its "objective" accomplishments were undeniably "impressive."[4] The debit side of the record "consisted largely, not of communist successes, which were few, but of mere manifestations of America's incapacity to roll Communism back: in North Korea, in Eastern Europe, at the Bay of Pigs."[5] Yet despite the long string of successes—the integration of the former Axis powers into the "American world system," Israel's regional military power, the Berlin blockade, the Congo crisis of 1960, the Cuban missile crisis, and the largely non-Communist decolonization process—by the late

1960s U.S. citizens felt "a sense of failure."[6] Although
this malaise could have been in part attributed to the
containment policy's failure to provide anything more
exalting than the indefinite pursuit of more containment,
Hoffmann argued that Vietnam had been the real cause, for
this blatant example of containment's misapplication had
succeeded in petrifying and paralyzing U.S. policy
everywhere. Vietnam "now appeared as the extreme but
logical, absurd but unavoidable end of the policy of
confrontation" and thus "put into question the policy
itself."[7] Huge means had led to inflated stakes and
spelled defeat for the entire strategy of containment. At
the root of the United States' failure in Vietnam lay the
same "neglect of local circumstances" that had doomed the
U.S. effort in China during the 1940s.[8]

Nevertheless, Henry Kissinger attempted to preserve
U.S. "primacy" by mapping a neo-Bismarckian course
ostensibly characterized by "moderation." He believed that

> primacy would be assured at less cost, in two ways.
> One was a modicum of disengagement from areas whose
> importance to the national interest could now be
> acknowledged as secondary. This was the meaning of
> the so-called Nixon doctrine. . . .
>
> A second way of reducing costs was a change in
> the instruments of primacy. There would be fewer
> overt military interventions, more covert action
> . . . , less food aid and assistance, more food and
> arms sales.[9]

Furthermore, Kissinger sought to move beyond containment to
a stable structure of peace grounded in the Sino-Soviet-
American triangular relationship and preserved by a
judicious admixture of carrot-and-stick diplomacy.

Hoffmann concluded, however, that Kissinger failed to
realize his vision of world order, and by 1976 U.S. foreign
policy had again lost its way.[10] Kissinger's policy
required execution that was too complex to retain domestic
support because the "web of dependencies" in which
Kissinger tried to enmesh the Soviet Union had actually
created a host of domestic U.S. interest groups; the health
of some groups rested on "carrots" and others demanded
"sticks." In the absence of a new foreign policy consensus
Kissinger discovered that he could not garner sufficient
support for a policy toward the Soviets that required a
subtle blending of carrots and sticks. His legacy was to
leave the United States at least as internally divided as

he had found it with "gloomy, grumpy, flamboyant"[11]
neoconservative anti-Communists accusing him of
appeasement; neo-Wilsonian "radicals" clamoring for the
United States to "purge itself of all the evil forces" that
had led to its "corruption" by proclaiming "a wholly new
moral and political order";[12] and "moderate activists,
without hegemonic pretenses, eager to draw on the reservoir
of American moralism on behalf of international
cooperation,"[13] by enthusiastically supporting Jimmy
Carter.

Hoffmann contended that Kissinger's world design was
"too simple for today's world," because it allegedly rested
on obsolete notions of world politics. That is, his vision
mistakenly presumed that the "diplomatic-strategic
chessboard" still contained the only significant
international "game," whereas Hoffmann argued that a series
of recent and momentous changes had transformed the nature
of the global environment. Now the classical chessboard
shared the spotlight with several new games, and although
these newcomers had not yet destroyed the ultimate
decisiveness of the older contest, they had created an
exceedingly ambiguous international system. No longer
could the United States define world order in terms of U.S.
hegemony, either overtly as in the Truman Doctrine or
covertly as in the Nixon Doctrine, but rather the nation
had to adjust to the post-Vietnam reality of "complex
interdependence." The United States remained the
"preponderant power," but this new age of "compulsory
bargaining and compromise" made concessions necessary.[14]
However, Hoffmann warned, in their search for a world order
policy, U.S. leaders could not rely on traditional
intellectual road maps, for this new world was unique and
classical political and historical theories and
prescriptions had only the barest relevance.[15] In short,
the past as described by Thucydides, Rousseau, Wilson, and
even Dean Acheson was dead.

What did the new world look like? First, there had
been a "change in the number and nature of actors."[16] In
addition to a tremendous increase in the number of states,
nonstate actors of many types who behaved "as if they had
. . . autonomy,"[17] had lately emerged. Furthermore, the
nature of states' objectives had altered so that foreign
policy was now "the external dimension of the universally
dominant concern for economic development and social
welfare."[18] Whereas "control" historically had been the
primary end of foreign policy, actors now sought "milieu
goals" through the achievement of "influence."[19] Hoffmann

had noted the same phenomena almost a decade earlier in
Gulliver's Troubles,[20] but what he had earlier identified
as a tendency had now become a compelling reality. Second,
through its "diffusion" (because of the growth in the
number of actors and foreign policy issues) and in its
"diversification" ("the kinds of supplies needed to exert
influence" were "so varied that the old quasiidentification
with military might" had "become absurd"), the nature of
power had undergone radical change. Moreover, the use of
power supplies had grown in complexity, and the existence
of new restraints on that use now affected the old logic of
interaction. To express the significance of this
extraordinary transformation, Hoffmann offered a homely
metaphor:

> in the traditional usage of power, states were like
> boiled eggs. War, the minute of truth, would reveal
> whether they (or which ones) were hard or soft.
> Interdependence breaks eggs into a vast omelet. It
> does not mean the end of conflict: I may want my egg
> to contribute a larger part of the omelet's size and
> flavor than your egg—or I may want you to break yours
> into it first, etc. . . . . But we all end in the same
> omelet.[21]

Third, the international hierarchy, which had formerly been
based exclusively on military or geomilitary power, now had
fragmented into "separate functional hierarchies, and in
each one the meaning of being 'top dog'" was "far from
simple."[22]   In contrast to the past when supremacy carried
with it umambiguous benefits, the new international system
had become "a trying world for top dogs, because of the
general difficulty (the interference of other actors and
one's own domestic accidents) of using one's might to
achieve desired results, because of the difficulty of
making might in one area affect outcomes in another
(linkage), and because of the handicaps proper to each
area."[23]   Fourth, not only had the traditional diplomatic-
strategic chessboard lost its previous monopoly over
international life, but its nature had been transformed as
well. The nuclear revolution had produced a "fear of
force," which made the "'minute of truth' more
hypothetical" but had also privileged "other kinds of
power."[24]   This presumably universal fear had changed the
"rules of the 'game of power'" by producing a "strange
blend of arms race and restraints," by subverting the
bipolar hierarchy of states through the proliferation of

nonnuclear forms of violence, and by worsening strains
among allies.[25]
Finally, the allegedly unprecedented political
significance of economic interdependence had spawned
"extraordinarily complex" games in which the "use of force"
was very "unlikely."[26] For Hoffmann, "this
interdependence, the possibility or obligation to weave
one's power into the web," was "both an opportunity for and
a restraint on the actor." But, as it turned out,
interdependence had disproportionately crippled giants and
empowered pygmies. The United States remained atop "almost
every hierarchy of economic power, but here, as in the
strategic realm, it is a Gulliver tied, not a master with
free hands."[27] In short, interdependence had so altered
the conditions of interaction that "rules prescribing
states what to do and what not to do," such as those
decided at the Bretton Woods Conference, were "no longer
enough." These rules needed to be replaced by
"international organizations with considerable powers
either of administration or even of policy making."[28]
Needless to say, the United States would find it impossible
to control these new institutions.
Momentous as these changes were, however, they had not
yet caused the demise of the nation-state as the world's
primary political unit. The concept of the national
interest may have splintered into "many alternatives," but
Hoffmann advised "prudence" and concluded that "the present
scene" was a "triumph of ambiguity."[29] Despite these
enormous changes the state retained surprising resilience;
it had been "neither superseded nor tamed"; and individuals
still turned to it for "protection, welfare, and
justice."[30]
In place of the traditional containment policy,
Hoffmann urged "moderation plus,"[31] a policy that would, in
effect, graft the new complexities (and constraints) of
interdependence onto the moderation of men like George
Kennan and Walter Lippmann.[32] But the task would not be
easy, because "the passion for control, so deeply rooted in
American history, the universal moralism, so deeply
expressive of America's civil religion, must now yield to
an external policy of extreme delicacy."[33] Patience,
compromise, cooperation, sensitivity, and nuance were
required. Yet

> the experience of the recent past—eight years of
> [Kissinger's] "amorality" tacked onto the long
> immorality of Vietnam—will make the curbing [of

aggressive idealism] difficult. If historical
activism is strong, historical memory is weak. The
instinctive desire to save the former creates the
legend that Vietnam was merely a product of cynicism
and elitism, rather than a catastrophe resulting from
misplaced idealism.[34]

Hoffmann warned that a world order policy must not become
an excuse for a crusade of neo-Wilsonianism, but must
reflect the complexity, ambiguity, and intractability of
the real world.

   To a remarkable degree many in the Carter
administration shared Hoffmann's outlook. Jimmy Carter
brought to the White House the most ambitious foreign
policy agenda of any president since John F. Kennedy.
Freed at last from Vietnam, U.S. diplomacy, the
administration argued, could now address a wide variety of
problems neglected for too long by Presidents Johnson,
Nixon, and Ford. The termination of the war thus provided
the United States an opportunity to construct a "complex"
foreign policy responsive to the several ongoing
technological revolutions that were delivering rapid change
to most of the world.

   President Carter outlined his global agenda at the
United Nations in March 1977 and at the University of Notre
Dame two months later, but the most comprehensive early
articulation was offered in Boston in June 1977 by Anthony
Lake, director of the State Department's Policy Planning
Staff.[35] He announced that six themes and ten subthemes
would be the major foci of the Carter foreign policies.
Ranging from detente and arms control to energy,
overpopulation, pollution, human rights, and the
North-South dialogue, all the themes and subthemes were
apparently to be given roughly equal attention and together
they defined a complex approach to a pluralistic world.
Echoing Hoffmann, Lake argued that the significant growth
in political and economic interdependence and the
dispersion of international power in the wake of
decolonization and the emergence of the non-aligned
movement had helped to inaugurate a newly diverse world.[36]
It was the task of the United States to participate "in the
construction of a pluralistic world order in which all
states, of necessity, must join."[37] In addition to
supporting its security alliances, upon which world peace
would continue to rest, the United States was obliged to
assist in the construction of new "global coalitions, . . .
which will be in constant motion, coming together on one

issue, but moving apart on another. Any state will belong
to many different coalitions, with loyalties and interests
that cut across traditional lines."[38] Fortunately, this
post-Vietnam role was neatly tailored to the nation's
domestic strengths: "No other people has so well learned
the workings of a pluralist world and the political skills
needed to keep it working. No other nation is composed of
such diverse groups and shifting coalitions as the United
States. Our domestic tradition is now our greatest
international asset."[39] In effect, Lake pledged the Carter
administration to an enormously ambitious program
underwritten by the unique domestic attributes of the
United States.

Yet if the size of the agenda was impressively large,
the number of foreign policy instruments that the United
States might employ to achieve these goals was more limited
than at any other time since World War II. Indeed, in its
apparent unwillingness to use or threaten military force,
the Carter administration shared more with Herbert Hoover
than with the Kennedy New Frontier, although after mid-1978
Zbigniew Brzezinski and most of the National Security
Council (NSC) staff became noticeably more enthusiastic
about the utility of military power than their State
Department colleagues.

Carter's world order policy was given coherence by the
concepts of complexity and change. Frequently
administration spokespersons articulated these notions and
applied them to the entire fabric of U.S. diplomacy. In
East-West relations, complexity implied a multidimensional
approach geared to both competition and cooperation with
Moscow. In a North-South context, it emphasized the wide
range of global issues that needed to become part of a
negotiating agenda. Brzezinski, Cyrus Vance, and other
senior officials continually noted that the world was now
one of unprecedented change and that the central task was
for the United States to become constructively relevant to
this new reality. Such a policy ostensibly required great
sensitivity to deep historical trends and forces lest the
chaotic nature of daily events become overwhelming.

U.S.-Caribbean Relations

The Carter administration's early Caribbean initiative
certainly reflected its world order instincts. Indeed,
much of its Caribbean agenda had been anticipated in two
reports issued in 1974 and 1976 by the blue-ribbon

Commission on United States–Latin American relations,
chaired by Sol M. Linowitz and prominently advised by
Hoffmann.[40]

The 1974 report, entitled "The Americas in a Changing
World," began with the assertion that "the United States
should change its basic approach to Latin America and the
Caribbean."[41] Dramatic global and regional transformations
had combined to undermine the assumptions that had governed
U.S. policy in the Americas since the Monroe Doctrine. A
revised hemispheric policy had to reflect four new regional
conditions. First, "Latin American countries are and will
remain extremely diverse in their ideologies, political
systems, economic systems, and levels of development."
Second, these nations "are playing and will continue to
play increasingly active and independent roles in
international organizations and other arenas of world
politics." Third, "nonhemispheric states will play
increasingly important roles in Latin American affairs."
And fourth, "the principal issues of U.S. policy towards
Latin America will increasingly be issues which are not
peculiar to U.S.–Latin American relations but rather
involve global economic and political relationships."[42]
The Linowitz commission then made thirty-three
recommendations dealing with political, cultural, and
economic issues. For example, it declared:

- The United States should refrain from unilateral
  military interventions and should cease covert
  interventions in the internal affairs of hemispheric
  states.
- The United States should take concrete steps to
  strengthen its commitment to human rights in the
  region.
- The United States should take the initiative in
  seeking a more normal relationship with Cuba by
  ending its trade embargo, dropping travel
  restrictions, encouraging non-official exchanges,
  and, depending on Cuban responses, should consider
  the renewal of diplomatic relations.
- The United States should sign and ratify a new
  Panama Canal Treaty.
- The United States should encourage conventional arms
  limitation agreements among supplier and consumer
  nations, should terminate grant military assistance
  programs and Military Assistance Advisory Groups in
  Latin America, and should not actively encourage the
  purchase of arms by Latin American countries.

- The United States should abandon the threat or application of unilateral measures of economic coercion against Latin American states.
- The United States should ease its restrictions against Latin American exports and should liberalize and multilateralize its economic assistance programs.

The report concluded that the countries of Latin America and the Caribbean should no longer be treated as a U.S. "sphere of influence" and insulated from extrahemispheric relationships. The "realities of global interdependence" require that the United States not "neglect, exploit, or patronize its hemispheric neighbors." "Justice and decency, not disparities in wealth and power should be the guiding forces in hemispheric relations," as the critical issues of "economic and political security in an uncertain world" replaced military security as the focus of mutual concerns.[43]

Jimmy Carter and his advisers evinced great sympathy for many of the Linowitz commission's assumptions and recommendations, and in August 1977 the administration created an interagency Caribbean task force composed of fifteen different offices and agencies. In October 1977 the task force made the following recommendations:

- Encourage greater regional cooperation in the Caribbean to build links among the countries which will increase political stability;
- Strengthen the multilateral framework for assistance for the area so that assistance can be used more efficiently, constructively, and systematically;
- Encourage the IFIs [international financial institutions], especially the World Bank, to play a leading role in this effort;
- Use foreign assistance for development as the key building block for cooperation among the Caribbean nations and for multilateralizing their relationships with outside countries;
- Support a major increase in U.S. assistance to the area;
- Recognize that this assistance must be more comprehensive than the AID [Agency for International Development] worldwide concentration on health, education, nutrition, and agriculture for the poorest groups.[44]

In addition, the Carter administration repeatedly stressed its firm commitment to democratic practices and human rights, its acceptance of ideological pluralism, and its respect for the national sovereignty of all Caribbean states.[45]

Early in his term President Carter sent his wife, Rosalynn Carter, Secretary of State Cyrus Vance, and United Nations Ambassador Andrew Young, on trips to the Caribbean to underscore his determination to give the region a new priority; the quality of U.S. diplomatic representation in the Caribbean was upgraded as career professionals replaced party loyalists; and steps were taken to implement many of the Linowitz and Caribbean task force recommendations. In the economic realm the Carter administration helped launch the Caribbean Group for Co-operation in Economic Development, a consortium of some thirty donor and recipient nations under World Bank auspices and including eleven international and regional organizations. By 1979 the U.S. contribution to the Caribbean group had reached $612 million, while additional development assistance and food aid climbed from about $70 million in 1976 to $130 million three years later, making the Caribbean the highest per capita recipient of U.S. aid of all developing areas. Furthermore, the multilateral nature of much of this assistance eliminated ideological affinity as a criterion for these programs. Politically, President Carter moved to initiate a dialogue with Cuba (as well as other Communist states like Vietnam). Before long the U.S. Department of State ended its ban on travel to Cuba, granted visas to Cuban citizens, established an interest section in the Swiss Embassy in Havana and allowed Castro to have one in Washington, opened discussions about airplane hijackings, drug traffic, and offshore rescue operations, negotiated the release of some political prisoners from Cuban jails, and allowed U.S.-Cuban trade through third parties.

Similarly, whereas the Nixon and Ford administrations had "punished" Jamaica's Michael Manley for his warm ties with Castro and for his espousal of socialism, Jimmy Carter took steps to ease U.S.-Jamaican relations. Rosalynn Carter, Andrew Young, and Assistant Secretary of State for Inter-American Affairs Terence Todman visited Manley. Soon Jamaica agreed to the demands of the International Monetary Fund (IMF) for budgetary austerity and higher domestic prices in return for a loan, and the Carter administration responded by including the island in the new Caribbean group assistance mechanism. In late 1977 Manley even visited the White House where he was enthusiastically welcomed.

Conflicting Outlooks and Priorities in the Carter Administration

But these world order initiatives, both globally and in the Caribbean, became increasingly difficult for the Carter administration to sustain. The rhetoric of world order politics had from the beginning only partly submerged differences among Carter's advisers, and by 1978 they threatened to paralyze U.S. foreign policy. Personalities aside—though they were important—Andrew Young, Zbigniew Brzezinski and Cyrus Vance had significant intellectual disagreements.[46] For Young, the idealist, the U.S. commitment to human rights had to be absolute, the ultimate goal of the U.S. was the elimination of all nuclear weapons, and a humane foreign policy required openness and honesty. He tenaciously opposed viewing Third World countries and movements "as pawns in the U.S.-Soviet rivalry—a policy he branded as a form of racist condescension—and argued instead for giving the benefit of the doubt to Third World 'progressives' as people whose judgements about their own interests should be respected,"[47] even if they accepted Cuban and Russian assistance. Thus Young, an old friend of Michael Manley, was untroubled by Jamaica's Havana connection and saw the Caribbean region—"with its relatively high level of education, democratic political traditions, and natural waterways for trade—as part of a Third World 'growth engine' for the American economy."[48]

Brzezinski agreed with Young that the United States should put itself on the "right side of change" in the Third World, but he had different reasons for doing so, for "he tended to shape his human rights and Third World policies to serve the geopolitical imperatives of the U.S.-Soviet competition rather than as ends in themselves."[49] The Soviet Union lay at the center of Brzezinski's world, and he insisted on linking detente to Soviet behavior in Africa and in the Gulf and the Mideast even to the point of threatening Moscow with a Sino-American alliance.

Vance, perhaps more deeply affected by Vietnam than any other of Carter's senior advisers, had grown "skeptical of grand designs, reformist or geopolitical, urging rather that each international situation be examined on a case-by-case basis."[50] By deemphasizing the centrality of U.S.-Soviet relations, Vance favored quiet diplomacy to deal with countries "'on the merits' of the particular needs of each country and the capacity of the United States

to relate to these needs."[51] Although he was not unmindful
of Soviet expansionism, he believed that the prudent use of
U.S. economic assistance to support indigenous nationalisms
would frustrate Soviet designs without damaging superpower
relations.

In short, Carter's world order approach was threatened
with incoherence from these distinct outlooks.
Furthermore, the administration was thrown more and more on
the defensive by two sets of developments. First, an
increasingly vociferous and influential group of
"neoconservative" critics mounted a powerful assault on
Carter's brand of post-Vietnam "appeasement." Carl
Gershman, later to become a top aide to Jeane Kirkpatrick,
leveled a typical attack in the July 1980 issue of
Commentary.[52] There he claimed that the practitioners of
world order politics (and he included Brzezinski in this
group) constituted a new foreign policy establishment
allegedly committed to the repudiation of postwar U.S.
diplomacy and the total rejection of containment. This
cabal had "devalued the importance of national-security
concerns . . . , saturating American foreign policy with
defeatism masquerading as optimism and 'maturity' and
'restraint'" while "cravenly following international
political fashion" and condoning virtually any Soviet
action.[53] Composed mostly of members of the Cold War
foreign policy establishment who had lost their nerve in
the wake of Vietnam; radical intellectuals who prized
equality more than liberty even if the price was
totalitarianism; and neo-Wilsonian academics and foreign
policy analysts who wished to breathe new purpose into a
nation staggered by Vietnam and Watergate, this elite,
according to Gershman, formed the core of a
"liberal-populist" governing coalition "wherein a Southern
President who campaigned as a populist staffed his
foreign-policy bureaucracy with members of . . . the new
foreign policy establishment."[54]

Ostensibly wracked by guilt and paralyzed by
tendencies that bordered on isolationism and appeasement,
the group held the conviction that military force was no
longer a suitable foreign policy instrument for the United
States. Rejecting the bases of thirty years of U.S.
foreign policy--the containment of communism and the
"lessons of Munich"--this new elite embraced the lessons of
Vietnam as the foundation of a new U.S. diplomacy. And
from the primary Vietnam lesson--that containment was
counterproductive, unfeasible, and unnecessary--this
establishment, Gershman claimed, drew several corollaries.

First, world order must replace national security as the
organizing concept of U.S. diplomacy. Second, the United
States should adopt an attitude of equanimity toward
changes in the world that previously would have been
considered injurious to its interests. Third, because the
Soviet Union was essentially a status quo power, U.S.
foreign policy ought not to be preoccupied with relations
with Moscow. Fourth, to avoid isolation in a world filled
with revolutionary change, the United States had to learn
to become more flexible and less ideological in its
dealings with the Third World. Finally, U.S. moral
strength, rather than a primary reliance on military power,
should be used to help alleviate global problems: e.g.,
hunger, racial hatred, and the arms race. Neoconservative
thrusts of this kind enjoyed important parainstitutional
elite support as organizations like the Committee on the
Present Danger and the American Security Council became
unrelenting critics of the Carter foreign policy record.[55]

The second set of developments that threatened
Carter's world policy concerned Brzezinski's fears, which
seemed to gain progressively greater vindication as the
Soviet Union, with Cuban support in some cases, showed more
of an appetite for Third World "adventurism." By 1978 the
national security adviser was able to discern an "arc of
crisis" stretching from the Horn of Africa to the Persian
Gulf, and by the next year the arc had reached Iran and
Afghanistan. In early 1980 Brzezinski, explicitly invoking
the Truman Doctrine as a model, persuaded Carter to issue
his own doctrine for the Gulf. The SALT II Treaty, which
the president had come to defend as a rearmament
opportunity, was withdrawn from Senate consideration, and
Carter fought Edward M. Kennedy for the Democratic
nomination as a hard-liner more in the mold of Harry Truman
than George McGovern.

Not surprisingly, the Carter administration's
Caribbean policy began to reflect its altered global
priorities. From the beginning Carter and his advisers had
hoped that the initial steps taken to normalize Cuban-U.S.
relations would eventually lead to a withdrawal of Havana's
armed forces from Angola. Not only did Cuban troops remain
there, but in January 1978 they were sent to Ethiopia as
well in order to turn back the Somali invasion of the
Ogaden. Brzezinski seized on this action as evidence that
Castro, far from desiring rapprochement with Washington,
had fully joined the ranks of Soviet adventurers. Later
that year U.S. intelligence found that Moscow had supplied
Cuba with a squadron of new MG-23s, which were capable of

carrying nuclear weapons. The Soviets assured Washington that they would not be so equipped, but President Carter ordered the resumption of aerial-photo reconnaissance missions over Cuba.

Then, in September 1979, at the height of the SALT II ratification debate, Foreign Relations Committee Chairman Frank Church released information that indicated the presence of a Soviet "combat brigade" in Cuba. Brzezinski and his staff wanted Carter to demand that the Russians withdraw their troops and to use the occasion to condemn Cuban and Soviet actions in the Third World. But after initially reacting with alarm to the reports, President Carter in a nationwide address sought to detach the issue from SALT. Conceding that the brigade "contributes to tension in the Caribbean and the Central American region" and "raises the level of the responsibility that the Soviet Union must take for escalating Cuban military actions abroad," Carter argued that "this is not a large force, nor an assault force. It presents no direct threat to us. It has no airborne or seaborne capability. In contrast to the 1962 crisis, no nuclear threat to the U.S. is involved." He declared that the Soviets had assured him that the troops would not be used in a combat role, but that he had ordered additional surveillance of Cuba to monitor the brigade and had expanded regular U.S. military maneuvers in the Caribbean. The president ended by noting that "the brigade issue is certainly no reason for a return to the Cold War."[56] Notwithstanding these reassurances, however, the clumsy and contradictory handling of the issue further worsened relations with Cuba and signaled a shift in administration rhetoric as the Caribbean now became a trouble spot.

The Nicaraguan revolution also presented Carter with a dilemma. Since early 1977 Washington had alternately reprimanded and rewarded the government of Anastasio Somoza Debayle for its human rights record. Conservative critics like Jeane Kirkpatrick claimed that the aid cutoffs had "destabilized" Somoza by bolstering the waning morale of the Sandinista rebels; liberal human rights activists argued that the aid resumptions had demoralized moderate opponents and driven them in desperation into an alliance with the radicals. In any event, by September 1978 Nicaragua had become thoroughly polarized, and for the first time in twenty years the United States faced the real prospect of the overthrow of a Latin American government by left-wing guerrillas.

In its search for a response to the Nicaraguan revolution, the Carter administration found four courses of action open in principle: (1) the rapid abandonment of Somoza, the quick recognition of the Sandinistas (while still belligerents), and the adoption of a generous economic and military aid program for the rebels; (2) a posture of genuine disinterest on the grounds that the outcome of the Nicaraguan civil war did not threaten the vital interests of the United States; (3) a policy of staunch support (including military assistance) for Somoza to help ensure the defeat or moderation of the Sandinistas; and (4) an attempt to steer a "middle course" between Somoza and the Sandinistas by identifying and encouraging popular and pliant moderates. The evidence shows, however, that the Carter administration seriously considered only the latter two policy options. Its ultimate adoption of the "search for moderates" alternative indicated a willingness to follow a quite traditional U.S. policy of "liberal interventionism," a policy that was unusual only in the clumsiness of its implementation.

A few NSC staffers apparently would have preferred a more conservative course entailing substantial aid and strong moral support for Somoza in a manner reminiscent of the Eisenhower administration's treatment of the Castillo Armas regime in Guatemala, but in light of Carter's censure of Somoza's human rights record, such actions would, if nothing else, have raised even more questions about the administration's consistency. Furthermore, many advisers firmly believed with Stanley Hoffmann that the United States "had to get on the right side of change," and, if it was hard to embrace the Sandinistas, so too was it difficult to cradle Somoza. Many officials, especially in the State Department, had been outraged by Nixon's support of Augusto Pinochet in Chile and were determined to avoid a replication of that situation. What ensued, therefore, was a halting, unsteady, and increasingly unrealistic search for a "moderate" alternative to the Left and the Right. When this search failed, Secretary Vance embarked on a futile last-ditch, Dominican-like effort to send an OAS "peacekeeping" force to Nicaragua.

It was not until after the fall of Somoza that members of the administration became concerned about avoiding "another Cuba." As one senior State Department official put it, "There was quite a lot of likening of this situation in Cuba in 1959. The lessons that liberals have learned from Cuba is that you don't force them into the hands of the Soviets, although even some liberals in

government would say that Castro probably had this up his
sleeve the whole time. . . . I think that people were
conscious of not letting this be a second Cuba."[57] Not
that the Sandinistas were greeted with enthusiasm even by
the State Department: "Nobody was pleased. It was clearly
a defeat for U.S. policy. But there was probably a sense
that . . . we were acting . . . in a mature way by
ultimately accepting the fait accompli. There were some
younger FSOs [foreign service officers] in the Latin
American Bureau who did look on the Sandinistas as maybe
not so bad, but none was in a policy position."[58]

It was this decision to "get on the right side of
change," if only after the fact, that distinguished the
Carter administration's policy during the postrevolutionary
phase. Far from reflecting a "revisionist" understanding
of U.S.-Latin American relations, this approach to
Nicaragua was "profoundly interventionist,"[59] very
sensitive to East-West ramifications, favorably impressed
(at least in June 1979) by the lessons of the Dominican
episode, and only belatedly aware of the Cuban analogy.
Nevertheless, to Jeane Kirkpatrick, soon to become
President Reagan's ambassador to the United Nations,
Carter's misplaced desire to avoid a second Cuba
constituted "a posture of continuous self-abasement and
apology vis-a-vis the Third World" that was "neither
morally necessary, nor politically appropriate."[60] Instead
of vigorously supporting Somoza, admittedly an autocrat but
also a firm friend of the United States, the Carter
administration allegedly adopted "an oddly uncompromising
posture" in dealing with him, "even though the State
Department knew that the top Sandinista leaders had close
personal ties and were in continuing contact with
Havana."[61] Kirkpatrick claimed that the administration had
forsaken a traditional understanding of the national
interest in order to impose on Nicaragua a "deterministic
and apolitical" theory of modernization that justified
(indeed demanded) U.S. passivity in the face of
"complicated, inexorable, impersonal processes."[62]

The Carter administration's Nicaraguan policy was, in
fact, far from passive. In its long and unsuccessful
search for a "democratic" alternative it became deeply
enmeshed in Nicaraguan politics. If, in the end, it rushed
to be on the "right side of change," this dash was largely
an exercise in damage control and hardly signified a new
definition of the national interest despite Hoffmann's
claim that the old one had become obsolete. Guided in its
course by doubts about Eisenhower's handling of Castro, its

admiration of Johnson's decisive Dominican intervention,
and a determination to prevent transforming Somoza into
another Pinochet, the Carter administration pursued a
rather traditional, if liberal, policy that was unusual
only insofar as it never seriously contemplated the use of
military force to achieve a solution.[63] The refusal to
consider military intervention had more to do with Vietnam,
however, than with Nicaragua.

Events in Grenada: 1979

The nearly bloodless coup d'etat that ousted the
Grenada government of Eric Gairy on March 13, 1979,
occurred within the context of heightened sensitivity to
Cuban activities in Africa and the Caribbean, yet the
Carter administration's reaction to Maurice Bishop and the
New Jewel Movement (NJM) was initially ambivalent. Many in
the State Department's Bureau of Inter-American Affairs had
been appalled by Gairy's human rights record, which
included the frequent use of his so-called Mongoose Gang to
assault and occasionally kill his opponents. Indeed, these
thugs had severely beaten Bishop and had murdered his
father, Rupert. Though technically a democratically
elected leader of a Westminster-type regime, Gairy,
according to the British commission of enquiry, had rigged
the 1976 elections and generally trampled on constitutional
procedures (see Chapter 2, note 12). In the words of one
State Department official he "was a blemish not only on the
face of Grenada, but also on the Caribbean. [His]
departure was probably a blessing for Grenada. It is
unfortunate that his removal was by extraconstitutional
means but, let's face it, this is probably the only way he
would have gone."[64]
The U.S. embassy in Barbardos, with accreditation to
all the small states of the eastern Caribbean, had had
contact with Bishop for many years. Indeed, a week before
the coup Ambassador Frank V. Ortiz wrote the following
letter to him:

The President's Day reception on February 19, 1979
. . . is a fresh, pleasant memory made especially so
by the honor now accorded us by your presence. Your
words on the quality of democratic ideals in Grenada
and your obvious respect for legitimate opposition
suited the spirit of the occasion perfectly. I know
all were inspired by the expression of your firm

intention to assure the protection and welfare of
Americans and their property.[65]

And according to Ortiz, in telephone conversations held
with Bishop immediately after the coup, the new prime
minister "solemnly assured me that U.S. lives and property
would be protected, that good relations with the United
States were a basic aim of his government, and that there
would be prompt and free election of a legally constituted
government."[66]

The State Department was simultaneously pleased with
the opportunity to try and get on "the right side of
change" in Grenada and relieved to see the tyrant Gairy
ousted, but concerned that Cuba may have helped Bishop take
power and worried lest the left-leaning New Jewel Movement
begin to move close to Havana. Relations between
Washington and Bishop, however, began to deteriorate
immediately. The ambassador, the embassy economic officer,
an AID representative, and the U.S. consul met several
times with Bishop and his ministers. According to Ortiz,
"Bishop was advised that the U.S. accepted his assurances
and wanted good relations."[67] The U.S. officials outlined
the details of previously approved Caribbean Development
Bank (CDB) funds for Grenada, reassured Bishop that his
government would receive them--plus additional money for
agricultural research pending his agreement--but cautioned
that this was slow-disbursing assistance. Ortiz also
advised him that "for quick impact in the interim the
embassy could immediately make available . . . several
grants from the Special Development Activities (SDA)
fund"[68] of $5,000 each for small-scale community-initiated
projects. Bishop expressed interest in the CDB, the SDA
grants, and in keeping the Peace Corps, but "in all our
meetings he was noncommittal about discussion of new U.S.
assistance and never responded to my urgings that he
initiate specific talks with us."[69]

By early April the U.S. embassy in Barbados already
saw disturbing signs. On April 7 eight Cubans had
surreptitiously entered Grenada; on April 9 the Guyanese
ship _Jaimito_ delivered Cuban arms hidden in rice; that same
day PRG soldiers fired at a small private plane over the
main tourist beach; and on April 14 arms arrived from Cuba
by sea.[70] During this time, according to Ambassador Ortiz,
"Grenada was in a state of ferment induced by Bishop's wild
allegations that U.S. assassination squads were after him
and that deposed Prime Minister Gairy and a mercenary army
was poised to invade Grenada."[71] On April 10 Ortiz met

separately with Deputy Prime Minister Bernard Coard and
Bishop. Ortiz allegedly told Coard that firing on private
planes would not be a help to Grenadian tourism. Three
days later Bishop condemned U.S. "threats" to the tourist
industry.

Ortiz said that Washington had directed him to raise
eleven points with the prime minister. Ortiz assured
Bishop that the U.S. Neutrality Act guaranteed that Gairy
could not invade Grenada from the United States, provided
evidence to show that Gairy was in San Diego, and asked
Bishop to make this information public. Bishop allegedly
refused. Ortiz also "pressed Bishop again on elections and
reviewed specific offers of economic assistance."[72] Bishop
promised to send representatives to the U.S. embassy in
Barbados to discuss aid but never did. According to Ortiz,
during the next few weeks the PRG "avoided several
occasions to consult on assistance."[73] Bishop subsequently
portrayed this meeting solely as an attempt by the United
States to prevent him from receiving Cuban assistance while
at the same time refusing his desperate pleas for military
aid. Ortiz, however, claimed that only one of his eleven
points concerned Cuba, and he allegedly told Bishop that
"Grenada's relationship with the United States and its
island neighbors would be complicated if it developed close
ties with Cuba."[74] Although it is not surprising that
Bishop interpreted Ortiz's statement as an unwarranted
infringement on Grenadian sovereignty, Bishop's expectation
that the Carter administration would arm him against a
Gairy countercoup was exceedingly naive. The PRG was
extended diplomatic recognition after Bishop promised
CARICOM that early elections would be held.

By the summer of 1979 the PRG had clearly become a
"problem" for middle-level officials at the State
Department. For instance, in late July, when Deputy
Assistant Secretary for Inter-American Affairs John A.
Bushnell testified before Congress on the administration's
eastern Caribbean policy,[75] he focused on Grenada. Noting
that until the mid-1970s Cuba had played a negligible role
in the Caribbean, Bushnell argued that although Havana had
no master plan for expanding its regional influence, it
(like Moscow) took advantage of targets of opportunity as
in Jamaica, Guyana, and, most recently, Grenada. Following
the March coup Cuba had "moved quickly to respond to
Grenadian requests for security assistance and now has a
significant presence" there. Bushnell added that there
also appeared to be "a drawing together of young radicals
and radical movements in the Caribbean, encouraged by the

recent events in Grenada and perhaps also by Cuban
leadership." Describing the young leaders of the New Jewel
Movement as influenced "as much by the black power and
antiwar movements in the United States as by the precepts
of world communism," the deputy assistant secretary stated
repeatedly that the United States had "no evidence that the
Cubans were directly involved in the coup, although they
may have had prior knowledge of it." In order to protect
itself against "real or imagined" internal and external
threats, Bishop turned to Cuba and Guyana for help, and
"we, in turn became concerned about the growing Cuban
presence in Grenada."

Bushnell noted that the U.S. ambassador had visited
Grenada "in the last two days, and our relations may be
improving." He reminded the subcommittee members that U.S.
assistance was disbursed through the Caribbean Development
Bank on a nondiscriminatory basis and said that he expected
Grenada to continue to receive these funds. But,
significantly, Bushnell acknowledged the administration had
gradually concluded that such programs by themselves--
constructed without regard to political and ideological
considerations--were "not sufficient to protect U.S.
interests or address emergent problems." The nation's
Caribbean friends had been sidestepped in favor of
recipients like Jamiaca and Guyana with which "we have had
some important differences in political and ideological
outlook."

Furthermore, Bushnell contended that the Grenadian
coup and several attempted coups in Dominica and St. Lucia
had "triggered concern among Caribbean leaders themselves
about the security of the region, and led them to approach
us and others for help." Although legislative restrictions
and limited resources had allegedly hindered the
administration's security efforts, Bushnell announced that
increases in regional military training and arms sales were
being considered along with a proposal for a coast guard
under the auspices of the newly formed Organization of
Eastern Caribbean States.

The hoped-for improved U.S. ties with Grenada did not,
however, materialize. According to Sally A. Shelton,
nominated as Carter's ambassador to Barbados, Grenada,
Dominica, St. Vincent, and St. Lucia on April 13, 1979,
although the administration initially wanted "to try to
work with, rather than against, the PRG," three major
issues proved irresolvable: economic assistance, the
extradition of Eric Gairy, and the extradition of two
Grenadian gunrunners.[76] Despite the fact that the PRG "was

told repeatedly that substantial amounts of U.S. aid were
in fact flowing into Grenada "through the Caribbean Group
the Bishop Government chose to perpetuate the myth that it
had been offered only $5,000." Second, Ambassador Shelton
stated that she had explained U.S. extradition procedures
to Bishop, but found to her "dismay" that the PRG
subsequently submitted as evidence against Gairy a brief
that largely consisted of newspaper clippings.
Furthermore, when Shelton took the unusual step of offering
to send a State Department legal specialist to help Bishop
prepare a stronger extradition case, the prime minister
fobbed the official off on "a middle-level functionary with
no real authority." Nevertheless, the PRG continued to
castigate Washington for refusing to cooperate in
extraditing Gairy.

Finally, when the March 13 coup occurred, two
Grenadians were arrested in Baltimore and charged with
illegally exporting arms from the United States to Grenada.
The PRG continually demanded their release, but Shelton
explained to Bishop that the State Department could not put
pressure on the U.S. judicial system. Subsequently,
Grenada jailed a U.S. citizen living on the island and
suggested that she would be released if the two Grenadians
in Baltimore were allowed to return. Ambassador Shelton
viewed it as a "a hostage situation"--a view that was
strengthened by the quick release of the U.S. citizen after
the Grenadians jumped bond and left the United States.
Shelton grew "extremely skeptical" that "a more sustained
experiment with a positive U.S. policy would have
succeeded," but she remained convinced that "we should have
tried, if for no other reason than it might have convinced
our friends and allies that we were willing to try to work
with revolutionary change and would work against it only as
a last resort after all else had failed."

Notwithstanding Shelton's preferences, however, the
Carter administration soon began to distance itself from
Bishop. Indeed, Brzezinski's first reaction to the coup
had been briefly to consider blockading Grenada,[77] and soon
he began to see the entire region as a "circle of crisis."
Some officials began to worry about "the possibility of
upheaval producing radically inclined regimes on the
smaller islands that might spread to larger countries like
Jamaica, Haiti, and the Dominican Republic and balkanize
the region with antagonistic political and economic
systems."[78] According to one Carter adviser in mid-1979,
"There's not an island in the Caribbean that couldn't go
the way of Grenada within five years."[79] Beyond these

geopolitical concerns Carter officials grew increasingly
disturbed by the PRG's human rights behavior as the
government suspended the constitution and the parliament,
detained about one hundred political prisoners, shut down
the only independent newspaper, suspended the write of
habeus corpus, and refused to schedule elections. At the
same time Bishop and his representatives frequently and
loudly denounced the United States in international forums.
Then in early 1980 Grenada refused to condemn the Soviet
invasion of Afghanistan at the United Nations.

It was this action, at a time when Washington was busy
looking for ways to punish the Soviet Union, that
apparently led the Carter administration to reduce official
contact with Grenada. The State Department had never
accepted the credentials of Grenadian Ambassador-designate
Dessima Williams, but now it constrained Sally Shelton from
visiting Grenada, though she met several more times with
Bishop in Barbados. Yet overwhelmed as it was with Iran,
Afghanistan, and Ronald Reagan, the administration never
viewed Grenada as a major issue. Neither the president nor
his secretaries of state ever made public statements about
it; Grenada was handled at the assistant secretary level.

Thus if the international shocks and domestic
political attacks of 1978 and 1979 had moved Carter's
Caribbean policy some distance away from its early world
order initiatives, the administration never fully embraced
the "Cuba-phobia" of its predecessors. Even in 1980 the
State Department's director of Cuban affairs was able to
assure Congress that "the Sandinista movement was and is
basically an indigenous movement with roots in Nicaragua.
While Cuban support was important to the FSLN [National
Sandinista Liberation Front] it was but one element in the
equation that produced Somoza's downfall."[80] Similarly,
the administration, while troubled by Grenada's close Cuban
ties and human rights abuses, did not believe the PRG
represented a serious threat to the eastern Caribbean.[81]

7
Reagan, "Neocontainment," and the Caribbean

The Neoconservatives and Foreign Policy

If the Carter administration's early Caribbean initiatives reflected the general concepts of world order politics and the specific recommendations of the Linowitz commission, Reagan's early approach to the region embodied the anti-Communist weltanschauung of neoconservative intellectuals like Jeane Kirkpatrick, Norman Podhoretz, Paul H. Nitze, and Eugene V. Rostow, and the more detailed advice of the Sante Fe committee.

According to Podhoretz, by 1980 the United States had been in moral and material decline for well over a decade. The failure in Vietnam, the nonreciprocal nature of detente, Watergate and the subsequent crippling of the presidency, the pathetic responses to OPEC and Third World radicalism, and, most importantly, the U.S. inability and unwillingness to counter the massive Soviet arms buildup were but the most dramatic examples of a profound and pervasive erosion of U.S. power. This decline had to be seen as part of a more general deterioration of traditional liberal values. As blacks, homosexuals, other minorities, and women sought rights through such devices as affirmative action, illiberal extremism replaced liberal democracy as the reigning intellectual ideology. The family became fragmented, traditional religions were eclipsed, pornography and drugs became middle-class entertainments, a psychoanalytic elite emerged, and a political culture of appeasement gripped the nation, according to Podhoretz. Anti-Communist containment, grounded in liberal, internationalist values and a progressive economy, had been assaulted by the "neo-isolationism, Malthusianism, and redistributionist egalitarianism"[1] of McGovernism and its friends. Instead of refurbishing containment to deal effectively with a now strategically superior Soviet Union, successive U.S. administrations had pursued a policy of detente verging on appeasement.

Podhoretz correctly realized that before any president could again seriously consider anti-Communist containment, the country's collective memory of Vietnam would have to be revised. The Carter administration had allegedly been incredibly naive about the war's anticipated effects, for instead of the pluralistic and complex world the administration had so confidently predicted, a much simpler, bleaker, and more traditional reality had emerged. Despite the undeniable growth of interdependence in the West and polycentrism in the East, the world remained essentially bipolar with one crucial change: Now the Soviet Union exercised strategic superiority, while the United States seemed unwilling and increasingly unable to use its military power. Moreover, the domestic attitudes produced by the war—an antidefense outlook, a "hypermorality" that judged the United States and its leaders by a double standard, and an apparently unshakable psychological malaise—had underwritten a shocking decline in U.S. military capabilities.[2]

Podhoretz and allies like Carl Gershman identified other problems as well. All of Southeast Asia had succumbed to an unspeakably barbaric form of communism: South Vietnam was transformed into a gulag, Cambodia became a vast Auschwitz, and Vietnamese imperialism threatened to engulf Thailand.[3] Faced with peril and unable to rely on a paralyzed United States for help, the remaining free states of the region might be forced to come to terms with Hanoi. Nations in other parts of the world also felt the crush of the totalitarian boot: Angola, South Yemen, Ethiopia, Afghanistan, and Nicaragua were now ruled by unsavory regimes that owed their power, directly or indirectly, to the U.S. defeat in Vietnam. Yet despite this disastrous series of setbacks, the Carter administration evidently continued to fear the exercise of U.S. power and believed that its emasculation would prevent future Vietnams.[4]

Podhoretz had grown increasingly optimistic that "the culture of appeasement," allegedly sustained by the Carter administration, could soon be swept away by a "new nationalism." In April 1980 Irving Kristol contended that "what we are witnessing is a powerful nationalist revival in this nation, a revival that coincides with the twitching deaththroes of an American foreign policy that has always regarded American nationalism more as a problem than as an ally."[5] Nevertheless, Podhoretz feared that despite several promising signs the new nationalism did not yet possess a moral core, for the nation's grass-roots responses to outrages like Iran and Afghanistan had been muted by selfish economic considerations. Before a real policy of containment could be inaugurated, "communism" had to be readmitted to the U.S. political vocabulary. Only then, Podhoretz warned, would the people recognize that the conflict with the Soviet Union was a "struggle for freedom and against Communism."[6]

But he did detect in the public mood the first stirrings of a "repressed strain of internationalist idealism," which could launch the nation on a new Wilsonian crusade to make the 1980s safe for democracy. The neoconservatives, however, professed not to be mere populists. Kristol, for example, observed that "precisely because it lacked intellectual guidance and articulation, popular sentiment on foreign affairs has frequently degenerated into crude chauvinism, isolation, or even downright paranoia."[7] To avoid these "democratic excesses" the United States allegedly needed a new foreign policy establishment, dedicated not to a world order ideology that shunned the use of force but, rather, committed to a nationalist perspective, intent on reasserting U.S. global leadership. Reagan's landslide victory demonstrated to Podhoretz the existence of a new and powerful consensus that demanded actions significantly more assertive than even Carter's post-Afghanistan initiatives and that could serve as the intellectual basis for a new foreign policy establishment.[8] Vietnam, according to Podhoretz, had actually proven that public support was "impossible to maintain in the absence of a convincing moral rationale for our effort there."[9] Having intervened in Vietnam

for idealistic reasons (in the strict sense that there was no vital geopolitical or material interest at stake, and that what we were actually trying to do was save the South Vietnamese from the horrors of Communist rule that have now befallen them), we tried to justify our involvement in the language of Realpolitik. But no good case could be made in that language for American military intervention; and even if it could, it would not in the long run have convinced the American people.[10]

Likewise, "the Nixon, Ford, and Carter Administrations robbed the Soviet-American conflict of the moral and political dimension for the sake of which sacrifices could be intelligibly demanded by the government and willingly made by the people."[11] Thus, "a strategy of containment centered on considerations of _Realpolitik_ would be unable to count indefinitely on popular support. Sooner or later (probably sooner rather than later) it would succumb to a resurgence of isolationism, leaving a free field for the expansion of Soviet power."[12] What was required, therefore, was "a strategy aimed at containing the expansion of Communism."[13] Only such a policy could satisfy the new consensus and slow the growth of Soviet power.

But would not a new strategy of anti-Communist containment run the risk of future Vietnams? Podhoretz admitted the possibility but thought it remote for three reasons. First, to reject such a policy for its alleged indiscriminate interventionism was a bit like the "Pope in Latin America warning people who have only just begun to afford wearing shoes about the dangers of consumerism and rampant materialism."[14] A country suffering from a decade-long paralysis need not yet worry about more Vietnams. Second, the "rule of prudence," although not able to guarantee absolutely against future Vietnams, would offer a good deal of protection against rash U.S. behavior. Eisenhower, for instance, had eschewed intervention in Indochina in 1954 while remaining faithful to global containment. Thus, Podhoretz's version of anti-Communist containment, in direct contrast to the Johnson-Dean Rusk formulation, would apparently allow U.S. presidents "to pick and choose" where and where not to intervene. What such exercises in realpolitik would do to the moral core of his preferred strategy or to public support for it remained unclear. After all, could Johnson have refused to intervene in Vietnam and still preserved the Cold War consensus that had legitimated anti-Communist containment? And had not Eisenhower's "prudent" decision of 1954 merely laid the entire problem in Kennedy's lap? Furthermore, Podhoretz's rule of prudence bore an ironic resemblance to orthodoxy's chief lesson of Vietnam: It seemed to accept Stanley Hoffmann's conclusion that the United States had tragically neglected local circumstances in Vietnam. In short, the intervention in Vietnam had been imprudent. Third (and this point was only implied by Podhoretz), perhaps another massive, anti-Communist intervention would not be an unalloyed disaster. The United States, after all, might have won in Vietnam if not for self-imposed restraints. A new war strategy, supported by the new and

increasingly powerful domestic consensus and led by a
determined and popular president, might silence dissent the
next time.[15]

The Reagan Foreign Policy Outlook

Ronald Reagan assumed the presidency with an electoral
mandate to reverse the domestic and international decline
of the United States. A stagflationary economy had
combined with setbacks in Iran, Afghanistan, and Central
America to defeat Jimmy Carter. Since the mid-1970s public
opinion polls had shown with increasing clarity that the
tide of antidefense sentiment that had helped Carter in
1976 had ebbed significantly. In 1979 the Chicago Council
on Foreign Relations released the results of a
comprehensive survey that had been completed before the
Iranian Shah's overthrow and the Soviet invasion of
Afghanistan. Nevertheless, the data indicated the growth
of a mood that rejected the introspective guilt of the
post-Vietnam period without, however, fully reembracing the
liberal internationalism of the Cold War consensus. This
disposition could, perhaps, best be described as
"conservative nationalism," for it was informed by several
defense-oriented, yet anti-interventionist tendencies.
Higher defense budgets, more military (but not economic)
aid, a willingness to protect NATO allies and Japan (but
not Taiwan), and more support for CIA covert activities
were responses that appeared with higher frequency than in
a similar 1974 survey. No clear national consensus had
emerged; however, the trends pointed to "a mood of
increasing insecurity in the American public . . . [it]
shows an increasing attraction toward such 'conservative'
symbols as military power and anti-Communism, but not
toward extending our commitments abroad or renewing the
tradition of Cold War interventionism. It is this
defensive and self-interested quality that distinguishes
the current mood from that of the Cold War."[16] The sense
of vulnerability, the desire for security, the
preoccupation with Soviet military power, the
disinclination for a global crusade, and the somewhat
contradictory dual wishes for U.S. world leadership with
reduced and restrained foreign commitments characterized
the tendencies in public attitudes about foreign policy
shortly before the 1980 election.
In these circumstances Carter's conversion to
anti-Soviet, if not anti-Communist, containment "only

reinforced the politically fatal image of an indecisive,
somewhat schizoid President presiding over an erratic,
incoherent policy."[17]   Reagan capitalized on this mood by
promising to modernize the nation's defenses and to conduct
an assertive, if largely unspecified, foreign policy.
Despite the president's refusal to enunciate a
comprehensive Reagan Doctrine, the main outlines of the
administration's program to revitalize U.S. diplomacy
became reasonably clear during its first two years in
office. First, proposals for a $1.6 trillion, five-year
defense program—by far the largest in U.S. history and
undertaken in tandem with domestic budget cuts—were
designed to make a global strategy feasible. That is, this
ambitious goal was initially announced in the absence of
the usual comprehensive strategic review undertaken by new
administrations; the goal, moreover, depended primarily on
equally ambitious domestic recovery forecasts. According
to one sympathetic observer, "The scatter-shot approach to
defense spending, along with Secretary of Defense Caspar
Weinberger's decentralization of the management of programs
and resources into the hands of the separate armed
services, meant that defense expenditures would be
undisciplined by strategic guidance until budgetary and
other constraints compelled choices among priorities."[18]
Nevertheless, the groundwork was laid for a significant
reassertion of U.S. power. Second, Weinberger's
articulation of a "three-war" strategy aimed at fighting
protracted, nonnuclear wars in several theaters
simultaneously around the Soviet periphery represented the
most ambitious operational concept since, perhaps, NSC-68
sanctioned global containment in 1950. At the very least,
it envisioned the containment of the Soviets at the
conventional level and in regions other than Europe, the
Gulf in the Mideast, Japan, and Central America.[19]   Third,
Secretary of the Navy John F. Lehman Jr.'s announcement
(and Weinberger's endorsement) of plans to achieve
"unquestioned maritime superiority" based on a
six-hundred-ship fleet with fifteen battle groups built
around large aircraft carriers, surface ships armed with
cruise missiles, and improved amphibious capabilities,
further indicated movement toward a global strategy.
According to Lehman, "We have a whole new geopolitical
situation. What's new is a consensus within the
administration that the Soviet threat is global. It's not
just central Europe."[20]   As Robert E. Osgood put it, "If
nothing else, these intimations of all-purpose strategic
goals indicated the Administration's firm intention to

change what a number of its officials had criticized as America's 'Euro-centered' strategy and to prepare the armed forces, for once to support the nation's global commitments with truly flexible, global capabilities."[21] Fourth, the Reagan administration did or said nothing to suggest that it contemplated any diminution in the number or extent of U.S. interests and commitments. Far from embracing an outlook that justified a strategy of selective or limited containment, as some of Reagan's academic supporters had urged,[22] the administration showed no inclination to rope off or stand aloof from any Soviet or Soviet-supported geopolitical or ideological initiative, and since it identified Moscow as the source of virtually all global instability, this attitude effectively placed every issue in an East-West context.

Reagan's Latin American Policy

The role of the Linowitz commission in setting much of the Carter administration's Latin American agenda was paralleled under Reagan by the Committee of Santa Fe's, which produced "A New Inter-American Policy for the Eighties," and like the Linowitz commission, which subsequently contributed several of its members to Carter as important advisers, so too did some of the authors of the Santa Fe report later join the Reagan team. For instance, Roger Fontaine became the National Security Council's Latin American specialist, Lt. General Gordon Sumner, Jr., served as special adviser to the assistant secretary of state for Inter-American Affairs, and in March 1984 President Reagan appointed as ambassador to Peru David C. Jordan, a professor of government at the University of Virginia. Released in July 1980, the Santa Fe report bluntly rejected President's Carter's Latin American policy as indecisive and naive and charged that the effort "to socialize the Soviets and their Hispanic-American puppets" was "merely a camouflaged cover for accommodation to aggression."[23] The report claimed that Latin America was being "overrun by Soviet supported and supplied satellites and surrogates," and argued that "decisive action, such as the occupation of the Dominican Republic in 1965" had been "replaced by retrograde reaction, as exemplified by the Carter-Torrijos Treaties of 1978, and by anxious accommodation," such as President Carter's cancellation of the sea-air exercise "Solid Shield '80" after the Panamanian president objected.[24] The Committee of Santa Fe

urged instead that the United States "take the strategic
and diplomatic initiative by revitalizing the Rio Treaty
and the Organization of American States; reproclaiming the
Monroe Doctrine; tightening ties with key countries; and,
aiding independent nations to survive subversion."[25] It
concluded that "in war there is no substitute for victory;
and the United States is engaged in World War III." Thus,
"containment of the Soviet Union is not enough. . . . Only
the United States can, as a partner, protect the
independent nations of Latin America from Communist
conquest and help preserve Hispanic-American culture from
sterilization by international Marxist materialism."[26]
    At his Senate confirmation hearing in January 1981,
Secretary of State-designate Alexander Haig argued that

> Imaginative remedies might have prevented the current
> danger. Unfortunately, . . . over the last decade,
> America's confidence in itself was shaken, and
> American leadership faltered. The United States
> seemed unable or unwilling to act when our strategic
> interests were threatened. We earned a reputation for
> "strategic passivity," and that reputation still
> weighs heavily upon us and cannot be wished away by
> rhetoric. What we once took for granted abroad--
> confidence in the United States--must be reestablished
> through a steady accumulation of prudent and
> successful actions.[27]

What would "a steady accumulation of prudent and successful
actions" entail? Haig did not say at the time, but it soon
became clear that the Secretary did not propose to
challenge the Soviets directly in Eastern Europe or
Afghanistan. Rather, Haig immediately sounded a Caribbean
Basin tocsin about a Soviet-Cuban axis and targeted El
Salvador as his top priority. In part, Haig thought that
El Salvador would provide an opportunity for a modest and
immediate reassertion of U.S. power in circumstances
ostensibly very different from Vietnam. The Johnson
administration had defended its Vietnam policy primarily on
psychological and moral grounds by stressing U.S.
credibility with its allies, obligation to create and
sustain a stable international order, the need to contain
the expansionistic dimensions of the Chinese Revolution,
and the right of South Vietnam to determine its future free
from aggression. Johnson's defense of the Dominican
intervention was similarly laden with global symbolism.
Haig, on the other hand, attempted to justify the dispatch

of military aid and advisors to El Salvador by more
restrictive arguments. He emphasized, for example, the
relatively small size and geographical proximity of El
Salvador, and not only underlined the allegedly crucial
outside support received by the insurrectionaries, but also
identified the specific security interests ostensibly at
stake in Central America: The Panama Canal and Mexican and
Venezuelan oil.

But the secretary of state felt that U.S. aid to El
Salvador could not save its government if the "source" of
rebel assistance remained immune to pressure: "There could
not be the slightest doubt that Cuba was at once the source
of supply and the catechist of the Salvadoran insurgency.
Cuba, in turn, could not act on the scale of the rebellion
in El Salvador without the approval and the material
support of the U.S.S.R."[28] The implications were clear: "I
believe that our policy should carry the consequences of
this relationship directly to Moscow and Havana, and
through the application of a full range of economic,
political, and security measures, convince them to put an
end to Havana's bloody activities in the hemisphere and
elsewhere in the world."[29] Yet despite the fact that
"President Reagan knew that a failure to carry through on
this challenge at the heart of our sphere of influence
would result in a loss of credibility in all our dealings
with the Soviets,"[30] his advisers cautioned him about
another Vietnam. A few "mild" measures were taken--naval
maneuvers around Cuba, a Caribbean naval exercise (the
first in twenty-three years) with an amphibious landing at
Vieques, the upgrading of the Key West task force to the
status of Caribbean command--but even these, according to
Haig, "produced results."[31]

It remained unclear exactly what the secretary had in
mind. In his memoirs he argued that "direct military
action was neither required nor justified, and, I repeat, I
never contemplated it." Rather, Haig wrote mysteriously of
applying "geostrategic assets" in a "firm, prudent" way so
that our military strength "could not be disregarded."
Haig's administration opponents were much clearer. They
needed congressional cooperation for their top priority--
tax and budget cuts--and they refused to risk its loss in
the spring of 1981 by challenging Cuba. Indeed the outcry
raised against the sending of a few dozen U.S. military
advisers in February 1981 was sufficient to prompt the
White House to silence Haig for fear of diverting attention
and enthusiasm from Reagan's economic initiatives. During
the summer of 1981 the State Department apparently

undertook negotiations with Cuba and Nicaragua in order to dry up the alleged "source" of Salvadoran support. But by the autumn these talks had broken down, and Haig again rang alarm bells in Central America. What began as an opportunity for a quick victory now threatened to engulf the administration in a Vietnam-type domestic and international controversy.

Public opinion polls taken in February and March 1982 reflected Reagan's dilemma. More than anything else, they indicated the continued attractiveness of at least part of the orthodox explanation of Vietnam, and it was significant that the administration did little to try to alter the public's perception of that war. An astonishing 89 percent of those polled by Gallup in mid-February opposed sending any U.S. troops to El Salvador, and 74 percent believed the U.S. involvement there was very or fairly likely to turn into a Vietnam-like quagmire demanding more and more U.S. resources.[32] At the same time, a New York Times-CBS News poll indicated that although 57 percent thought that El Salvador and Central America were "very important to U.S. defense interests," 63 percent urged the administration to send no aid at all.[33] Finally, a Washington Post-ABC News survey revealed that although a solid majority of those polled believed that a Communist victory in El Salvador would endanger U.S. security, and although 81 percent predicted that the loss of that country would probably trigger a domino effect throughout Latin America, fully 51 percent said that they would support U.S. draftees who refused to fight in El Salvador.[34] The result of these polls, of course, stood in direct contrast to those conducted as late as early 1966 when public support for Johnson's escalation in Vietnam ran 3 to 1.

Public hostility was matched by congressional skepticism and allied criticism. In early March 1982 Senate Minority Leader Robert C. Byrd introduced an amendment to the War Powers Act to require prior congressional concurrence before combat troops could be sent to El Salvador.[35] Several senators and representatives toured El Salvador and returned with warnings against U.S. support for the ruling junta, and congressional reaction to the Caribbean Basin plan was subdued at best. International enthusiasm was similarly muted: West European Christian Democrats generally applauded President Jose Napoleon Duarte's reform efforts, but Social Democrats urged negotiations with the Left; France recognized the belligerent status of the guerrillas in August 1981; and only a handful of nations agreed to

send observers to supervise the March 1982 Constituent
Assembly elections. Finally, the region's most powerful
nations, Mexico and Venezuela, offered to moderate the
dispute between Washington and Havana.

In the face of these circumstances the Reagan
administration could no longer ignore the legacy of Vietnam
but steadfastly refused to defend its conduct in El
Salvador by attempting to rehabilitate Vietnam. Rather, it
went to great lengths to distinguish between the two cases
and to argue that Cuba constituted the real historical
analogy. For example, Haig tried to deal with the Vietnam
analogy by claiming that it had always been questionable
whether Southeast Asia constituted "a vital challenge to
fundamental American interests"; in El Salvador, by
contrast, "we're talking about the strategic vulnerability
of the Canal. . . . We are, in effect, at the very core of
United States hemispheric interests."[36] On the other hand,
some former Vietnam planners advised Reagan to equate
Vietnam with El Salvador openly. Walt Rostow suggested
that "It's the same bunch of 'left-intellectuals' and
journalists who undermined the Vietnam war effort who are
at work now undermining our effort to help Salvador. 'I
fear for my country.'"[37] But the administration showed no
signs of adopting Rostow's strategy. Although leaks
reporting a $19 million covert operations program to
"destabilize" Nicaragua reminded some observers of John
Foster Dulles' campaign against Jacobo Arbenz Guzman's
Guatemala in 1954, by early March 1982 the Reagan
administration had evidently ruled out the use of U.S.
troops in El Salvador.[38]

The Caribbean Basin Initiative

Indeed, by this time President Reagan had apparently
concluded that a regional policy of security assistance
needed to be complemented by a program of economic aid.
The result was the Caribbean Basin Initiative (CBI),
unveiled on February 24, 1982. Alexander Haig had
discussed the idea of a "Mini-Marshall Plan" with his
Canadian, Mexican, and Venezuelan counterparts in July 1981
when it was agreed to consult the countries of the
Caribbean and Central America about their development
needs. The Reagan administration relied heavily for advice
on Jamaican Prime Minister Edward Seaga, long a White House
favorite, who argued that U.S. assistance should be
tailored to halt the Communist offensive in the Caribbean.

According to one Carter official, "Having just emerged from his own election where the smear of Communism had worked so effectively, Seaga thought that the United States needed to be frightened if it were going to extend massive aid to the region."[39]

President Reagan needed little convincing about the Communist threat. For example, in late March 1982 he called Michael Manley's former government "virtually Communist." This ideological focus soon alienated Mexico, Canada, Colombia, and Venezuela from the emerging Reagan plan. Mexico, in particular, objected to the exclusion of Havana, Nicaragua, and Grenada, and when the Caribbean Basin Initiative was finally announced, it was a unilateral program in marked contrast to the Caribbean group of the Carter years. President Reagan asked for congressional authority to grant duty-free treatment for twelve years on the export by Caribbean Basin nations of all products save for textiles and certain apparel items. Sugar would not be taxed, but the import fee was to remain. He also asked for the power to add more countries to the free-trade area so long as they were not Communist, had not expropriated U.S. property without just compensation, or discriminated against U.S. exports. Furthermore, Reagan announced support for tax incentives to encourage foreign investment in the region and a strengthened Overseas Private Investment Corporation to protect U.S. entrepreneurs. The price tag for U.S. economic assistance for fiscal 1982 was to total $350 million, but El Salvador was to receive $128 million of these funds, while the eastern Caribbean was allotted only $10 million. Military assistance was treated separately with $112.1 million for fiscal 1983. El Salvador would receive 70 percent of this aid.

The president articulated his program squarely in the context of the Soviet-Cuban axis: "A new kind of colonialism stalks the world today and threatens our independence. It is brutal and totalitarian. It is not of our hemisphere but threatens our hemisphere." His Manichean imagery recalled the Truman Doctrine: "The positive opportunity is illustrated by the two-thirds of the nations in the area which have democratic governments. The dark future is foreshadowed by the poverty and repression of Castro's Cuba, the tightening grip of the totalitarian left in Grenada and Nicaragua, and the expansion of Soviet-backed Cuban-managed support for violent revolution in Central America."[40] What did the Cubans and the Soviets hope to accomplish in Central America?

Very simply, guerrillas armed and supported by
and through Cuba are attempting to impose a Marxist-
Leninist dictatorship on the people of El Salvador as
part of a larger imperialistic plan.

If we do not act promptly and decisively in
defense of freedom, new Cubas will arise from the
ruins of today's conflicts.

We will face more totalitarian regimes, more
regimes tied militarily to the Soviet Union, more
regimes exporting revolution.[41]

But if sufficient U.S. economic and military assistance
helped to check the totalitarian threat to Central America,
Reagan predicted a happy future:

I have always believed that this hemisphere was a
special place with a special destiny. I believe we
are destined to be the beacon of hope for all mankind.

With God's help we can make it so; we can create
a peaceful free and prospering hemisphere based on
shared ideals and reaching from pole to pole of what
we proudly call the New World.[42]

Yet this providential rhetoric did not deliver the
Caribbean Basin Initiative from congressional controversy.
First, some critics, particularly the Black Caucus,
objected to the very notion of a Caribbean Basin as an
artificial geopolitical construct that did violence to the
racial, cultural, linguistic, historical, economic, and
political diversity of Central America and the Caribbean.
By invoking the democratic traditions of the eastern
Caribbean, the Reagan administration was allegedly trying
to win support for its program of military assistance for
the repressive regimes of Central America. Furthermore, by
describing the basin as an undifferentiated entity subject
to Soviet and Cuban subversion and intimidation, the
administration risked antagonizing the nationalist
sensibility of the region. Most Caribbean leaders, these
representatives claimed, found the crude East-West focus of
the CBI irrelevant and condescending. Second, the
additional $350 million, while a substantial increase over
the $474 million initially earmarked for the area in fiscal
1982, nevertheless represented less than 10 percent of the
amount needed for these countries' balance-of-payments
deficits. Third, many objected to the disproportionate
share of these funds targeted for Central America; in the
Caribbean itself only Jamaica and the Dominican Republic

would be major recipients. In its final version, aid to El
Salvador was reduced to $75 million, funds for the eastern
Caribbean were doubled, and Secretary of State George
Shultz promised to spend 12.5 percent of the total on basic
development projects. Finally, domestic U.S. economic
interests expressed fears about the impact of the CBI on
the textile, petroleum, leather goods, footwear, and sugar
industries. Even so, the free-trade area affected only
slightly more than 5 percent of the area's exports to the
United States. After many delays and some additional
changes in the trade and tax portions of the bill, Congress
passed the CBI on August 5, 1983.

Reagan and the Bishop Regime in Grenada

But if the Caribbean Basin Initiative represented, in
part, an acknowledgment by the administration that it could
not conduct just a policy of militant containment against
Cuba, its approach to tiny Grenada betrayed no such second
thoughts. The Carter administration, particularly after
the PRG's UN vote on Afghanistan, adopted a policy of
"distancing" toward Grenada, but the Reagan team entered
office determined to isolate, punish, and perhaps even
overthrow Bishop. To repeat, the Reagan administration's
Grenada policy closely resembled what Haig had hoped would
be the approach to Cuba.
This policy featured several components and, again in
contrast to the situation during the Carter administration,
was evidently coordinated at the most senior governmental
levels. Upon taking office Secretary Alexander Haig
ordered officials at the Bureau of Inter-American Affairs
to make sure that Grenada would not receive "one penny"
from any international financial institution (IFI).[43]
Accordingly, Grenada was added to an informal "hit list" of
countries that the State Department tries to prevent for
political reasons from receiving IFI loans. In the words
of one analyst, "Whenever a loan for one of these countries
comes under consideration at an IFI"--in 1981 the list
reportedly included Vietnam, Cuba, Nicaragua, Afghanistan,
and Grenada--experts prepare "a negative critique in the
technical, economic language that IFIs use to evaluate
proposals." Then U.S. officials rely on these critiques
"to lobby against the loan with the . . . IFI and other
countries' foreign ministers and representatives on [the]
IFI's executive board."[44] Apparently the U.S. executive
director to the International Monetary Fund used these

"technical" arguments to try to deny loans to Grenada in 1981 and 1983. In November 1979 the PRG announced plans to construct an international airport at Point Salines to encourage tourism. The Carter administration, while skeptical, did nothing, but Reagan's advisers feared that the airport's 10,000-foot runway would be used by Cuban and Soviet military planes and tried vainly to persuade the European Economic Community (EEC) to refuse the PRG's request for assistance. Arguing that large loans to Grenada would add excessively to its external debt, United States officials evidently helped convince the IMF to reduce the loans from $9 million over three years to $3 million for one year. In August 1983 the United States again tried to stop or at least reduce a three-year IMF loan of $14.1 million to Grenada, but this time the other executive directors supported the staff's decision to offer the aid.[45] More than two years earlier, in June 1981, the State Department had put intense pressure on the Caribbean Development Bank to eliminate Grenada from a $4 million U.S. grant for basic human needs projects.[46] Moreover, the U.S. pressured the World Bank's International Development Agency to refuse a Grenadian request for a $3 million loan.[47] Yet despite these vigorous efforts the PRG was extremely successful in obtaining international assistance. For example, the $23 million it received from Cuba, East Germany, the EEC, and Canada in 1982 was more than twice the amount that President Reagan proposed for the entire eastern Caribbean in his Caribbean Basin Initiative.

Covert operations against the Bishop government had been discussed by the Carter administration in the wake of Grenada's UN vote on Afghanistan, but after reviewing options the president apparently "rejected all but propaganda measures." In July 1981, however, the CIA approached the Senate Select Intelligence Committee with a plan to cause the PRG economic hardship. The details have not yet been made public, but the Washington Post reported in February 1983 that one unnamed CIA official denied that it sought to oust Bishop: "We may cause a little economic trouble, a little publicity, and [give] aid [to opposition groups], but we don't overthrow governments."[48] One member of the committee, however, characterized the proposal as "economic destabilization affecting the political viability of the government." In any case it found little support among the senators. Lloyd Bentsen, for example, exclaimed, "You've got to be kidding!" when told of the plan.

Military pressure, however, was exerted against Grenada. From August 1 to October 15, 1981, the United

States staged Caribbean maneuvers. In large part, of
course, they were designed to intimidate Cuba. On Vieques
Island, a military installation near Puerto Rico, more than
200,000 U.S. and NATO personnel not only invaded "Red,"
described as "a mythical island interfering in the region
and shipping arms to Central America," but also "Amber and
the Amberdines," which, according to the Defense
Department, was "our enemy in the Eastern Caribbean where
U.S. hostages were in need of rescue." According to the
fictional scenario, the U.S. troops, after rescuing the
hostages, would remain on Amber to "install a regime
favorable to the way of life we espouse."[49]

Members of the Black Caucus in Congress grew
increasingly critical of the Reagan administration's
largely quiet but persistent efforts to isolate and punish
Grenada. In June 1982 they persuaded Michael Barnes,
chairman of the House Subcommittee on Inter-American
Affairs to hold hearings on the issue.[50] Stephen D.
Bosworth, principal deputy assistant secretary of state for
Inter-American affairs, laid out the administration's case
against the PRG:

- In stark contrast to its CARICOM neighbors, Grenada
  supported Cuba on the South Atlantic crisis by
  attacking British "colonialism and will no doubt
  repay its debt to Cuba with more than verbal
  support" by providing Cuba access to the Point
  Salines Airport for transit flights to Africa and
  other military bases.
- The PRG "has become a center for solidarity meetings
  and established close ties to small, radical
  movements elsewhere in the Caribbean."
- Cuba has provided training to Grenada's "vastly
  expanded security forces" and has stationed small
  numbers of military advisers there.
- Cuba and the USSR have provided arms, transportation
  and communications equipment to the PRG's security
  forces.
- Cuba's role in the construction of an airport that
  will be capable of handling "advanced military
  aircraft" adds "a new and serious dimension to our
  security concerns," for it is "difficult, if not
  impossible to identify any economic justification"
  for the "enormous investment" involved.
- Despite the PRG's "professed interest in a high
  level dialog," its anti-American statements typified
  by Bishop's calling President Reagan a "fascist" and

the CBI as "chicken feed," seem, "designed to foster a climate of confrontation."
- PRG officials continue to ridicule Westminster-style "democracy for five seconds when votes are cast every five years."
- The human rights situation has continued to deteriorate: there is no independent press, no freedom of assembly, no due process of law, while over one hundred political prisoners remain under detention.

Relations between the United States and Grenada would not improve, Bosworth warned, unless the PRG (1) halted "its unrelenting stream of anti-American propaganda and false statements about U.S. policies and actions"; (2) moved to "restore constitutional democracy, including prompt, free, and fair elections"; (3) returned to "the high standard of human rights observance that is typical" of the CARICOM states; and (4) practiced "growing nonalinement rather than continuing its present role as a surrogate of Cuba."[51]

These statements constituted the most detailed public indictment that would be brought against the Bishop government by the administration, but President Reagan on several occasions offered sharp and vivid denunciations of Grenada's policies. He made passing reference to "the tightening grip of the totalitarian left in Grenada" when announcing the Caribbean Basin Initiative in February 1982, but he lingered longer in remarks made in Barbados on April 8, 1982, while on a "working vacation": "El Salvador isn't the only country that's being threatened with Marxism, and I think all of us are concerned with the overturn of Westminster parliamentary democracy in Grenada. That country now bears the Soviet and Cuban trademark, which means that it will attempt to spread the virus among its neighbors."[52] Then in a speech on Central America and El Salvador to the annual meeting of the National Association of Manufacturers in Washington on March 10, 1983, Reagan presented Grenada in the context of a geopolitical nightmare:

Grenada, that tiny little island—with Cuba at the west end of the Caribbean, Grenada at the east end— that tiny little island is building now, or having built for it, on its soil and shores, a naval base, a superior air base, storage bases and facilities for the storage of munitions, barracks, and training

ground for the military. I'm sure all of that is
simply to encourage the export of nutmeg.

People who make these arguments haven't taken a
good look at a map lately or followed the
extraordinary buildup of Soviet and Cuban military
power in the region or read the Soviets' discussions
about why the region is important to them and how they
intend to use it.

It isn't nutmeg that's at stake in the Caribbean
and Central America; it is the United States national
security.

Soviet military theorists want to destroy our
capacity to resupply Western Europe in case of an
emergency. They want to tie down our attention and
forces on our own southern border and so limit our
capacity to act in more distant places, such as
Europe, the Persian Gulf, the Indian Ocean, the Sea of
Japan.

Those Soviet theorists noticed what we failed to
notice: that the Caribbean Sea and Central America
constitute this nation's fourth border. If we must
defend ourselves against large, hostile military
presence on our border, our freedom to act elsewhere
to help others and to protect strategically vital
sealanes and resources has been drastically
diminished. They know this; they've written about
this.

We've been slow to understand that the defense of
the Caribbean and Central America against Marxist-
Leninist takeover is vital to our national security in
ways we're not accustomed to thinking about.[53]

Finally, and most spectacularly, in a nationwide address on
national security on the evening of March 23, 1983, the
president unveiled aerial-reconnaisance photographs of
Cuba, Nicaragua, and Grenada:

On the small island of Grenada, at the southern end of
the Caribbean chain, the Cubans with Soviet financing
and backing, are in the process of building an
airfield with a 10,000-foot runway. Grenada doesn't
even have an air force. Who is it intended for? The
Caribbean is a very important passageway for our
international commerce and military lines of
communication. More than half of all American oil
imports now pass through the Caribbean. The rapid
buildup of Grenada's military potential is unrelated

to any conceivable threat to this island country of under 110,000 people and totally at odds with the pattern of other eastern Caribbean states, most of which are unarmed.

The Soviet-Cuban militarization of Grenada, in short, can only be seen as power projection into the region. And it is in this important economic and strategic area that we're trying to help the Governments of El Salvador, Costa Rica, Honduras, and others in their struggles for democracy against guerrillas supported through Cuba and Nicaragua.

These pictures only tell a small part of the story. I wish I could show you more without compromising our most sensitive intelligence sources and methods. But the Soviet Union is also supporting Cuban military forces in Angola and Ethiopia. They have bases in Ethiopia and South Yemen, near the Persian Gulf oil fields. They've taken over the port that we built at Cam Ranh Bay in Vietnam. And now for the first time in history, the Soviet Navy is a force to be reckoned with in the South Pacific.[54]

Thus by the spring of 1983 the Reagan administration had elevated Grenada to the status of a serious security threat to the United States and its allies. Its strategic position in the eastern Caribbean allegedly formed the third point on a geopolitical triangle that stretched to Cuba and Nicaragua; its new airport would soon allow the Cubans and Soviets to threaten the Caribbean sealanes; and Havana could use the island as a military bridge to Africa and as an ideological bridge to the eastern Caribbean. Finally, the administration even raised the spectre of another Cuban missile crisis. For example, Nestor D. Sanchez, deputy assistant secretary of state for Inter-American affairs, claimed in February 1983 that Grenada's new military facilities "would provide air and naval bases . . . for the recovery of Soviet aircraft after strategic missions. It might also furnish missile sites for launching attacks against the United States with short and intermediate range missiles."[55]

The administration had virtually ended formal diplomatic relations with Grenada in 1981 by excluding it from the list of states to which the U.S. ambassador in Barbados was accredited. Occasionally, however, Grenadian Foreign Minister Unison Whiteman or an assistant was able to meet with mid-level U.S. embassy personnel in Bridgetown. Bishop wrote several letters to President

Reagan asking for more normal diplomatic relations, but all went unanswered. Rumors about a U.S. or U.S.-supported invasion of Grenada, usually fueled by PRG statements, had routinely swept the island since the 1979 coup, but Reagan's March 23, 1983, speech seems to have genuinely alarmed Bishop. At this point it is likely that Fidel Castro personally urged Bishop to try to talk to President Reagan. In any case, at the invitation of Transafrica, self-described as "the Black American Lobby for Africa and the Caribbean," and with the support of the Black Caucus, Prime Minister Bishop came to Washington in early June to attempt to see the president. Not only was he unable to see Reagan, but he was apparently rebuffed by the State Department as well until two senators, Claiborne Pell and Lowell Weicker, intervened on his behalf. Soon thereafter, Bishop met for forty minutes with National Security Advisor William Clark and Deputy Secretary of State Kenneth Dam.[56] Bishop termed the meeting "a useful first step in the recommencement of dialogue between the governments," and evidently promised to hold elections within two years. He added that the talks had "delayed" an invasion but admitted that "we do not think the threat has been entirely removed."[57] No such dialogue with Grenada, of course, began until November, after Bishop had been overthrown and killed by his PRG rivals, and the island had been invaded by the United States and several eastern Caribbean countries.

8
The Grenada Intervention
and U.S. Foreign Policy

Ronald Reagan's astonishing announcement of October 25, 1983, that a "rescue mission" in Grenada was underway raised a host of serious questions about U.S. foreign policy. Would the public support this first use of U.S. combat troops in the Caribbean in almost twenty years? If so, would that support signal the beginning of a new domestic consensus about the purposes and limits of U.S. power? What role had concern about Cuba and Nicaragua played in the administration's decision? Did it represent a return to "gunboat diplomacy"? Did the invasion constitute a Reagan Doctrine for the Caribbean that would countenance future interventions? How had a host of historical analogies--from the abortive Bay of Pigs invasion to the Iranian hostage crisis--affected the decision? Had the OECS really invited the United States to intervene, and if so, why? The following is an attempt to answer these questions.

The decision by five members of the Organization of Eastern Caribbean States plus Jamaica and Barbados to cooperate with the United States in the Grenada intervention must be understood, at least in part, in the context of CARICOM relations and traditions. Despite periodic electoral abuses and recurrent government corruption, the English-speaking Caribbean has long taken collective pride in its democratic institutions and peaceful transfer of power. Hence, although Eric Gairy was generally perceived as an unstable, petty tyrant, his removal represented the first violent, unconstitutional change of government in the region and caused considerable consternation. CARICOM leaders gathered in Barbados to try to decide how to respond to this situation. Barbadian Prime Minister Tom Adams, in particular, had qualms about

137

the way in which the PRG had come to power. But CARICOM, eager to present a united front and under pressure from Michael Manley of Jamaica and Forbes Burnham of Guyana, recognized the Bishop government after assurance that early elections would be held.

However, Grenada's relations with the small states of the eastern Caribbean never became cordial. By mid-1979 Dominica and St. Lucia were experiencing political instability and a leftward political drift. These nations' new leaders went to Grenada in July and signed the Declaration of St. George's, which seemed to reinforce the anti-imperialistic rhetoric and radical social goals of the PRG. Furthermore, placards displayed by some participants during the conference urged the overthrow of the Robert Cato government on St. Vincent.

Soon, however, the political situation had changed drastically. In July 1980 Dominican elections produced a victory for the conservative Freedom party of Eugenia Charles; in November Michael Manley was ousted in Jamaica by the militantly anti-Communist Edward Seaga. Then in May 1982 the conservative John Compton returned to power in St. Lucia. These leaders, along with Tom Adams, frequently expressed criticism of the PRG's failure to hold elections, its human rights record, and its continuing military buildup. When a formal CARICOM summit was convened at Ocho Rios, Jamaica, in November 1982, Adams announced that he would propose an amendment to the organization's treaty to set human rights standards for member-states. Moreover, he argued that the CARICOM rule of unanimity for treaty changes should be altered in favor of a simple majority. Maurice Bishop tried to preempt this effort by proposing a set of social and economic rights to be protected by all CARICOM states, while at the same time warning that "Grenada will never again see Westminster parliamentary elections. That is dead in our country."[1] In any case, the conference never formally discussed the issue. Afterward, Trinidadian Prime Minsiter George Chambers claimed that Bishop had privately told him of a timetable for a constitutional referendum and an election—though not a traditional one. Bishop also released twenty-eight political prisoners and promised to allow CARICOM observers to ensure that leftist guerrillas were not being trained on the island.[2]

CARICOM's membership includes the relatively large states of Jamaica, Trinidad, Guyana, and Belize, as well as the microstates of the eastern Caribbean; the latter group had for some time felt that their security and economic

problems could not be fully addressed by such a
heterogeneous organization. Not only were these tiny
islands virtually impossible to defend against traditional
forms of international aggression, but they were hard
pressed to offer resistance by themselves to private
takeovers as well. In the late-1970s the Mafia, the Ku
Klux Klan, and a group of Rastafarians had each attempted
to establish redoubts in the region. In addition, these
little states believed that "giants" like Jamaica and
Trinidad had practiced economic discrimination against
their products. To meet these concerns, Antigua, Dominica,
Grenada, Montserrat, St. Kitts-Nevis, St. Lucia, and St.
Vincent established the Organization of Eastern Caribbean
States on June 4, 1981.

Yet the combined security forces of these territories
--except for Grenada--were negligible, and Grenada was
perceived as a threat, particularly by the conservative
governments of Eugenia Charles and John Compton. To ensure
their protection further, these leaders, along with those
of Antigua and St. Vincent, signed a Memorandum of
Understanding with Barbados on October 29, 1982, "to
prepare contingency plans and assist one another on request
in national emergencies; prevention of smuggling; search
and rescue; maritime policing duties, and threats to
national security." While pointing toward the
establishment of an eastern Caribbean regional security
organization, this agreement represented a theoretical,
essentially paper framework. The PRG, nevertheless,
severely criticized it. It was against this background,
then, that CARICOM and the OECS responded to Bishop's
overthrow and murder in October 1983.

Events in Grenada: October 12-28, 1983

On October 12, 1983, Prime Minister Bishop challenged
a September 14 decision of the New Jewel Movement's Central
Committee that he share his leadership with Bernard Coard.
Two days later Bishop was placed under house arrest. On
October 15, Milan Bish, the U.S. ambassador to Barbados,
apparently initiated talks with an aide to Tom Adams about
rescuing Bishop. It is unclear whether Bish took this step
on his own or acting under State Department instructions.
On October 17 a representative of the Bureau of Inter-
American Affairs, supported by Under Secretary for
Political Affairs Lawrence Eagleburger, argued at an
interagency meeting that serious thought be given to the

evacuation of U.S. citizens from Grenada.

Representatives of the Joint Chiefs of Staff did not even want to begin contingency planning for such an operation, but after news reached Washington on October 19 that Bishop had been killed, they agreed to discuss plans for an evacuation. At the same time Barbados and other eastern Caribbean states held preliminary consultations. Now, however, the State Department officials argued that the entire island had to be secured in order "to save Americans lives and to serve broader goals."[3] On the nineteenth, "or soon after," Secretary of State George Shultz "got to" President Reagan to nudge the Pentagon into "full swing" for contingency planning. According to State Department officials, they found "to their dismay" that the Defense Department had done no prior contingency planning or intelligence gathering for a move against Grenada."[4] Also on October 19 the U.S. embassy in Barbados attempted to send two foreign service officers to Grenada to assess the situation, but their plane was turned back. Then, according to Assistant Secretary of State for Inter-American Affairs Langhorne Motley, Ambassador Bish sent a red-coded warning to the State Department, that the necessity for a sudden evacuation might arise at any time.

> There appears to be imminent danger to U.S. citizens resident on Grenada due to the current deteriorating situation, which includes reports of rioting, personnel casualties (possibly deaths), automatic weapons being discharged, Soviet-built armored personnel carriers in the Grenadian streets, and some loss of water and electricity on the island. . . . AmEmbassy Bridgetown recommends that the United States should now be prepared to conduct an emergency evacuation of U.S. citizens residing in Grenada.[5]

On Thursday, October 20, Barbadian Prime Minister Adams publicly condemned the Grenadian murders and privately asked Ambassador Bish for a U.S. invasion force. Later that afternoon Vice President George Bush convened an urgent meeting in the White House situation room to consider Adams's request. Secretary Shultz and Langhorne Motley arrived during the session, at which the participants also discussed intelligence reports on Bishop's successors, formally ordered the Joint Chiefs to prepare a contingency plan for evacuations, and diverted to the Caribbean a ten-ship marine amphibious force that had been on its way to Beirut.[6] Some participants suggested

that Grenada's new rulers, especially General Hudson
Austin, reminded them of the Iranian militants who had
seized the U.S. citizens in Teheran.

Eugenia Charles of Dominica, who happened to be in
Washington, returned home the next day and immediately
requested a meeting of the OECS.[7] It is not known if she
spoke with U.S. officials before her departure, but some
evidence indicates "that discussions about possible
collaboration were held between U.S. officials and the
Barbadian Government and OECS leaders no later than the
evening of Thursday 20 October."[8] The Reagan
administration, however, contended that neither the OECS
nor any Caribbean state approached it until after the
October 21 meeting. In any case, the OECS met in Barbados
(a non-OECS country) on Friday, October 21, and formally
decided to intervene militarily in Grenada and to invite
friendly governments to lend assistance. According to an
October 28, 1983, article by Tim Hector in Outlet, however,
Prime Minister Seaga and Ambassador Bish attended the
meeting and broke a deadlock by urging the OECS to "invite"
the United States to participate.[9] That evening
representatives of Barbados and Jamaica, and subsequently
Ambassador Bish, were orally informed of the decision. The
OECS apparently also decided to ask France, Canada,
Venezuela, and Britain for help.[10] None would accept the
invitations, which it seems were never formally presented.

Bish's cable was received in Washington at about 1:00
A.M. Saturday (October 22) by Deputy National Security
Adviser John Poindexter, who called Augusta, Georgia to
notify the president, the secretary of state, and the
national security adviser. Shultz was awakened at 2:45,
and he discussed the OECS request with Robert McFarlane.
The vice president and Secretary of Defense Caspar
Weinberger were called, and Shultz explained that the OECS
had brought Barbados and Jamaica into their counsels to
request aid. In fact, Prime Minister Adams had, along with
Eugenia Charles, taken the lead, but it is unclear if
Shultz knew that. Then President Reagan was awakened, and
he soon "gave the go-ahead to proceed with invasion
plans."[11] The vice president's crisis management team
reconvened in Washington, D.C., at 9:00 A.M. with Reagan,
Shultz, and McFarlane participating by telephone from
Augusta. Fears of a hostage situation were heightened when
it became clear that news of the fleet diversion had been
leaked to the press. The Joint Chiefs were ordered to
proceed with invasion planning on the basis of a "go
order,"[12] and it was decided to gather more intelligence

about the U.S. citizens' situation in Grenada by sending U.S. diplomats to the island. In addition, the group dispatched a special envoy, Frank McNeil, to Barbados with Major-General George Crist to clarify the OECS request and to arrange for military cooperation. They left early Sunday.

At 9:00 P.M., Saturday, the Cubans had sent a message to Washington reminding U.S. officials of Havana's condemnation of Bishop's death and indicating their awareness of U.S. concern about the safety of its citizens. The message also said that Havana was concerned about its own workers in Grenada and about reports that U.S. ships had been diverted to the island. But Cuba sought to reassure Washington by noting that "according to our reports, no U.S. or foreign citizens has run into any problem, nor has our personnel met with problems."[13]

Also on October 22 the leaders of CARICOM assembled at Port of Spain, Trinidad, and by 3:00 A.M. on Sunday, the twenty-third, they had agreed to communicate to Sir Paul Scoon, the Grenadian governor-general, the following demands:

1. the immediate establishment of a broad-based civilian government of national reconciliation acceptable to Scoon. This government would make arrangements for holding early elections
2. acceptance of a CARICOM fact-finding mission
3. arrangements to assure the safety of foreign nationals and/or their evacuation where desired
4. acceptance of a CARICOM peace-keeping force.[14]

When the second session began later on Sunday morning it became clear that some of the members believed that military force was inevitable and wished to dissociate themselves from the agreement. The leaders of Trinidad, Guyana, Belize, and the Bahamas explained that they were not in favor of military intervention "as a first resort."[15] A majority of members then voted to suspend Grenada from CARICOM and to impose the following sanctions:

1. no official contact with the existing regime
2. no sea and air communications links with Grenada
3. no new issues of currency to the regime by the East Carribean Central Bank
4. no trade or other economic cooperation with the regime

But apparently neither Adams, Seaga, nor the OECS
representatives informed the other CARICOM members of their
October 21 meeting or the decisions reached there.[16]
On Saturday, October 22, the British deputy high
commissioner in Barbados, David Montgomery, and two U.S.
consular officials landed in Grenada, and the following day
Montgomery met with Sir Paul Scoon. The U.S. diplomats had
found the Grenadian officials they had met "obstructionist
and uncooperative," but Montgomery's "assessment of the
danger to foreign nationals on Grenada was markedly
different." Sir Paul, "although evidently worried about
the situation of his country, . . . did not make any
request to the Deputy High Commissioner for help."[17]
Meanwhile in Barbados, the U.S special emissary, Ambassador
Frank McNeil, met with Charles, Adams, and Seaga and
received a formal invitation to help. There was no mention
of any external threat as required under Article 8 of the
OECS treaty, nor did anyone mention a request from Sir
Paul. The letter was not sent to the British presumably
because Charles knew that Britain opposed military action
at that time.[18] It is also <u>possible</u> that the OECS letter
had actually been drafted in Washington and given to Seaga,
Adams, and Charles by McNeil. In any case, according to
Kenneth Dam's later testimony, "Ambassador McNeil found
these three Caribbean leaders unanimous—and I repeat,
unanimous—in their conviction that the deteriorating
conditions on Grenada were a threat to the entire region
that required immediate and forceful action."[19]
Early that morning, of course, the massacre of U.S.
Marines had occurred in Beirut, and the presidential party
immediately returned to Washington from Augusta. All-day
meetings of Reagan and his advisers ensued. By afternoon,
discussions shifted from Lebanon to Grenada, and "when it
did, the President's overriding concern was over possible
hostages. Depressed and exhausted, he was haunted by his
predecessor's predicament in 1980, bewailing at one point,
'I'm no better off than Jimmy Carter.'"[20] The State
Department was especially eager for action. One
participant recalled that "The overriding principle was not
to allow something to happen worse than what we were
proposing to do. The purpose was to deny the
Russians/Cubans a feeling of potency in grabbing small
vulnerable states in the region. It had to be nipped in
the bud before it developed into another Cuba.[21] Shortly
before 7:00 P.M. the president made what Secretary Shultz
described as "his tentative decision that we should respond
to this urgent request." It was also agreed to consult no

allies. Lawrence Eagleburger assured the meeting that
Prime Minister Margaret Thatcher was likely to support the
intervention.

In Grenada, meanwhile, two more U.S. diplomats had
arrived and were apparently given assurances that Pearls
Airport would be reopened the next day, Monday, October 24,
for an evacuation flight. White House officials later
claimed that these promises were not kept--Pearls remained
closed to commercial traffic. Furthermore, on Monday the
Grenadian military rulers "changed their tone" and now
demanded six hours' advance notice for any evacuation
flights and warned that they could not guarantee the safety
of foreigners on the ride from their residences to the
airport. Ambassador Bish feared that the Revolutionary
Council was planning to use the safety issue as a
bargaining chip. He was also apparently concerned about
reports that, contrary to earlier assurances, the
Grenadians had turned back a forty-five-seat chartered
Canadian airliner. But, in fact, Canadian efforts to
charter a plane from the Leeward Islands Air Transport
Company had been scuttled by CARICOM's decision to cut all
transportation links with Grenada. Canadian officials also
later asserted that at least four small charter flights
left Pearls on Monday with about thirty passengers. One of
them, an OAS technical expert, Robert J. Myers,
subsequently said that airport operations seemed fairly
routine on Monday afternoon with Grenadian customs officals
"processing departures, normally stamping passports and
collecting airport taxes." Nor had Myers encountered any
violence en route to Pearls.[22]

On Sunday evening in New York the parents of about
five hundred of the students at St. George's Medical School
had gathered for a previously scheduled reception.
Naturally, Bishop's murder and the military takeover became
the focus of discussions. The group heard from parents who
had been in touch by telephone with their children, and
they discussed a cable that had just been received
summarizing a meeting earlier on Sunday at the school, at
which only about 10 percent of the students had expressed a
wish to be evacuated. The parents then sent a cable to the
White House informing the president of their children's
safety and asking him "not to move too quickly or to take
any precipitous action at this time."[23] Prior to the
parents' gathering, the chancellor of St. George's, Charles
Modica, who was in New York, had been telephoned by
Ambassador Bish and other State Department officials asking
him to state publicly that the students were in jeopardy.

The chancellor refused, citing his contrary evidence.
Earlier in the day in Grenada, Hudson Austin had called
Geoffrey Bourne, the vice chancellor, to offer jeeps and
other transportation for students wishing to go to the
airport, and he had promised to reopen the supermarket for
students who were staying. He also gave Dr. Bourne his
home phone number in case of any trouble.[24] In his
subsequent congressional testimony Kenneth Dam admitted
that he had "no information" that any U.S. citizens had
been threatened or harmed during the entire period.

Dr. Bourne, at his congressional appearance on
November 16, 1983, painted a rather different picture. He
revealed that on October 20 General Austin had assured him
that the students were in no danger and would not be
harmed. Two days later Bourne told Austin that only 10
percent of the students wanted to leave. Later that night
Austin called to express concern that the U.S. diplomats
had demanded helicopters and transport planes to evacuate
all the students, but he seemed satisfied after Bourne
talked with one of the U.S. officials. Bourne concluded,
however, "from General Austin's reaction when he thought
the embassy group was going to take all the students out, I
had grave doubts if they could have got out."[25] Vice
Chancellor Bourne apparently feared that although Austin
was not about to harm the students, any attempt by him
(Bourne) to cut a deal with the diplomats to evacuate large
numbers of students could have led to his (Austin's)
overthrow. As Bourne put it: "Would Bernard Coard . . .
have ordered the negotiations stopped? Would the Russians
and Cubans have taken the responsibility to pour in even
more arms and troops while diplomatic negotiations were
going on? The whole situation with the students may have
suddenly gone into reverse and the school have found itself
in a hostage situation. . . . We had a volatile and highly
dangerous situation . . . which could have become
disastrous at any minute."[26]

In any case, U.S. diplomats in Grenada ended their
efforts to arrange an evacuation at midnight Monday when
the embassy in Barbados sent General Austin a telex message
repeating concerns about the safety of U.S. citizens.

Sometime on Monday, according to Deputy Secretary
Dam's subsequent testimony, Washington was informed by
Prime Minster Adams that Governor-General Scoon "had used a
confidential channel to transmit an appeal for action by
the OECS and other regional states to restore order on the
island." The invitation, "which we were unable to refer to
publicly until the Governor-General's safety could be

assured, was an important element--legally as well as
politically--in the United States decision to intervene."[27]

According to a painstaking House of Commons report
released in March 1984, "both the timing and the nature of
this request remain shrouded in mystery, and it is
evidently the intention of the parties directly involved
that the mystery should not be dispelled."[28] This report,
however, concluded that Sir Paul's request "appears to have
been made orally to 'emissaries'" sent by Tom Adams, and,
although dated October 24, the confirmation in writing was
not received until after the intervention. Second, the
report found "considerable circumstantial evidence to
suggest that the Governor-General was aware of the
possibility of the intervention at some time earlier than
Sunday, October 23, and possibly as early as Friday,
October 21." Yet Sir Paul did not notify the British
deputy high commissioner of any need for assistance when
the two met on Sunday.[29] Furthermore, Prime Minister Adams
never mentioned any such invitation to Giles Bullard, the
British high commissioner in Barbados. Finally, when
Washington did inform London of the impending invasion on
Monday evening, no U.S. official--including the president--
mentioned Sir Paul's request despite the importance that
Britain would have obviously attached to such a plea.

This omission becomes even more puzzling in view of
London's negative reaction to the news. Sir Paul later
told the BBC that he did not consider assistance necessary
until late Sunday evening (the twenty-third), and what he
asked for was "not an invasion but help from the outside."
Indeed, the London _Economist_ even suggested that "the Scoon
request was almost certainly a fabrication concocted
between the OECS and Washington to calm the post-invasion
storm."[30]

President Reagan met from 2:15 to 3:00 P.M. Monday
with Weinberger and the Joint Chiefs. He signed the
directive at about 6:00 P.M. According to the State
Department's bulletin on the news conference,[31] early on
Tuesday morning, a combined force of troops ultimately
totaling 7,000 (from the United States, Jamaica, Barbados,
and the OECS states of Antigua, Dominica, St. Nevis/Kitts,
St. Lucia, and St. Vincent) landed on Grenada by sea--south
of Pearls Airport in northeast Grenada and by air--at the
nearly completed Point Salines Airport in the southwest.
By Friday, October 28, the force had secured all
significant military objectives and had defeated the
People's Revolutionary Army and Militia and 784 Cuban
construction workers. Forty-five Grenadians (including

twenty-four civilians), twenty-four Cubans, and eighteen
U.S. personnel were killed. Forty-nine Russians, seventeen
Libyans, fifteen North Koreans, ten East Germans, and three
Bulgarians were found and quickly repatriated.

Justification for U.S. Action

For the first time since the Dominican intervention of
1965, U.S. troops had been ordered into combat in the
Caribbean. The administration, over a period of several
weeks, presented rather elaborate justifications for the
action--justifications that revealed a good deal about
Reagan's regional and global goals and priorities.

The president's first announcement at 9:00 A.M.
Tuesday, October 25, of the "rescue mission" briefly
outlined the main reasons for the operation: to ensure the
"personal safety" of between 800 and 1,000 U.S. citizens on
Grenada, to "forestall further chaos," and "to assist in a
joint effort to restore order and democracy" there. He
also strongly emphasized that the effort had been mounted
in response to "an urgent, formal request" from several
eastern Caribbean states.

Later the same day Secretary Shultz underlined and
elaborated upon Reagan's initial statement at the news
conference. He described "an atmosphere of violent
uncertainty" in Grenada since the house arrest of Prime
Minister Bishop on October 14 and asserted that he could
"see no responsible government in the country." Instead,
"we see arrests of leading figures, . . . a shoot-on-sight
curfew . . . , reports--their validity uncertain-- . . .
about arrests, deaths, and so forth and certainly random
sporadic firing that one could hear." This atmopshere
"caused anxiety among U.S. citizens and caused the
President to be very concerned." So "he felt that it is
better under the circumstances to act before they might be
hurt or be hostage than to take any chance, given the great
uncertainty clearly present in the situation." Secretary
Shultz reiterated that the OECS's "urgent request"
constituted the second reason for the landing. These
neighboring states, which had "followed these developments
very closely over a period of time, and intensively in
recent days, . . . determined for themselves that there
were developments of grave concern to their safety and
peace taking place." Thus, pursuant to Article 8 of the
OECS treaty, these countries requested U.S. help. In
response to reporters' questions the secretary reiterated

his contention that "for all intents and purposes, there is no semblance of a genuine government present. There is a vacuum of governmental authority—the only genuine evidence of governmental authority being a shoot-on-sight curfew. . . . Mr. Austin was not genuinely in charge as far as we could see." Shultz also stressed that the action "was not taken as a signal about anything else," although "those who want to receive a message will have to receive it."

On October 26, at a special meeting of the Permanent Council of the Organization of American States, U.S. Ambassador J. William Middendorf emphasized the parallel perceptions of the OECS and Washington.[32] He described the atmosphere in Grenada in words very similar to Shultz's: "this quality of menacing uncertainty—the violence, the disintegration of civilized governmental authority, the creation of a dynamic that held out the distinct prospect of further violence." But Middendorf also tried to make an international legal case for the intervention. Arguing that that action was "a reasonable and proportionate reaction to the deterioration of authority in Grenada and the threat this pose[d] to the peace and security of the eastern Caribbean," he affirmed its consistency with the regional security clause (Article 52) of the United Nations Charter,[33] Articles 22 and 28 of the OAS Charter,[34] and Article 8 of the OECS treaty.[35] According to the Ambassador, the OECS decision was "a measure adopted for the maintenance of peace and security in accordance with existing treaties, as contemplated by Article 19 of the OAS Charter." By the time Middendorf made his remarks, reports from Grenada had indicated that the bulk of the resistance was being mounted by Cubans. He used this circumstance to draw a "disturbing lesson," for "construction workers on that island suddenly transformed themselves into soldiers." "This development," Middendorf warned, "must be a source of concern to all states and cast doubt on the bona fides of Cuban 'civilian' advisers and contingents elsewhere."

The next day, October 27, at the Security Council, Ambassador Jeane Kirkpatrick delivered an ambitious speech that seemed to carve out further justification for the action while paying somewhat less attention to the rescue mission dimension.[36] She began by challenging an alleged perspective about world politics that "treats the prohibition against the use of force as an absolute; and the injunction against intervention in the internal affairs of other states as the only obligation of states under the U.N. Charter." Rather, Kirkpatrick argued, "the

prohibitions against the use of force in the U.N. Charter
are contextual, not absolute. They provide ample
justification for the use of force against force in pursuit
of other values also inscribed in the Charter—freedom,
democracy, peace." Thus, "the Charter does not require
that peoples submit supinely to terror, nor that their
neighbors be indifferent to their terrorization."

In evaluating the U.S. actions, one must begin, not
with the October 25 landing, the ambassador suggested, but
with the character of the Bishop government and the group
that supplanted it. Bishop's government came to power in a
coup, refused to hold elections, and "succumbed to superior
force" when, "with the complicity of certain powers. . . ,
it first arrested, then murdered Bishop and his ministers.
Thus began what can only be called an authentic reign of
terror in Grenada." Political violence, then, had gripped
the island well before the arrival of the task force on
October 25.

Furthermore, the people of Grenada had been subjected
to "foreign intervention" because Maurice Bishop had
"freely offered his island as a base for the projection of
Soviet military power in this hemisphere. The familiar
pattern of militarization and Cubanization was already far
advanced in Grenada." In effect, "Grenada's internal
affairs had fallen under the permanent intervention of one
neighboring and one remote tyranny. Its people were
helpless in the grip of terror."

But why was the U.S. action different from other
interventions that under the guise of restoring self-
determination actually deny it? Because, she answered, "we
in the task force intend . . . to leave Grenada just as
soon as law is restored and the instrumentalities of self-
government—democratic government—have been put in place."
But don't all contemporary governments claim to be
democratic? What will ensure that this new Grenadian
government will represent the authentic expression of the
people any more than the "gang of thugs" from which the
island was delivered? "There is," Kirkpatrick asserted, "a
simple test," because free institutions—a free press, free
trade unions, free elections, representative, responsible
government—will be clearly in evidence.

Kirkpatrick then attempted to show that the "U.S.
response was fully compatible with relevant international
law and practice." Here she largely repeated the
statements of Shultz and Middendorf, but she added a few
important embellishments. Reagan's "brutal gang of leftist
thugs" became "madmen" and "terrorists," who, the United

States reasonably concluded, could at any moment decide to hold 1,000 U.S. citizens hostage in a replay of Iran. The ambassador admitted that in normal circumstances "concern for the safety of a state's nationals in a foreign country" does not justify military measures against that country. But in the Grenadian case no new government had replaced the old one; anarchy prevailed; and terrorists had wantonly endangered the lives of its citizens, foreign nationals, and the security of neighboring states. In these circumstances, Kirkpartick claimed, military action to protect endangered nationals is legally justified.

Second, the OECS concluded that the heavily armed "madmen" who had engineered the coup possessed an oversized army--one and one-half times the size of Jamaica's-- supported by more than 600 armed Cubans and had ambitions for using Grenada as a center for subversion, sabotage, and infiltration. Lacking sufficient security forces, the OECS asked the United States to join the effort to restore order to Grenada and to remove it as a security threat.

Finally, Kirkpatrick vehemently denied that the U.S. action was somehow counterrevolutionary. "The issue was not revolution . . . nor was it the type of government Grenada possessed," for neither the OECS nor the United States had ever attempted "to affect the composition or character" of the Bishop government. Rather, military power that Grenada had "amassed with Cuban and Soviet backing had fallen into the hands of individuals who could reasonably be expected to wield that awesome power against its neighbors." At the same time, however, "the coup leaders had no arguable claim to being the responsible government," as the failure of other states to recognize them, the governor-general's request, and their own declarations made clear. Kirkpatrick concluded that "in the context of these very particular, very unusual, perhaps unique circumstances, the United States decided to accede to the request of the OECS for aiding its collective efforts aimed at securing peace and stability in the Caribbean region."

That same evening President Reagan addressed the nation in an effort to defend his policies in Lebanon and Grenada.[37] He claimed that the nation's will was being tested by Soviet-backed terrorism in both the Middle East and the Caribbean. After asserting that the United States as a global power had a variety of vital interests in the Middle East, the president warned that "if terrorism and intimidation succeed, it'll be a devastating blow to the peace process and to Israel's search for genuine security."

Pointing to a massive Soviet military presence in Syria he asked, "Can the United States, or the free world, for that matter, stand by and see the Middle East incorporated into the Soviet bloc?"

Then Reagan turned to Grenada and reminded his audience that Maurice Bishop, "a protege of Fidel Castro," had overthrown a government elected under a "constitution left to the people by the British," sought Cuban help to build an airport, "which looks suspiciously suitable for military aircraft including Soviet-built long-range bombers," and alarmed his neighbors with a large army. Bishop, in turn, was ousted and subsequently killed by a group "even more radical and more devoted to Castro's Cuba that he had been." Now "Grenada was without a government, its only authority exercised by a self-proclaimed band of military men." Concerned that about 1,000 U.S. citizens on Grenada might "be harmed or held hostage," the president recounted how he had ordered a marine flotilla headed for Lebanon to be diverted to "the vicinity of Grenada in case there should be a need to evacuate our people." Then the OECS sent "an urgent request that we join them in a military operation to restore order and democracy to Grenada. These small peaceful nations needed our help." Hence Reagan acceded to their legitimate request and to his own concern for the U.S. citizens on the island. Resurrecting a theme from his inaugral address, he asserted that "the nightmare of our hostages in Iran must never be repeated."

President Reagan raised another issue connected with the landing, but did not exactly offer it as a reason for the intervention: "[W]e have discovered a complete base with weapons and communications equipment which makes it clear a Cuban occupation of the island had been planned." A warehouse of military equipment, stacked with enough weapons and ammunition to supply "thousands of terrorists" had been discovered. The president was unequivocal: Grenada "was a Soviet-Cuban colony being readied as a major military base to export terror and undermine democracy. We got there just in time."

Nor did Reagan leave any doubt about the relationship between Lebanon and Grenada: "Not only has Moscow assisted and encouraged the violence in both countries, but it provides direct support through a network of surrogates and terrorists. It is no coincidence that when the thugs tried to wrest control of Grenada, there were 30 Soviet advisers and hundreds of Cuban military and paramilitary forces on the island."

This speech was instrumental in gaining overwhelming public and congressional support for the U.S. action in Grenada, though, interestingly, Reagan's Lebanon policy remained controversial and unpopular. Indeed, the administration made only a handful of additional statements about the Caribbean intervention. Two of them, however, are noteworthy. In a November 2 address to the General Assembly--an anti-U.S. vote without debate had aleady been taken--Jeane Kirkpatrick sought to counter critics who equated the U.S. intervention in Grenada with Moscow's intervention in Afghanistan.[38] She agreed that there was a certain similarity:

> The United States believes, as some nations have suggested, that a parallel can be drawn between the action in Grenada and the Soviet action in Afghanistan--a very meaningful parallel. Just as Maurice Bishop was murdered in Grenada because he tried to free himself from the Soviet stranglehold, so too was Mohammed Daud murdered in Afghanistan. They too discovered that the only thing more dangerous than embracing the Soviet bear is trying to break loose from its deathly grip. They too learned that the price of trying to "reverse" Soviet conquest is violent death. This, and this alone, is the parallel between Grenada and Afghanistan. The difference is that the people of Grenada have now been spared the cruel fate of the people of Afghanistan.

Deputy Secretary of State Dam on November 4 cataloged what U.S. forces had found on Grenada: five secret treaties--three with the Soviet Union, one with North Korea, one with Cuba--"under which these communist countries were to donate military equipment in amounts without precedent for a population of 110,000; . . . artillery, antiaircraft weapons, armored personnel carriers, and rocket launchers; . . . thousands of rifles, thousands of fuses, tons of TNT, and millions of rounds of ammunition; . . . communications gear and cryptographic devices"; and agreements that authorized the secret presence of Cuban military advisers on the island. Dam then drew four broader lessons from the events in Grenada. First, the administration had been guilty of understating the dangers of Soviet-Cuban penetration of the Caribbean. In light of what was found in Grenada, Dam invited Americans and Europeans to "reassess their estimates of the security concerns of the American government and of the

non-Communist countries of the Caribbean." Second, by
looking at Maurice Bishop's fate when he accepted Cuban and
Soviet help but then tried to remain unaligned, "the nine
commandantes of Nicaragua might . . . wish to ponder their
relationship with their Soviet and Cuban mentors." Third,
the Sandinistas ought to learn from Grenada that in the
absence of democracy and free elections "policy differences
tend to degenerate into violence." And finally, Grenada
showed that "neighbors have a clear, ongoing responsibility
to act in ways consistent with each other's legitimate
security concerns." Dam called on Nicaragua to negotiate
seriously, reduce its reliance on military power, and "stop
its belligerent behavior" toward its neightbors. The
deputy secretary did not, however, speculate about the
consequences of a Nicarguan failure to heed the "lessons"
of Grenada.[39]

Reaction in the United States to the Grenada Invasion

Despite the administration's elaborate efforts to
portray the Grenada intervention as a humanitarian rescue
mission, a compassionate response to an urgent request for
help by small, friendly, democratic neighbors, and the
successful foiling of a Soviet-Cuban colony, the U.S.
public supported the action because it was swift,
conclusive, and relatively free of cost. Several polls
conducted in the immediate aftermath of the operation
affirm the overwhelmingly pragmatic nature of the public's
reactions. The November ABC-Washington Post survey, for
example, showed 71 percent in favor and only 22 percent
opposed to the Grenada landing. Yet although most people--
50 percent to 35 percent in the New York Times poll taken
after Reagan's October 27 speech--thought the United States
had intervened to protect U.S. lives rather than to .
overthrow a Marxist government, most people also believed
that the U.S. citizens in Grenada had not been in a "great
deal of danger." And in a Newsweek-Gallup canvass more
respondents favored the withdrawal of U.S. troops as soon
as the safety of the U.S. nationals was assured than those
who wanted the troops to stay until Grenada was able to
install a democratic government. Consistent with this
finding was a New York Times-CBS survey that indicated that
the public opposed by a 60 percent to 21 percent margin
U.S. support for the Nicaraguan contras. Furthermore, at
the same time that the public supported the president on
Grenada, a plurality--47 percent to 43 percent--continued

to believe that he was "too quick to employ U.S. forces,"
and another plurality—49 percent to 44 percent—felt more
"uneasy" than "confident" about Reagan's ability to handle
international crises.[40] The public, in short, liked the
Grenada invasion because it worked but was unwilling to
read "broader lessons" into the affair.

Initial congressional reaction was largely negative.
The Senate was not in session on October 25, but in the
House several representatives voiced sharp criticism. For
example, Don Bonker accused the administration of "a
cavalier attitude about using military force to deal with
diplomatic problems" and claimed that "it flies in the face
of the President's condemnation of Soviet interference in
other countries."[41] Howard Wolpe called the action an
example of "gunboat diplomacy in direct contradiction to
American ideals, traditions, and interests."[42] Edward J.
Markey asked the president: "where does all this military
intervention end? Are the Marines going to become our new
Foreign Service officers?"[43] And George Miller maligned[44]
Reagan for refusing to meet with Maurice Bishop in June.

The next day, in the Senate, Gary Hart introduced a
resolution to invoke the War Powers Act and "vowed to
oppose any further extension of U.S. military involvement
in this small island country."[45] The rest of the Senate,
though, had virtually nothing to say about Grenada, and
John Melcher warned that the intervention "should not
distract us from the timely and urgently needed correction
of a disastrous Lebanon policy."[46]

The Democrats continued the offensive in the House on
October 26. Bob Edgar argued that U.S. lives were not
endangered in Grenada, that the people of Grenada had not
been consulted, and that the Congress had been
circumvented. Noting that bloody coups-d'etat were a
common occurrence in the world, he asked, "Are we to send
in our marines and rangers every time there is an
international disturbance?"[47] Major R. Owens called the
invasion "illegal, immoral, and a wasteful expenditure of
resources and human lives" and predicted that "the United
states will now become a scapegoat" as the poor and
unemployed throughout the Caribbean will blame this country
for their condition.[48] Jim Leach reminded his colleagues
that "our most loyal ally, Great Britain, strongly objects
to our decision." Questioning the legality of the action,
Leach complained that "we have reconstituted gunboat
diplomacy in an era when the efficacy as well as the
morality of great power intervention have come increasingly
into question."[49] Gus Savage was even more blunt. He

recalled Prime Minister Charles's briefing of the Black
Caucus the previous day and, terming her "this puppet of
the President" who "represents 'Aunt Jemimaism' in
geopolitics," claimed that the intervention had raised "to
an international level Reagan's ante-bellum attitude
towards blacks in this country."[50]
   Most Republicans had immediately leaped to the
president's defense, but by October 26 even some Democrats
began to offer support. Most notable in this regard was
Dante Fascell, soon to become chairman of the Foreign
Affairs Committee. Although deploring the administration's
failure to consult Congress prior to the invasion, he
stated that "under the circumstances which existed in that
region, which is virtually in our backyard, I believe the
U.S. was justified."[51] Speaker Thomas P. ("Tip") O'Neill's
first reaction was to urge national unity while the
fighting was in progress, though he soon suggested that
unless U.S. citizens had been in actual danger, the
invasion would represent gunboat diplomacy.
   As the medical students began returning from Grenada
on Tuesday night, however, and as U.S. forces began to
uncover evidence of Cuban and Soviet weapons, criticism of
Reagan diminished markedly. Tim Valentine exclaimed:
"What a beautiful sight to see . . . our youthful
countrymen kiss the soil of South Carolina with praise and
thanks on their lips. Thank God for our Armed Forces."[52]
And Dan Burton echoed: "We have heard the terms
'warmonger' and 'gunboat diplomacy' used. Well, last night
we saw the results of that action. Students were geting
off the plane. They were kissing the ground. They were
saying 'God bless America.' They were thanking the
President for sending in the marines and the rangers."[53]
For William S. Broomfield, the ranking Republican on the
Foreign Affairs Committee: "It appears obvious. . . that
the Soviets and Cubans had definite plans for turning
Grenada into another Cuba. With yet another base in that
area, the Soviets could continue to export revolution and
terrorism to the small countries of the region."[54]
   On October 28 the Senate voted 64 to 20 to invoke the
War Powers Act in Grenada, but most of those who favored
the resolution were careful to explain that their support
did not imply criticism of the invasion. A few senators
such as Gary Hart and Paul Sarbanes did use the resolution
as the occasion to attack Reagan's action, but even Senator
Hart tried to narrow its meaning: "This amendment . . .
has nothing to do with whether the U.S. citizens were in
danger. It does not question the authority of the

President . . . . Whether we could have adopted some different remedy . . . is not an issue." The House also voted overwhelmingly (403 to 23) on November 1 to apply the War Powers Act to Grenada on these restricted legal grounds.

Faced with massive public support of the action, the apparent evidence of danger in Grenada provided by the returning students, the discovery of Cuban and Soviet weapons, and the popularity of Reagan's October 27 speech, congressional criticism became more muted, and its emphasis tended to shift to other issues. The administration had clamped a news blackout on the military operation, prohibited journalists from going to the island until several days later, and incarcerated those who sought to evade this rule. The Defense Department, partly because of its conviction that the media had hurt the war effort in Vietnam, and partly because of the evident success of the British news blackout during the Falklands invasion, was behind the ban. The networks, wire services, and major newspapers expressed predictable outrage, and a few congressional critics of the intervention took up the issue. Senator Edward M. Kennedy, for example, expressed "concern about the administration's continuing effort to manage the news from Grenada" and announced that he formally asked Senator John Tower, chairman of the Armed Services Committee, to undertake an investigation of the press policies "imposed during the Grenada invasion."[55] And Partick J. Leahy proclaimed that "Rarely have reporters been treated with the cynicism and contempt they have experienced since our troops went ashore on Grenada."[56] Other critics bemoaned the accidental bombing of a mental hospital that claimed several lives, and a few emphasized the largely negative assessment of the intervention by European allies and Latin American countries, but by October 28 supporters of the actions had begun to dominate congressional debate.

One particularly interesting exchange occurred in the Senate on that day. Senator Howard Baker, with strong backing form the White House, introduced the following:

> The Congress commends the President for his swift and effective action in protecting the lives of American citizens in Grenada. Moreover, the Congress commends the professionalism and valor of the combined U.S. forces who are participating in this operaton.
> Finally, the Congress expresses its appreciation to the Organization of Eastern Caribbean States and to

the states of Jamaica and Barbados for their
dedication to freedom and democratic government in the
region.[57]

Steven D. Symms rose to propose a "slight modification"
that would have said "swift and effective action in
enforcing the Monroe Doctrine and protecting the lives of
American citizens in Grenada." He explained that "the
Monroe Doctrine is the most fundamental principle of
American foreign policy, and it is the very best
justification for the President's decision to intervene in
Grenada." Professing to "have no problem at all" with
Symm's suggested change, Baker admitted that the language
of his amendment had first been cleared "in other quarters"
and insisted that it ought not be altered. Symms
reluctantly agreed, but added: "The Grenada relief
operation is the first time the Brezhnev doctrine has been
stopped by the Monroe Doctrine. It is the first time that
we have done anything to destroy a military base
established by Cuba." Baker ended by saying, perhaps
sincerely, "Had I thought of it I would have included that
language because I believe in the position asserted by the
Senator from Idaho."[58]

Minority Leader Robert C. Byrd then introduced a Sense
of the Senate resolution that called on the president to

1. provide immediate, maximum protection and security
   for U.S. forces in Lebanon;
2. vigorously pursue, in coordination with our allies
   in the Multinational Peacekeeping Force, every
   possible avenue to facilitate the orderly
   transferral of the peacekeeping responsibilities in
   Lebanon to a United Nations peacekeeping presence,
   or to other forces from neutral countries, in order
   to hasten the withdrawal of U.S. groundforces; and
3. prepare and transmit to the Congress a report
   setting forth the measure he has taken to carry out
   paragraphs (1) and (2).
   Sec. 2. The Secretary of the Senate shall transmit a
   copy of this resolution to the President.[59]

In the course of the ensuing debate Byrd acknowledged that
he supported the Grenada decision, but Baker countered that
in tying a Lebanon clause to the Grenada amendment, "we are
talking about two things that are very similar but very
different."[60] Byrd, not surprisingly, asked "If the
President ties them together, why does it not make sense

for the U.S. Senate to tie them together?"[61] Confronted
with a stalemate, Senator Charles McC. Mathias, Jr.,
suggested that both resolutions be withdrawn. There the
matter rested. In the House two Republicans introduced a
concurrent resolution. It was promptly sent to the Armed
Services Committee where it was buried.[62] In contrast, a
bill submitted by Ted Weiss to impeach the president failed
to win a single cosponsor.

Meanwhile, Speaker O'Neill appointed a fourteen-member
commission to conduct a fact-finding mission to Grenada and
Barbados. Chaired by the Democratic whip, Thomas S. Foley,
the group returned from a four-day trip on November 7.
According to Foley, "Under the circumstances, the majority-
-and I would say, the very large majority--feels that . .
the President acted correctly to protect American lives."[63]
But, Foley warned that "if I conceived this to be a
precedent for other interventions, I would be frightened."
Not all the members of the commission agreed. Ronald V.
Dellums, a leader of the Black Caucus, asserted that
"because the administration wanted to strike out against
the government of Grenada and its Cuban advisers, the
presence of the students was used as an excuse to launch
the invasion."[64] More representative, however, was Robert
B. Torricelli's acknowledgement that "Public opinion is
what's behind things here. Years of frustration were
vented by the Grenada invasion. I hardly get a call in my
office about Grenada where people don't mention the Iranian
hostage situation. So people feel their frustration
relieved and members of Congress sense that."[65] After
being briefed by Foley and the commission, Speaker O'Neill
reversed his earlier criticism--a switch that some
Democrats called a "strategic retreat"--and called the
intervention "justified" to rescue U.S. citizens.[66]

Most of those commentators, newspapers, and opinion
journals that generally supported the Reagan foreign policy
liked the Grenada action, while those that had been
bothered by recent U.S. foreign policy were troubled by the
intervention. A partial, but important, exception was the
influential Norman Podhoretz, who had been repeatedly
disappointed by Ronald Reagan but showed great enthusiasm
for the Grenada affair. In May 1982 he had written a piece
for the New York Times Magazine,[67] entitled "The Neo-
Conservative Anguish Over Reagan's Foreign Policy," which
bemoaned the administration's cancellation of the Soviet
grain embargo, its hesitation in response to martial law in
Poland, its "retreat" in Central America, and its
capitulation to public pressure for arms control talks.

Podhoretz sadly concluded that "the Administration . . . loves commerce more than it loathes Communism." Furthermore, he claimed that Reagan was pursuing a policy of detente--"not the corrupted adaptation, so often indistinguishable from appeasement, pursued by the Carter Administration"--but detente "in the sophisticated Nixon-Kissinger form." Indeed, Reagan's alleged failure to implement a strategy of anti-Communist containment signified "the slipping away of a precious political opportunity that may never come again."

Podhoretz's depression deepened in the wake of the Israeli invasion of Lebanon in June 1982: "Indeed, American Marines were sent into Lebanon in the first place not to cooperate with the Israelis in clearing the P.L.O. out of Beirut but to prevent the Israelis from doing the job themselves."[68] For Podhoretz, "the result has inevitably been an incoherent political strategy, and it is this incoherence that is reflected in the mission of the Marines in Lebanon." But Grenada "tells a different story, and the contrast is both instructive and inspiring." The administration approached Grenada "with a clarity of political and moral purpose that we have been utterly unable to achieve in Lebanon" and "has managed to brush aside pre-emptive rationalizations of the kind that were invoked to justify our impotence over the hostages in Iran." Podhoretz claimed that "Grenada by itself cannot be taken to signify a resurgence of American power," but Grenada points the way back to recovery and health "after the shell-shocked condition that has muddled our minds and paralyzed our national will since Vietnam."[69]

The Wall Street Journal, a consistent supporter of the administration on most foreign and domestic issues, evinced similar enthusiasm for Grenada.[70] An editorial on October 26 contended that the real reason for the intervention was the prospect of a "Soviet-Cuban puppet state" among the tiny democracies of the eastern Caribbean, and the "real question is whether the U.S. has the will to protect its friends." The Journal admonished, "there is little time for the moral complexities that perplex Georgetown salons," for "we are likely to learn that the American people are not opposed to any use of force, only to the use of force for no obtainable purpose." Hence, "if no one will say that what happened in Grenada is wrong, why should a different morality apply in the rest of Latin America and in the rest of the world?" Clearly, the Journal relished the notion, given the appropriate circumstances, of more Grenadas.

A few regional examples should suffice to convey the tone of editorial support. According to the Columbus Citizen-Journal, "President Reagan has been bolstered by the facts in defending his military intervention in Grenada. . . . Reagan moved in time to prevent an Iran-style hostage crisis that could have embarrassed and weakened the United States." Now, "if things work out" as the United States hopes, "Grenadians will enjoy rights they never would have had under the murderous thugs who terrorized them in recent weeks."[71] And the Jacksonville Journal was even more assertive: Grenada "is of great strategic importance to the Soviet Union." It "is the third point in a triangle--Cuba and Nicaragua being the other two points--that can control shipping throughout the Caribbean." So "let the critics rave: Reagan has sent two clear messages to the Kremlin this week that he will not be content with mere U.S. handwringing while the Soviet Union uses every form of brutality to advance its imperialist policies."[72]

At the same time, radical and the majority of liberal commentators condemned the invasion. Ronald Steel, for instance, characterized Reagan as "hypocritical," for "we will wait in vain . . . for a liberation of Haiti, El Salvador and other friendly, thug-ruled countries."[73] The president "ordered the invasion of Grenada because he wanted to show that the United States will use force to get rid of marxist governments--thereby hoping to intimidate radicals in other Caribbean countries." Steel concluded that "this Administration still has not grown up, and at this point probably never will." Similarly, the Boston Globe asserted that "pretending that this unilateral move was a 'joint maneuver' insults the intelligence of Americans. Pretending that the United States has suddenly developed a lively interest in the democracy that it has ignored in the rest of Latin America insults the rest of the world." Grenada's real threat "was not military but ideological."[74] The New York Times was only slightly less acid in its observation that

> when all is done, pacifying Grenada will prove only the obvious about American power. The enduring test for Americans is not whether we have the will to use that power but the skill to avoid having to. A President who felt he had no other choice last Monday night should not be celebrating a victory. He should be repairing the prior political failures and forestalling the bitter harvest to come.[75]

The Washington Post and the Nation also deplored the
invasion, and the Coalition for a New Foreign and Military
Policy called it illegal and unnecessary.[76] Transafrica
went even further:

> The resort to military force reflects a failure on the
> part of our government to exercise any available
> diplomatic options to promote democracy in Grenada.
> We denied any receptive audience to Prime Minister
> Maurice Bishop or other representatives of the New
> Jewel Movement when they requested dialogue. The
> efforts of Bishop himself to create a representative
> government were given no credibility by the
> administration. The United States encouraged his
> demiseby ignoring him. Meanwhile, American officials
> planned an invasion of Grenada as long as two years
> ago. This particular invasion was in the planning
> stages as early as two weeks before the mililtary coup
> occurred. All of this suggests a covert U.S. role in
> the overthrow of the civilian government.[77]

But more significant, perhaps, than these rather
unsurprising reactions were those of two relatively liberal
observers, Carl T. Rowan and Morton Kondracke, both of whom
firmly supported the intervention. Rowan noted that "there
was no outpouring of black denunciation [in the U.S.]--just
a lot of black ambivalence." Some blacks, Rowan admitted,
were disgusted "over two leaders of small Caribbean
countries sitting in 'photo opportunities' where Reagan
posed as their savior, even at the time Reagan was firing
three members of the U.S. Civil Rights Commission," and
others initially doubted that the OECS's urgent request was
anything more than a way to get more U.S. aid. But, Rowan
concluded, "in deciding whether to support or condemn the
invasion, I think a lot of liberals and blacks put
ourselves in the place of these Caribbean leaders." And
when they did that and closely followed the chronology of
events in Grenada from October 12 to October 19, "a
remarkable number of liberals and blacks" decided that they
too would have joined in a call for U.S. military
intervention.[78]
  Kondracke, then executive editor of the New Republic,
acknowledged that "we liberals oppose the use of force on
principle and prefer the rule of law, [b]ut honest people
have to admit that, unfortunately, force has its place in
this world." He agreed with the people who thought the
saving-lives argument was just a pretext because "Reagan

was . . . itching to take a shot at some leftist regime to prove that the United States could win this one." Nevertheless, Kondracke still offered his support, for "if liberalism values self-determination, peaceful change, and democracy, then liberal values are being threatened in the Caribbean and around the world. They need to be defended, and Reagan defended them." And like Podhoretz, Kondracke expressed the belief that the invasion "will warn the Soviets, Cubans, Sandinistas, and other aggressive leftists that the United States has overcome its Vietnam-bred reluctance to use military power to defend its interests and its values."[79]

International Reaction to the Grenada Invasion

If domestic opinion tended to support the intervention, international opinion did not. The UN Security Council quickly took up the issue as Guyana, Nicaragua, and Zimbabwe orchestrated a drive against the United States and the OECS. Despite a U.S. request for a twenty-four-hour postponement, debate began on the evening of October 25 with a strong attack by Mexico's representative, Porfirio Munoz Ledo, who called it a "clear violation of the rules of international law . . . totally lacking in justification."[80] Of the sixty-three countries that spoke over the next two days, only the United States and the OECS participants defended the action, though many of the speakers asserted that they opposed all interventions, including those in Afghanistan, Namibia, and Kampuchea. The resolution, which "deeply deplored the armed intervention in Grenada" as "a flagrant violation of international law and of the independence, sovereignty and territorial integrity of that state," was passed early on October 28 by a vote of 11-1-3, with Britain, Togo, and Zaire abstaining. France, the Netherlands, and Pakistan were among those who supported it, and the United States, of course, cast a veto.[81] An identical resolution was then introduced in the General Assembly and passed without debate on November 2 with well over one hundred states voting yes. The South Yemen motion to stifle debate, however, squeaked through by only 60-54-24, and the United States strongly supported a successful Belgian resolution calling for "the holding of elections in Grenada as soon as possible." South Yemen's attempt to set aside this motion failed, and the Belgian amendment was then approved 71-23-41.[82] This amendment implied that U.S. intentions in

Grenada were quite different from those of the Soviet Union
in Afghanistan. Indeed, one senior U.S. official at the
United Nations claimed that the outcome "wasn't an
unmitigated disaster for U.S. policy."[83]

The OAS Permanent Council first considered Grenada on
October 26, and although most of the twenty-nne delegates
who spoke assailed the action as a violation of
international law and of the principle of nonintervention,
no resolution was introduced. At the annual meeting of the
OAS General Assembly, which convened in Washington, D.C.,
on November 14, Mexico led the attack against the invasion.
Many states joined in the assault, but at least some
delegates privately admitted that they were somewhat
reassured by Deputy Secretary of State Dam's statement of
November 15 that the allegedly unique circumstances in
Grenada meant that the intervention did not represent a
precedent.[84] Again, no resolution was offered.

The European allies of the United States evinced
strong initial disapproval of the intervention—disapproval
made even more embarrassing by Prime Minister Margaret
Thatcher's outspoken opposition. But as the Reagan
administration continued to produce evidence allegedly
showing that the U.S. students had been in danger and that
Grenada had become a Soviet outpost, European opinion began
to soften. West German Chancellor Helmut Kohl told a Tokyo
news conference in early November that he "understood" the
reasons for the invasion, former French President Valery
Giscard d'Estaing announced his approval, and Le Monde
called the affair a "failure for Cuba."[85] In Britain,
Labour remained highly critical, but many Conservative MPs,
Thatcher's reservations notwithstanding, proclaimed their
support and criticized the government for ignoring its
eastern Caribbean obligation. On balance, then, when
placed in the context of other postwar U.S. interventions
in the Caribbean, the international reaction, while
certainly negative, was not without precedent.

9
U.S. Foreign
Policy Implications

President Reagan's decision to send U.S. troops to
Grenada in October 1983 rekindled an ancient, if episodic,
debate in U.S. foreign policy about the proper use of
military power. More specifically, it raised anew the issue
of intervention in the affairs of other states--an issue
that has periodically confronted the United States not only
in the Western Hemisphere but also in much of the world ever
since Edmond-Charles Genet directly petitioned the United
States for help against Britain in the 1790s. And since
Washington's farewell address, U.S. presidents have tried to
face the issue of intervention by providing broad guidelines
defining U.S. interests. The Monroe Doctrine, the Roosevelt
Corollary, and more recently the so-called doctrines of
Truman, Eisenhower, Johnson, Nixon, and Carter all staked
out either regional or global interests for the United
States. Indeed, postwar presidents have evidently felt, in
part, that affixing their names to these doctrines ensured
historical greatness. Such self-consciousness certainly
affected Jimmy Carter and his doctrine for the Persian
Gulf.

Notwithstanding these efforts to articulate U.S.
interests, however, more or less grand national debates have
frequently erupted over the intervention issue. As long as
U.S. power remained limited, as it did during the Latin
American revolutions of the 1820s and the liberal
revolutions in Europe twenty years later, the prospect of
actual military intervention was extremely remote; when
revolution broke out in Cuba--on the doorstep of a rapidly
industrializing United States--the issue became much less
abstract. And when Europe went to war in 1914 President
Woodrow Wilson was faced with the agonizing decision of
whether to commit U.S. forces to a nonhemispheric conflict.

The debilitating isolationist-internationalist clash of the 1930s concerned, of course, the advisability of U.S. intervention in a new European war. World War II and the Truman Doctrine apparently settled the issue--the United States was a global power with global responsibilities--but then Vietnam spawned a new and divisive national debate.

It was this complex legacy that Ronald Reagan inherited. In view of his loudly and frequently proclaimed anticommunism and his overwhelming 1980 electoral mandate, President Reagan might have been expected to announce some sweeping foreign policy doctrine early in his administration. Haig's efforts to interest the president in El Salvador and Cuba in 1981, however, were defeated by the White House's domestic economic priorities. But by late 1983 the economy was experiencing a strong, if uneven, recovery, and Reagan had made the Caribbean Basin a focal point of his foreign policy. Military advisers had been sent to El Salvador, Honduras was being transformed into a base camp, the CIA was actively supporting the anti-Sandinist contras, and Congress had just passed the Caribbean Basin Initiative. Yet the president firmly resisted all temptations to use the Grenada affair to lay down broad guidelines for U.S. military power, if not globally, at least for the Caribbean. Whereas in 1965 Lyndon Johnson had defiantly asserted that "the American nations cannot, must not, and will not permit the establishment of another Communist government in the Western Hemisphere" as he ordered U.S. troops into the Dominican Republic, Ronald Reagan and his spokespersons generally defended the Grenada intervention as a highly unusual response to probably unique circumstances.

For example, when asked by a congressional representative if the United States would have intervened if U.S. lives had not been endangered and if there had been no OECS request for aid, Deputy Secretary Dam replied, "That is correct."[1] Another representative asked Dam if the United States would use the Grenada precedent to invade Nicaragua if invited to do so by the members of the Consejo de Defensa Centro Americana (CONDECA), he answered, "you would have a different situation from the standpoint of the United States reaction because there were several factors [in Grenada], most particularly the threat to American lives."[2] And when Representative Gerry Studds asked Dam if the Cuban buildup did not in fact constitute one of the principal reasons for the Grenada intervention, he reiterated that the only reasons had been the issue of U.S. lives and the OECS request and added, "We had been aware of a Cuban-Soviet

buildup earlier, but we had not gone in."[3] The point here
is not whether the administration was being wholly
truthful--this dimension will be discussed later--but the
rather narrow grounds that it chose to justify the invasion.

President Reagan declined to proclaim a sweeping
"Grenada doctrine" largely because of the continuing lack of
a domestic consensus about the purposes and limits of U.S.
power. The absence of such a consensus, which had been
destroyed in the late 1960s during the Vietnam War, is often
noted. Furthermore, this lack can explain a good deal about
U.S. foreign policy since 1970. A review of some basic
features of the U.S. public's foreign policy attitudes may
clarify Reagan's defense of the Grenada invasion. Public
opinion analysts frequently distinguish "valence" from
"position" issues.[4] Position issues, because they pit
alternatives such as dove and hawk against each other, are
inherently divisive; valence issues involve only one
position or value, which can possess either a negative or
positive "valence." Thus voters value positively peace,
prosperity, strength, and honest government but attach
negative valences to unemployment, military weakness, and
corruption. Valence issues unify the electorate--the only
question is how important the value is in relation to other
ones. Thus valence issues entail competition to associate
one's policy position with the preferred value. For
instance, whereas both Carter and Reagan in 1980 identified
themselves with military strength, the incumbent Carter
claimed that he had reversed the decline in defenses
allegedly begun under Nixon, but candidate Reagan blamed
Carter for U.S. weakness.

Political scientists have also for many years
differentiated the attentive from the uninformed public.
The attentive public is better educated and follows foreign
affairs regularly. Since World War II--or perhaps more
accurately, since Eisenhower's victory over Robert Taft at
the 1952 Republican Convention--a very high percentage of
the attentive audience has possessed an internationalist
outlook, and until the late 1960s this outlook formed the
core of the Cold War consensus. Supportive of an active
world role for the United States, this group, which has
always consisted of more than half of the overall
electorate, applauded initiatives like the Marshall Plan,
the Truman Doctrine, NATO, and, initially at least, the
Korean War. Needless to say, the attentive public was
anti-Communist and deeply suspicion of the Soviet Union but
also supported efforts like Atoms for Peace, allegedly
designed to improve superpower relations.

In contrast, the uninformed audience has been, and
continues to be, overwhelmingly composed of people with
noninternationalist attitudes. Although not isolationist in
the sense of a principled opposition to U.S. participation
in international affairs, this group nevertheless has been
unsupportive of much of U.S. foreign policy. Distrustful of
involvement in the world, these voters believe that "most of
what the United States does for the world is senseless,
wasteful, and unappreciated."[5]

In the late 1960s, however, the internationally minded
attentive public broke up and after a few years of
incoherence, arrayed itself into two attitude groups of
roughly equal strength: conservative and liberal
internationalists. Broadly speaking, the former group was
promilitary and antidetente while the latter held
antimilitary and prodetente convictions. Each group, in
short, reflected different aspects of the old consensus.
Conservative internationalists viewed the world in the
context of the East-West conflict and attached traditional
ideological categories--freedom versus repression, democracy
versus totalitarianism, capitalism versus communism--to
international relations. Furthermore, they celebrated
military power, maligned detente, and strongly supported an
expanded defense budget. The intellectuals and foreign
policy specialists holding these views are neoconservatives.
Liberal internationalists, in contrast, rejected the
East-West focus on security issues and military power and
emphasized economic and humanitarian concerns. Stressing
concepts like interdependence and change, they applauded
detente as a useful beginning toward a safer world. And the
intellectuals and experts who evinced this outlook became
known as "world order" advocates. Interestingly, however,
both groups not only favor sustained U.S. involvement in
world affairs but also perceive foreign policy in highly
ideological ways.

Noninternationalists do not believe that U.S. foreign
policy should serve higher interests or noble causes whether
of the left or the right. Since the late 1960s they have
allied with the liberal internationalists on the issue of
intervention and with the conservative internationalists on
the issue of military strength. Their "basic impulse is
defensive";[6] they want a strong United States that does not
give "foreign aid handouts" and does not get "bogged down"
in other countries' wars. They oppose U.S. involvement
"unless a clear and compelling issue of national interest or
national security is at stake."[7] If so, then
noninternationalists favor swift, decisive action to defend

the country's interests. Thus, although this group gradually turned against Vietnam when the United States showed that it was unable or unwilling to win the war, by the mid-1970s it had begun to worry about the apparent decline of U.S. military strength. Not surprisingly, noninternationalists voted strongly for Reagan in 1980, partly because of his promise to rearm the nation, though they simultaneously worried about his "gunslinger" and "trigger happy" reputation.

For all intents and purposes the Reagan administration, in my view, had no _foreign_ policy during its first year in office. What it had was a _defense_ policy--or, rather, a defense posture--and polls indicated wide public approval of increased defense spending. But by 1982 the number of people favoring a further expansion had fallen from 56 to 29 percent, and for the first time since 1976 more people thought that the United States was spending too much on defense than those who believed it was spending too little.[8] In February 1982 the public's overall approval of Reagan's foreign policy performance fell below 50 percent, and after a series of foreign crises erupted in El Salvador, the Falklands, and Lebanon, it dipped even lower. Public opposition to Reagan's El Salvador policy was sizable in March 1981 when U.S. advisers were sent in, but the public's general enthusiasm for foreign interventions dropped dramatically from a crest at the time of the Iranian hostage crisis and the Soviet invasion of Afghanistan. For example, the public's willingness to send U.S. troops to defend Western Europe if it were attacked by Russia fell from 70 percent in February 1980 to 50 percent in July 1981.

In short, fear of voter reprisal certainly played a large role in constraining President Reagan from proclaiming a grand Grenada doctrine. In the absence of a public consensus about military interventions--even in areas deemed vital to U.S. security--Reagan would have risked electoral punishment if he had declared Grenada a precedent for future actions. Indeed, as the opinion polls cited earlier suggest, people supported the invasion on the narrow, pragmatic grounds of swiftness and success. No doubt they would have similarly celebrated a successful rescue of the Iranian hostages in 1980.

But the administration's refusal to attach wider meanings to Grenada should not be exaggerated. Even though Reagan hesitated to issue a presidential doctrine about future military interventions in the Caribbean, he and his advisers were not loath to make (or imply) certain rather broad claims. The administration argued that the Grenada

situation was highly unusual because of the simultaneous
presence of three elements: the reasonable likelihood that
U.S. citizens would be harmed or taken hostage; a
governmental vacuum resulting in an atmosphere of terror,
anarchy, and chaos in Grenada; and an urgent request for
U.S. assistance by a group of neighboring democracies who
had a reasonable fear of a highly armed Grenada and lacked
the security forces to act alone. Moreover, the
administration steadfastly refused to say what it would have
done had any of these three elements been missing. In fact,
however, each of them contained sufficient ambiguity to
countenance future interventions in less than identical
circumstances.

For instance, in view of the country's recent,
traumatic experience with hostages in Iran, the
administration was bound to be extremely sensitive to this
possibility in Grenada. Given this peculiar experience,
what would have constituted an _unreasonable_ expectation by
Reagan that hostages would be taken? In short, the test of
reasonableness inevitably involves perceptions and
experience. British representatives in Grenada, who were
much more sanguine about the situation than their U.S.
counterparts, doubted that foreign nationals were in danger.
Furthermore, no U.S. official could cite any specific threat
or violent incident involving U.S. citizens. This fact does
not mean that they were not imperiled, but it does suggest
that with U.S. nationals scattered all around the world,
U.S. administrations might find it easy in other
circumstances to discover the reasonable likelihood of
danger. The problem, of course, is that the reasonable
likelihood test may be the only one available to
policymakers despite its susceptiblity to abuse.

Ambassador Kirkpatrick acknowledged this difficulty in
her Security Council speech but argued that the absence of a
government in Grenada after October 19--as evidenced by the
twenty-four-hour shoot-on-sight curfew--made administration
fears reasonable. But there are problems here as well.
What, after all, constitutes effective government? Theodore
Roosevelt offered some suggestions in his 1904 corollary to
the Monroe Doctrine, asserting that any Latin American
nation "whose people conduct themselves well can count upon
our hearty friendship. If a nation shows that it knows how
to act with reasonable efficiency and decency in social and
political matters, if it keeps order and pays its
obligations, it need fear no interference from the United
States." Most administration officials no doubt rejected
the Roosevelt Corollary as anachronistic, yet Kirkpatrick

claimed that the Revolutionary Military Council was not a government because the curfew indicated it could not maintain order. This constitutes a rather strange test of effective government and one that the United States has not ordinarily applied, for example, to African countries in the immediate aftermath of military coups.

The claims about anarchy and a vacuum of authority were probably made to anticipate criticism that the United States had overthrown a government. Rather, it was argued that U.S. forces had restored order and helped to create conditions for democracy. Then, too, if Grenada lacked a government--if it was anarchy, terror, and chaos that threatened the U.S. citizens there--then how could neighboring Caribbean countries have the reasonable fear of a Grenadian military threat? It should not be forgotten that this second reasonableness test allegedly convinced the administration to accede to the OECS request for assistance. According to Deputy Secretary Dam, "they certainly felt that their safety, the preservation of their democracies, was threatened from an external source operating through Grenada. In any event, it was their interpretation . . . that counts." By this "external source," Dam, no doubt, meant Cuba or the Soviet Union, but that implies that by October 21 Cuba and/or the Soviets had gained control of the situation in Grenada. Did that constitute no government or a government directed from abroad? If the latter is the case, then we are reminded of Lyndon Johnson's justification for his actions in the Dominican Republic.

We are left, however, with a rather ironic conclusion: President Reagan ordered the invasion because he reasonably believed that the lack of governmental authority threatened U.S. citizens and because the OECS states reasonably believed that an externally controlled Grenadian government threatened their security. Could not a similarly reasonable fear by other neighboring democracies prompt future U.S. interventions? The administration sought to avoid this conclusion, for fear of raising anew the broader issue of intervention. In sum, none of the three tests that the administration asserted it used before deciding to intervene is quite as restrictive as portrayed by Reagan and his advisers, and they were, moreover, in a state of some disagreement with each other. Nevertheless, Washington sought to emphasize the criteria's narrowness and their consistency.

Without congressional opposition to the CIA's destabilization plan, it is quite possible that the Reagan administration might have tried to topple the PRG in 1981.

Thus although Reagan and his advisers defended the invasion
on relatively narrow grounds, they did not hesitate to offer
certain lessons about the Grenada experience--lessons that
some feared might lead to more interventions in the
Caribbean Basin.

Some White House statements portrayed Maurice Bishop as
a would-be social democrat who was murdered because he
sought to free himself from Marxist-Leninist ideology and
Soviet-Cuban domination. What was the lesson? Leaders
should not ally their countries with Havana and Moscow at
all, for if the leaders suffer a change of heart they will
pay with their lives. This lesson required a rather
selective reading of the historical record. Ambassador
Kirkpatrick indicated that Grenada under the PRG "had fallen
under the permanent intervention of one neighboring and one
remote tyranny." It had, in effect, lost its sovereign
independence. What lesson was implied? States should rely
on the broad purposes of the UN Charter to restore the
sovereign independence of other states. The Charter, in
short, allows for preemptive interventions in the name of
human rights and national self-determination. President
Reagan claimed that both Grenada and Syria had become bases
for Soviet-supported terrorism. The lesson? The United
States must be willing to use military force to confront
this terrorism or risk endangering its vital interests.
Kenneth Dam, even while assuring the OAS that Grenada did
not constitute a precedent for future interventions, invited
the Sandinistas to look carefully at Bishop's fate and his
successors' belligerent behavior toward their neighbors.
Thus, although the main thrust of the administration's
defense of the intervention was designed to emphasize
prudence, restraint, and uniqueness, some of its dicta
sketched out extremely broad justifications for future uses
of U.S. military power.

Despite these only partly submerged ideological
instincts of the administration, however, the character of
public support and congressional opinion encouraged
Washington to present the Grenada intervention as a highly
pragmatic enterprise. Congressional Democrats in particular
initially raised a variety of objections to the invasion.
Some opponents softened or changed their attitude after the
administration produced evidence of substantial Cuban and
Soviet involvement in Grenada: Tip O'Neill, Tom Foley,
Michael Barnes, and other top House Democrats based their
belated and reluctant support on the issue of the physical
safety of the U.S. nationals, but continued to stress their
fear of setting a dangerous precedent. At the same time, a

number of Democrats in both houses, plus a handful of maverick Republicans, refused to blunt their criticism. This opposition took several forms: Some interpreted the invasion as the latest eruption of the "Cubaphobia" that had distorted the Caribbean policy of the United States for more than two decades; others saw it as the illegal and immoral use of military force; still others believed it represented a "premature" resort to force undertaken before diplomatic remedies had been exhausted; a few in the Black Caucus branded it as a racist exercise that reflected the administration's broader views on domestic minorities.

In reality, however, congressional reaction to Grenada, like its response to all major episodes in U.S. foreign policy since the late 1960s, demonstrated the absence of the old bipartisan consensus. The Republican party has largely embraced the outlook of conservative internationalism while the Democrats have been split since Vietnam, with important elements accepting the precepts of liberal internationalism, some aligning themselves more with the conservative internationalists, and a few moving close to a principled sort of isolationism. Although enthusiastic public support for the Grenada invasion compelled many congressional Democrats to beat a "strategic retreat" from outright opposition, Grenada has failed to unify the Democratic party around a foreign policy consensus. Zbigniew Brzezinski, hardly a neutral observer, claimed that the platform positions accepted by the party at its 1984 convention were to the left of Jimmy Carter's post-1978 position. In any case, it seems clear that the liberal anticommunism of the Truman and Kennedy presidencies no longer unites the Democratic party and that no comparable principle appears able to do so.

What, then, of Reagan's Caribbean Basin policy? Has the Grenada intervention helped the president to accomplish his regional goals, or has it proven to be a divisive legacy? Despite the administration's hopes for and critics' fears of wider lessons, the Grenada invasion has had surprisingly little impact on U.S. foreign policy. The states of the eastern Caribbean remain, of course, deeply affected by the events of October 1983. Suriname, perhaps fearing a similar fate, expelled its Cuban advisers shortly afterward, and CARICOM, meeting in July 1984, found itself still divided on the issue. But, had it not been for the imminent opening of the infamous airport at Port Salines—thanks to $71 million in U.S. aid—and the elections scheduled for late 1984—the Grenada invasion would have passed into oblivion in less than a year.

Doubtless the Reagan administration has encouraged this amnesia. Except for naming one of its Honduran military exercises "Grenadero," it has kept Grenada out of the public discourse even when plying Congress for aid to. El Salvador or the contras. The White House, recalling Secretary Haig's early enthusiasm for the "steady accumulation of prudent victories," could in principle have invoked Grenada to gain more support for its Central American policy. That it has chosen not to do so reflects the administration's appreciation of the very limited utility of a Grenadian analogy.

If a consensus about Central America has begun to take shape in Congress, its emergence has little to do with the issue of military force. Indeed, Congress remains deeply divided on the issue of covert aid to the anti-Sandinist guerrillas. Rather, Reagan has been able to piece together a coalition largely on the basis of Duarte's election as Salvadoran president. Armed with a legitimacy never enjoyed by El Salvador's juntas—or South Vietnam's military strongmen—President Duarte has begun to win key U.S. congressional support. In a July 1984 visit to Washington he was able to convince House majority leader Jim Wright that El Salvador deserved more U.S. aid and prompted Clarence D. Long, chairman of the House Appropriations Subcommittee on Foreign Operations, to remark: "He's persuaded me he's caught between the radical left and the radical right and needs some support. I think Duarte's a very straightforward guy, and I want to give him a chance."[10] The shift by Long, who had frequently likened El Salvador to Vietnam, seemed to indicate a significant change in congressional sentiments, though he continued to condition his support on Duarte's progress in curbing the death squads. At the same time, the head of the U.S. Southern Command, General Paul F. Gorman, told Congress that he "could foresee no circumstances when it would be useful "to commit American combat troops to El Salvador. Even if the Salvadoran government was in danger of being defeated by the rebels, Gorman argued that the use of U.S. forces would likely "transform the conflict from an indigenous struggle into a very different kind of fighting in which nationalism might cut against the United States."[11]

On the other hand, some observers professed to see a "Grenadian complex" at work in Reagan's Central American policy. For example, Wayne S. Smith, who served as chief of the U.S. Interests Section in Havana from 1979 to 1982, complained that although the Bishop government had been signaling its interest in reaching an accommodation with

Washington, it was rebuffed. The Reagan administration "had no more interest in a diplomatic process with the Grenadians than it has in one with the Nicaraguans and Cubans."[12] For Smith, military force did not work in Lebanon and it will not work in Central America, but the Reagan administration's refusal to negotiate with the Sandinistas, the Salvadoran rebels, and Castro indicated that the United States was misapplying the "lesson of Grenada." In short, critics of the invasion saw future Grenadas everywhere, and defenders of the operation could see no connection between it and the rest of the Caribbean Basin.

What, in fact, does Grenada teach us about the current state of U.S. foreign policy? What does it say about the Reagan administration's desire to practice neocontainment? And will Grenada prove to be a seed from which a new foreign policy consensus can sprout? First, Grenada obviously demonstrated the willingness of the administration to employ military force in certain circumstances. Even if Washington did use the hostage issue as a pretext and even if it did fabricate, at least in part, the invitations of the OECS and Scoon, the intervention showed that the United States would act to defend its perceived interests. However, the fact that Reagan did not invade until an elaborate justification was in place is in some contrast to the overthrow of Arbenz, the Bay of Pigs fiasco, and even the 1965 Dominican episode. Not only was Reagan careful not to invoke the Monroe Doctrine—and there he acted like his postwar predecessors— but he also tried to restrict the "meaning" of Grenada more than many of his congressional and journalistic supporters would have preferred and more than other presidents had done in similar circumstances. In other words, the Grenada intervention showed that U.S. military power could be employed prudently as long as the objectives were limited and could be achieved swiftly, decisively, and at a reasonably low cost. But whether that becomes the major lesson of Grenada remains to be seen.

Second, in the overall context of postwar U.S. foreign policy, the Grenada invasion was clearly closer to containment than to world order politics. Containment had never prohibited rolling back Communists from areas not in the Soviet sphere of influence at the end of World War II, i.e., Eastern Europe, as U.S. actions in Guatamala, Iran, the Congo, Cuba, and elsewhere attest. Thus the liberation of Grenada—given its location—is well within the parameters of containment. The Carter administration's foreign policy after 1978, of course, was also more reminiscent of containment than it was the application of world order politics--as the U.S. treatment of Bishop made clear, but Reagan's use of force in Grenada symbolized a return to containment--at least in the Caribbean--that was less ambiguous than Carter's revived anti-Sovietism.

If these conclusions are plausible, then will Grenada prove to be a turning point in the reconstruction of a foreign policy consensus? Perhaps, but only in a very limited way. Grenada, after all, has not enabled Reagan to rally public and congressional support for his more controversial Central American policies, nor has he tried to use it for this purpose. The report of the Kissinger commission did not invoke Grenada to garner support for its conclusions, and Grenada has done little to convince the Pentagon--at least publicly--that U.S. troops could prove beneficial in Central America. It did not signal the formation of a new anti-Communist consensus, and it did not reveal a public willingness to invade Cuba or to oust the Sandinistas.

The Grenada affair has compelled the Reagan administration to pay considerably more attention to the microstates of the Caribbean than it would probably prefer. Indeed, since the invasion, Grenada has become a virtual dependency of the United States. In an age of supposedly fierce nationalism, many Grenadians, exhausted after years of misrule by Gairy and the PRG, evidently favored annexation by the United States. For Washington it was much less difficult to invade Grenada than it has been to restore democracy. Moreover, with Britain unwilling to assist the eastern Caribbean states in security matters, and with conservative leaders like Seaga, Adams, and Charles asking the United States for a close and sustained presence in the region, the Reagan administration has discovered that invasions do have consequences. In short, Washington has been obliged to send substantially more aid to the eastern Caribbean in the months since the intervention, if only to make future interventions there less likely.

Finally, what does the Grenada invasion imply about Reagan's Cuba policy? Although the administration had been unwilling to apply against Castro the systematic military pressure favored by Secretary Haig, it did adopt toward Cuba the most militant policy of containment since the days of Kennedy and Johnson. Haig and his advisers made it clear to Castro that Cuban-U.S. relations could not improve until Havana significantly loosened its ties with Moscow, withdrew from Africa, ceased its material support of Nicaragua, the Salvadoran rebels and other anti-U.S. elements in Central America and the Caribbean, and allowed the repatriation of

some of the Mariel boat people who had come to the United
States in 1980. Castro refused to reconsider his Soviet
alliance and showed no signs of leaving Africa but did on
several occasions offer to participate in a joint U.S.-Cuban
withdrawal from Central America and to talk about the
refugees. The Reagan administration steadfastly ignored
Castro's offer to negotiate a mutual withdrawal from Central
America, though it did pursue efforts to begin Mariel
discussions. At the same time, by relentlessly
characterizing Cuba as an imperialistic, Soviet puppet with
a failed economy and a totalitarian political system, by
reimposing some of the travel and economic sanctions against
Havana that recent administrations had gradually removed,
and by pushing hard for the creation of "Radio Marti" (a
sort of Radio Free Europe for Cuba), President Reagan sought
to pressure and intimidate Castro without making overt
military threats.

In view of this history the only surprising thing about
the Grenada invasion is that Reagan waited so long to carry
it out. In fact, of course, the administration's approach
to Bishop was a small-scale duplicate of its approach to
Castro. Would Reagan intervene in Cuba if Castro were
overthrown, "chaos" broke out, and neighboring states
"urgently requested" U.S. assistance? What, if anything,
would the Soviets do? Although it is impossible to predict
these sorts of contingencies, such speculation does raise
important questions. What did Washington want from Bishop,
and what does it want from Castro? It demanded free
elections, the breaking of the Cuban connection, and the
cessation of anti-U.S. rhetoric from Bishop. It then
contended that Bishop's attempts to modify his behavior
directly led to his murder. Can that be the ultimate aim of
Reagan's Cuba policy? If so, then the Grenada invasion may
yet set an extremely important precedent--a precedent that
no one in the administration has dared to raise. But in the
absence of a domestic consensus about the purposes and
limits of U.S. power, the silence of the Reagan
administration about this issue should not be surprising.

Notes

Notes to Chapter 1

1. Even though these islands are called the Grenadines, they belong (with the exception of Carricou and Petit Martinique) to the nation of St. Vincent.

2. See, for instance, the large mural at the St. James Hotel at St. George's, Grenada.

3. Raymond Devas, _A History of the Island of Granada, 1498-1796_ (St. George's: Carenage Press, 1974).

4. Eric Williams, _From Columbus to Castro: The History of the Caribbean, 1492-1969_ (New York: Harper and Row, 1970), pp. 183-185.

5. Ibid., p. 134.

6. Edward Frederick, _From Camahogne to Free Grenada-- A Brief Introduction to the History of Grenada_ (St. George's: Grenada National Museum), pp. 2-3. After the revolution of March 13, 1979, Fort George was renamed Fort Rupert in honor of Maurice Bishop's father. Bishop himself was killed there on October 19, 1983.

7. Beverly A. Steele, "Grenada, an Island State, Its History and Its People," _Caribbean Quarterly_, 20, 1 (March 1974): 11.

8. Ken Lewis, "Fedon, Grenada's First Revolutionary," _Free West Indian_, March 21, 1981.

9. Frederick, _From Camahogne_, p. 5.

10. _Free West Indian_, September 25, 1982, p. 9.

11. E. Gittens-Knight, ed., _The Grenadian Handbook and Directory_ (Bridgetown, Barbados: The Advocate Co., Ltd., 1946), pp. 43-45.

12. Ecumenical Program for Interamerican Communication and Action (EPICA) Task Force, _Grenada--The Peaceful Revolution_ (Washington, D.C., 1982), p. 38.

13. Frederick, _From Camahogne_, p. 6.

14. Gordon K. Lewis, _The Growth of the Modern West_

Indies (New York: Monthly Review Press, 1968), pp. 88-96.

15. Epica Task Force, _Grenada,_ pp. 26-27.

16. T.A. Marryshow, _Cycles of Civilization_ (New York: Pathway Publishers, 1973), p. 4.

17. "Marryshow Day Address by Prime Minister Comrade Maurice Bishop delivered at York House, St. George's on November 7, 1982," hectograph, pp. 2-17. Much research remains to be done on Marryshow as well as Grendian history in general during his lifetime (1887-1958). The only scholarly works dealing with Grenada during the first half of the twentieth century are Patrick Emmanuel, _Crown Colony Politics in Grenada, 1917-1951_ (Cave Hill, Barbados: Institute for Social and Economic Research, University of the West Indies, 1978) and George Brizan, _The Grenadian Peasantry and Social Revolution 1930-1951_ (Kingston, Jamaica: ISER, University of the West Indies, 1979). It is interesting to note that both of these scholars have entered Grenadian politics since the U.S. intervention in October 1983. Patrick Emmanuel became the foreign minister of the interim government appointed by Governor-General Paul Scoon, and George Brizan has formed his own National Democratic Party.

18. The Rastafarian Cult, which grew out of the Garveyite Movement of the 1920s, has a considerable following among the lower class of Grenada as it does on the other Anglophone islands of the Caribbean.

19. These houses can still be seen in St. George's. They are located across from Marryshow's own former home on Tyrrel Street and next to the Empire Cinema on the Carenage.

20. It was in his honor that Prime Minister Maurice Bishop's office, located on a spectacular promontory at St. George's, was named Butler House. This building, dating from 1943 and formerly a hotel, was demolished during the U.S. intervention in October 1983.

21. _In the Spirit of Butler_ (Wildey, Barbados: Fedon Publishers, 1982), pp. 32-44.

22. Epica Task Force, _Grenada,_ pp. 31-32.

Notes to Chapter 2

1. Interview with W. Richard Jacobs on March 11, 1981, in Havana, Cuba.

2. In contrast to the French and Spanish colonizers, the English mixed little with the black subjects of their

Caribbean colonies. Grenada has an overwhelmingly black population. The small number of mulattoes trace their ancestry mostly to the French period of occupation. Some of the dislike for Eric Gairy on the part of the elite can be blamed on the color of his skin.

3. GULP was reconstituted upon Gairy's return to Grenada in 1984.

4. W. Richard Jacobs and Ian Jacobs, <u>Grenada: The Route to Revolution</u> (Havana: Casa de Las Americas, 1980), p. 17.

5. Sinclair D. DaBreo, <u>The Grenada Revolution</u> (Castries, St. Lucia: Management Advertising and Publicity Services, 1979), pp. 37-38.

6. Epica Task Force, <u>Grenada--The Peaceful Revolution</u> (Washington, D.C., 1982), p. 38.

7. The cross (although no longer illuminated) has survived both Gairy's demise in 1979 and the PRG's end in 1983.

8. Jacobs and Jacobs, <u>Grenada</u>, p. 60.

9. Epica Task Force, <u>Grenada</u>, p. 39.

10. Jacobs and Jacobs, <u>Grenada</u>, p. 69.

11. Ibid., p. 74; Epica Task Force, <u>Grenada</u>, p. 44.

12. <u>Commission on Enquiry into the Control of Public Expenditure in Grenada 1961 and Subsequently</u>, pp. 9-10.

13. DaBreo, <u>Grenada Revolution</u>, p. 46.

14. Epica Task Force, <u>Grenada</u>, p. 42.

15. Jacobs and Jacobs, <u>Grenada</u>, p. 71.

16. Epica Task Force, <u>Grenada</u>, pp. 42-50.

17. Jacobs and Jacobs, p. 47. East Caribbean dollars (EC $) are used by the small English-speaking islands of the Caribbean such as Anguilla, Antigua and Barbuda, St. Kitts and Nevis, Montserrat, Dominica, St. Lucia, St. Vincent, and Grenada. Barbardos, Jamaica, and Trinidad and Tobago all use their own currency.

18. Interviews with Jacqueline Creft and the prominent Grenadian lawyer Carroll Bristol. Zeek departed by speedboat the day after Gairy's overthrow on March 13, 1979. He is rumored to be on one of the British Virgin Islands. The author must look almost identical to Zeek because throughout his sojourn on Grenada (August 1982-May 1983), people would come up to him and exclaim: "Hey, Clancy, what are you doing back here?" The author once asked the late PRG minister of education, Jacqueline Creft, whether he really looked like Zeek. She replied: "Come to think of it, you do look like him, except that Zeek always wore white bucks!"

19. Fitzroy Ambursley and Robin Cohen, eds., Crisis in the Caribbean (New York: Monthly Review Press, 1983), p. 197.

20. Jorge Luna, Granada--La Nueva Joya Del Caribe, (Havana: Editorial de Ciencias Sociales, 1982), p. 22.

21. Epica Task Force, Grenada, p. 49.

22. One night Gairy had a dream of circles. The next day, according to several members of his government, he ordered the construction of traffic circles all over Grenada (personal commun.).

23. Interview with Jacqueline Creft, PRG minister of education, youth, sports, women, social affairs and community development, on November 15, 1982. See also Luna, Granada, pp. 170-171.

24. La Qua, which carries as its motto "Satisfaction Guaranteed," is Grenada's largest funeral home.

25. Epica Task Force, Grenada, p. 86. See also, Grenada is Not Alone (Wildey, Barbados: Fedon Publishers, 1982), p. 73.

26. Interview with PRG Minister of National Mobilization Selwyn Strachan on December 28, 1981.

27. "Maurice Bishop--Premier in the Spotlight," Caribbean Life and Times 1, no. 2 (December 1979): 11-15.

28. Interview with W. Richard Jacobs on March 8, 1982 in Havana, Cuba.

29. Interview with Prime Minister Maurice Bishop at the Office of the Prime Minister at Butler House in St. George's, Grenada, on September 27, 1982.

30. Frank J. Prial, "Exile's Return to Granada: A Has-Been or a Hero?" New York Times, February 23, 1984.

31. Forward Ever! Three Years of the Grenadian Revolution, Speeches by Maurice Bishop (Sidney: Pathfinder Press, 1982), p. 65.

32. Prime Minister Eric M. Gairy, "Black Power in Grenada," radio broadcast, May 23, 1970.

33. Jacobs and Jacobs, Grenada, p. 95.

34. Epica Task Force, Grenada, p. 45.

35. Interview with the minister of foreign affairs, Unison Whiteman, November 10, 1982. See also Jorge Luna, Granada, p. 73.

36. Forward Ever! Speeches of Maurice Bishop, p. 67.

37. Chris Searle, Grenada--The Struggle Against Destabilization (New York: W.W. Norton, 1983), p. 17, and Hugh O'Shaughnessy, Grenada: An Eyewitness Account of the U.S. Invasion and the Caribbean History that Provoked It (New York: Dodd, Mead & Co., 1984), p. 49.

38. Jacobs and Jacobs, p. 100. See also _Free West Indian_, November 17, 1982, p. 6. Gairy had devised his "54 reasons" by multiplying his "27 crimes" by two.

39. Each year during the Bishop regime (1979–1983), this "Bloody Sunday" (November 18, 1973) was commemorated by the PRG in a special ceremony. After the anniversary celebration, it was the custom of the Bholas to invite the NJM leadership to a reception at the family home. On Sunday, November 21, 1982, I was invited, along with entertainer Harry Belafonte and his wife Julie as well as Toledo, Ohio, lawyer and industrialist, Edward Lamb, to the above-mentioned reception at the Bholas, where the Bloody Sunday events had taken place. The man who had then been minister of national mobilization, Selwyn Strachan, related to us in detail what had transpired on that day, and the above account is based upon his description of the incident. See also Luna, _Granada_, pp. 65–69.

40. Jacobs and Jacobs, _Grenada_, pp. 105–108.

41. _Report of the Duffus Commission to Grenada_ by Sir Hubert Duffus, KT, Aubrey Fraser, Esq., and Archbishop Samuel Carter, February 27, 1975 (Kingston, Jamaica).

42. _Free West Indian_, January 19, 1983, p. 1; Merle Hodge and Chris Searle, _Is Freedom We Making_ (Government Information Service, Grenada, 1982), pp. 77–78; and Alister Hughes, "Violations of Human Rights in Grenada for Human Rights Research Project of the Caribbean Conference of Churches," August 1977.

43. Epica Task Force, _Grenada_, p. 47.

44. "His Excellency Sir Eric Matthew Gairy, Prime Minister of Grenada Addresses the Thirty-Second Session of the General Assembly of the United Nations on 7 October 1977," p. 9.

45. Jacobs and Jacobs, _Grenada_, p. 110.

46. _Caribbean Contact_, June 1977, p. 2.

47. _Forward Ever! Speeches of Maurice Bishop_, pp. 71–72.

48. Jacobs and Jacobs, _Grenada_, p. 115.

49. Epica Task Force, _Grenada_, p. 50.

50. The Hon. E.M. Gairy, _Address to the Nation_, October 1, 1976.

51. "For Human Rights Research Project of the Caribbean Conference of Churches," compiled by Colville McBarnette, p. 3.

52. For a description of the development of the trade union movement on Grenada under the PRG, see _In The Spirit of Butler_ (Wildey, Barbados: Fedon Publishers, 1982).

53. Vincent Noel was missing because he had been put in jail by Gairy before his departure.

54. On July 26, 1953, Fidel Castro staged an unsuccessful raid on Moncada barracks in the eastern part of Cuba, which resulted in his arrest and trial as well as the deaths of many of his companions.

55. The account of the assault on True Blue barracks and the seizure of Radio Grenada is based upon an interview with the former commander of the PRA and minister of labor, communication and public works, Hudson Austin, on November 21, 1982. See also Luna, Grenada, pp. 91-102.

56. Address to the nation delivered over Radio Free Grenada by Maurice Bishop on March 13, 1979.

Notes to Chapter 3

1. W. Richard Jacobs and Ian Jacobs, Grenada: The Route to Revolution (Havana: Casa de Las Americas, 1980), p. 126.

2. "New Jewel Movement's Manifesto," October 1973.

3. Washington Post, July 6, 1979.

4. The U.S. ambassador to the Eastern Carribean, who is stationed at the U.S. embassy on Barbados, also represents the United States on Antigua and Barbuda, St. Kitts and Nevis, Dominica, St. Lucia, St. Vincent and the Grenadines, and Grenada. The United States has separate embassies on Trinidad and Tobago, Haiti, the Dominican Republic, and Jamaica, as well as an Interest Section on Cuba. U.S. diplomats on Martinique belong to the U.S. embassy at Paris, France.

5. See, for example, Epica Task Force, Grenada--The Peaceful Revolution (Washington, D.C., 1982), p. 26. "The Ortiz visit set the U.S. and Grenada on a collision course in which the U.S. hostililty toward the PRG made Cuban and other Caribbean friendships all the more valuable and necessary for the fledgling revolutionary government."

6. Interview with Joseph D. McLaughlin, deputy chief of mission and chargé d'affaires" at the U.S. embassy at Santo Domingo in the Dominican Republic, June 1984. McLaughlin had previously served under U.S. Ambassadors Frank Ortiz and Sally Shelton at the U.S. embassy at Bridgetown, Barbados, and had participated in many negotiations with the PRG on Grenada. See also Ambassador Ortiz's version of the April 10, 1979, meeting as presented by Ambassador Frank V. Ortiz in a "Letter to the Editor," of The Atlantic, June 1984, pp. 7-12.

7. Richard Massing, "Grenada—Before and After," The Atlantic, February 1984, p. 81.

8. Maurice Bishop, broadcast over Radio Free Grenada, April 13, 1979.

9. Ortiz, "Letter to the Editor," p. 12.

10. It is an amazing fact that the Cuban government allowed one of its ambassadors to be married to a woman who still holds a U.S. passport! For a U.S. ambassador to be married to a Cuban who still holds a Cuban passport would be an impossibility. So, of course, would be the idea of a Soviet ambassador being married to anybody from a non-Communist nation. Gail Reed was very popular in Grenada. Driving her Soviet-built Lada with her little son Juliencito at her side, she would pick up hordes of Grenadian children on their way home from school. In contrast, the Soviet ambassador, Genady Sazhenev, drove around in a chaffeur-driven Mercedes-Benz (the only one on Grenada!), which created a very bad impression among the Grenadians, who did not expect a "people's representative" to be driven around in a capitalist luxury limousine!

11. Grenada—The World Against the Crime (Havana: Editorial de Ciencias Sociales, 1983), p. 14.

12. Interview with Joseph D. McLaughlin, June 1984.

13. Dessima Williams went to Washington anyway in her capacity as Grenadian ambassador to the Organization of American States. During a visit to Barbados in January 1983, I asked the the U.S. deputy chief of mission at Barbados, Kim "Flowers" Ludlow, why the State Department had refused to accept her credentials. His reply was in the form of a question: "Would you accept the credentials of a gun runner?" When I interviewed Dessima Williams in May 1984 in New York City, I brought up Ludlow's remark and asked her whether she had, indeed, ever been involved in arms smuggling in Grenada. Dessima Williams dismissed this accusation as "absurd" and commented that it was part of a deliberate campaign at the time by the United States to defame her character (She stated that another story, which described her as "a call girl," was planted). Williams sided with the Maurice Bishop faction during the fratricidal struggle within the NJM during October 1983, and today heads, together with Grenada's former ambassador to the United Nations, Caldwell Taylor, the Maurice Bishop and October 19, 1983, Martyrs Foundation in New York City.

14. Free West Indian, October 28, 1980. See also Epica, Grenada, p. 118. WINBAN—the Windward Islands Banana Growers Association, is composed of Grenada, St. Vincent, St. Lucia, and Dominica.

15. Interview with Joseph D. McLaughlin, June 1984.

16. OUTLET, November 5, 1982, pp. 1-5. Interview with the former prime minister of Dominica, Patrick John, on December 5, 1982 in Roseau, Dominica. I spoke with him in the morning. In the afternoon, he had been put back into jail. The Swedish journalist who happened to be interviewing Patrick John when the police came to arrest him was taken to the airport and expelled from Dominica.

17. CARICOM, the Caribbean Community, was founded in 1973 at Chaguaramas, Trinidad, and consists today of the following thirteen Anglophone Caribbean political entities: The Bahamas, Barbados, Belize, Antigua, Dominica, Grenada, Guyana, Jamaica, Montserrat, St. Lucia, St. Kitts and Nevis, St. Vincent, and Trinidad and Tobago.

18. Ortiz, "Letter to the Editor," p. 12.

19. Free West Indian, April 1, 1983. For greater details see, "An Outline of Grenada's Proposed National Insurance Scheme to be Introduced on 4th April 1983." St. George's, 1983.

20. The Torchlight, October 10, 1979.

21. The crackdown by the PRG could not have been very severe because the present writer during his stay on Grenada (August 1982-June 1983) often witnessed the selling and smoking of marijuana at St. George's places of public entertainment.

22. The above account of the Torchlight controversy is based upon conversations with Don Rojas, press secretary to prime minister Maurice Bishop. These conversations took place during September 1982.

23. Speech given by Prime Minister Maurice Bishop at the Heroes' Day Rally held in Queen's Park, St. George's, on June 19, 1981.

24. LIAT (Leeward Islands Air Transport) has a virtual monopoly on flights between the small Anglophone Caribbean islands. Its planes arrive and depart so notoriously late that the inhabitants of the Leeward and Windward Islands say that LIAT really stands for "Leave Island Any Time."

25. Paul McIsaac, "Revolutionary Suicide," Village Voice, November 22, 1983, p. 14.

26. Rickey Singh, "Caribbean Media and the Grenada Affair," Caribbean Contact, January/February 1984, p. 14.

27. A third nongovernmental newspaper, the Catholic Focus, was prohibited by the PRG in 1981.

28. Ortiz, "Letter to the Editor," p. 7.

29. Grenada Is Not Alone, Speeches by the People's Revolutionary Government at the First International Conference in Solidarity with Grenada, November 1981 (St. Georges: Fedon Publishers, 1982), pp. 81-84.

30. There are six parishes on Grenada all named after saints: St. George, St. John, St. Mark, St. Patrick, St. Andrews, and St. David. The capital, St. George's, is located in the Parish of St. George. The six stars of the Grenadian flag represent these six parishes. The parish councils, representing entire parishes, were larger than the zonal councils, which represented clusters of villages. The work of a parish council, the zonal councils and the mass organizations of a particular parish was supposed to be directed by a PCB (parish coordinating body).

31. The present writer, while on Grenada, witnessed many parish and zonal council meetings and can testify that they were both popular and productive.

32. By the end of the PRG's reign (October 1983), the unemployment rate had been reduced to 14 percent. With the dismantling of government industries and programs, the dissolution of the PRA and the purge from government service of thousands of NJM supporters, the unemployment rate had passed 33 percent by mid-1984.

33. Modified and Updated Version of Grenada's Report on Its Implementation of the "Regional Action Plan for the Decade of Women in the Americas of the CIM" Originally Presented at the Twentieth Assembly of the CIM in the Dominican Republic in November 1980. NWO Document, 1983, p. 5.

34. For the people's participation in the drawing up of the 1982 Budget, see To Construct From Morning—Making the People's Budget in Grenada (St. George's: Fedon Publishers, 1982). See also Report on the National Economy of 1981 and the Prospects for 1982, presented by Brother Bernard Coard, deputy prime minister and minister of planning, finance and trade (St. George's: Government Printing Office, 1982).

35. Report on the National Economy for 1982 and the Budget Plan for 1983 and Beyond, presented by Brother Bernard Coard, deputy prime minister and minister of planning, finance and trade (St. George's: Government Printing Office, 1983), pp. 55-63.

36. Interview with the Jamaican economist and director of NACDA, Robert Gordon, on December 2, 1982. See also Grenada Is Not Alone, pp. 93-102, and Sam Manuel and Andrew Pulley, Grenada—Revolution in the Caribbean (New York: Pathfinder Press, 1981), pp. 13-16.

37. Report On The National Economy For 1982, p. 49.

38. Interview with Richard Menezes, president of the Grenadian Chamber of Commerce, May 22, 1983.

39. Report On the National Economy For 1982, p. 47.

40. Grenada Is Not Alone, p. 51.

41. Chris Searle and Maurice Bishop, Grenada: Education Is A Must (London: Education Committee of the British-Grenadian Friendship Society, 1981), p. 28.

42. Address By Comrade Maurice Bishop, Prime Minister, People's Revolutionary Government of Grenada to Executive Board of UNESCO (Paris: UNESCO Headquarters, 1982), pp. 12-13.

43. Interview with Chris Searle, November 8, 1982.

44. Free West Indian, September 11, 1982.

45. For an account of the PRG's efforts to bring Carriacou and Petit Martinique into the mainstream of Grenadian life see: Carriacou and Petit Martinique--In The Mainstream of the Revolution (St. George's: Fedon Publishers, 1982).

46. Let Us Learn Together (Free Grenada: Center for Popular Education, 1980), p. 15.

47. Ibid., p. 31.

48. Free West Indian, November 1, 1980.

49. Interview with Jacqueline Creft, minister of education, youth, and social affairs, November 20, 1982.

50. Address by Comrade Maurice Bishop, p. 11.

51. Grenada is Not Alone, p. 59.

52. Free West Indian, October 30, 1982.

53. All Of Us, (Grenada: Center for Popular Education, 1982), p. 23.

54. Free West Indian, October 30, 1982.

55. We Work and Play Together, (Grenada: Center for Popular Education, 1982), pp. 34-38.

56. Education is Production Too! Speech by Comrade Prime Minister Maurice Bishop at the reopening of the second year of the National In-Service Teacher Education Program (NISTEP), delivered on October 15, 1981, at the Teachers' College. Ministry of Education, St. George's. 1981 Year of Agriculture and Agro-Industries, pp. 8-9.

57. Grenada Is Not Alone, p. 56.

58. Interview with Didacus Jules, permanent secretary of the ministry of education, March 30, 1983.

59. Massing, "Grenada," p. 82.

60. Interview with Ron Smith, airport project manager, November 21, 1982.

61. Documents Pertaining to Relations Between Grenada, The USSR and Cuba (henceforth to be referred to as DPR-GUC), USIA, Series 2, Document 100243, Central Committee Report on First Plenary Session, July 13-19, 1983, p. 15.

62. Speech given by President Fidel Castro at the funeral of the 24 Cubans killed in Grenada, at Havana on

November 14, 1983, as quoted in <u>Monthly Review</u>, January 1984, p. 11.

63. <u>Free West Indian</u>, March 26, 1983.

64. <u>Free West Indian</u>, April 1, 1983.

65. Massing, "Grenada," p. 82.

66. The True Blue Campus. The medical school's other campus was located right on the magnificent Grand Anse Beach.

67. He was referring to the former U.S. ambassador to the Eastern Caribbean, Sally Shelton, who had criticized the Reagan administration for vastly exaggerating the importance of the Bishop regime on Grenada.

68. <u>Miami Herald</u>, March 17, 1983.

69. In its attacks on Grenada's new airport, the Reagan administration implied that the length of the Point Salines runway was unusual for a Caribbean island airport. Yet there are 8 runways on Caribbean islands that have longer runways than the 9000 ft. runway of Grenada's new airport: The Bahamas (Nassau): 11,000 ft.; Barbados: 11,000 ft.; Curacao: 11,187 ft.; Guadeloupe: 11,499 ft.; Martinique: 10,827 ft.; Puerto Rico: 10,002 ft.; St. Lucia: 11,070 ft. and Trinidad: 9,500 ft.

70. <u>Grenada Is Not Alone</u>, pp. 120–121.

71. Not only was "Amber and the Amberines" chosen because it sounds like "Grenada and Grenadines," but there actually exists an Amber Beach on Grenada.

72. Epica Task Force, <u>Grenada</u>, p. 122.

73. Interview with Selwyn Strachan, January 7, 1983.

74. <u>Free West Indian</u>, March 19, 1983.

75. DPR-GUC, USIA, Series 2, Document 100285, Minutes of the Politburo, April 20, 1983, pp. 5–6.

Notes of Chapter 4

1. Epica Task Force, <u>Grenada</u>, pp. 106–109.

2. DPR-GUC, USIA, Series 2, Document 100243, Central Committee Report on First Plenary Session, July 13–19, 1983, p. 19.

3. DPR-GUC, USIA, Series 1, Document 100319, Minutes of Emergency Meeting of NJM Central Committee, August 26, 1983, p. 2.

4. DPR-GUC, USIA, Series 2, Document 000123, Extraordinary Meeting of the Central Committee NJM, September 14–16, 1983, p. 5.

5. Ibid., p. 10.

6. DPR–GUC, USIA, Series 2, Document 100243, p. 9.

7. DPR–GUC, USIA, Series 1, Document 100017, Summary of Prime Minister's Meeting with Soviet Ambassador, May 24, 1983, p. 5.

8. DPR–GUC, USIA, Series 1, Document 100291, Minutes of the Political Bureau, dated June 22, 1983.

9. Phyllis Coard, the Jamaican-born wife of Deputy Prime Minister Bernard Coard, was a member of the PRG and the Central Committee of the NJM as well as president of the NWO and vice-minister for women's affairs. Physically unprepossessing, she was thoroughly disliked by most Grenadians who, in all likelihood, resented the fact that a foreigner occupied such high positions in the Grenadian power structure. One persistent and probably apocryphal rumor stated that Phyllis Coard had declared that she had not become the wife of Bernard to end up simply as the spouse of the deputy prime minister. After the U.S. intervention in October 1983, she was captured along with her husband by U.S. troops and handcuffed and blindfolded, flown to the U.S. aircraft carrier Guam for interrogation. Thereafter, in spite of the fact that she was pregnant, she was thrown into Richmond Hill Prison where she has been held incommunicado and without a trial up to the time of this writing (May 1985). Her three children by Bernard Coard, Shola, 13; Abby, 11; and Neto, 5, have been taken to Jamaica to live with relatives.

10. For more information on Grenadian-Venezuelan relations, see Kai Schoenhals, "Venezuela Increases Aid to Grenada," Caribbean Contact, March 1983.

11. Interview wiuth Romulo Nucete Hubner, May 18, 1983.

12. Interview with Don Rojas, press secretary of prime minister Maurice Bishop, May 20, 1983.

13. DPR–GUC, USIA, Series 2, Document 000123, p. 7.

14. DPR–GUC, USIA, Series 1, Document 100319, p. 4.

15. Ibid., p. 1.

16. According to NWO documents captured during the U.S. invasion, Hudson Austin, a father of four children, often beat his wife mercilessly and was known to spend his nights with his girl friend.

17. DPR–GUC, USIA, Series 1, Document 100139, pp. 6–7.

18. DPR–GUC, USIA, Series 2, Document 000123, p. 21, and Document 000188, pp. 9–11.

19. Document 000123, p. 30.

20. Ibid., p. 33.

21. Ibid.

22. Ibid., p. 36.

23. Document 000123, pp. 37–38.

24. Cathy Sunshine and Philip Wheaton, Death of A Revolution (Washington, D.C.: Epica, 1983), p. 8.

25. A reference to the twenty-six prominent Grenadians who had attempted, even after the closing of the Torchlight, to publish an opposition newspaper.

26. Reference to the fact that Lt. Col. Ewart Layne was appointed to the third highest position (after Bishop and Austin) in the PRA over Major Einstein Louison, who was the PRA's chief of staff.

27. DPR-GUC, USIA, Series 2, Document 000123, pp. 43–46.

28. The minutes of the extraordinary general meeting of full members of the NJM on September 25, 1983, were not included in the three volumes of captured documents published by the U.S. government and much credit must be given to editor Barry B. Levine for getting hold of this important document and publishing it in Caribbean Review, no. 4, (Fall 1983), pp. 14–15, and pp. 48–58.

29. Anthony Payne, Paul Sutton, and Tony Thorndike, Grenada—Revolution and Invasion (New York: St. Martin's Press, 1984), p. 128.

30. DPR-GUC, USIA, Series 2, Document 000149, Report on the Meeting of the Politburo and Central Committee held on October 12, 1983, and given by Comrade Strachan, p. 1 and p. 4.

31. "Statements by the Party and Revolutionary Government of Cuba on the Events in Grenada" as quoted in Grenada: The World Against the Crime (Havana: Editorial de Ciencas Sociales, 1983), pp. 9–12.

32. Payne, Sutton, and Thorndike, Grenada, pp. 128–129.

33. DPR-GUC, USIA, Series 2, Document 000149, p. 2. See also: Document 100270, Letter by Victor Nazim Burke, p. 2. Jacqueline Crft had a four-year-old son by Bishop whom the prime minister named Vladimir in honor of Lenin. She was deeply hurt by the fact that Bishop had acquired another girlfriend by 1982 (the chief of protocol, Shehiba Strong). Nevertheless, Creft stood by Bishop until the end. She shared his house arrest and was executed at his side on October 19. Bishop's wife, Angela, had moved in 1981 to Canada, where she is still living together with her two teenage sons by Bishop.

34. Jo Thomas, "From a Grenadian Diplomat: How Party Wrangle Led to Premier's Death," New York Times, October 29, 1983.

35. DPR–GUC, USIA, Series 2, Document 000149, pp. 3 and 6.

36. The PRAF consisted of the PRA, the People's Militia and the Police.

37. DPR–GUC, USIA, Series 2, Document 000149, p. 2.

38. Miami Herald, October 16, 1983.

39. Miami Herald, October 19, 1983.

40. Bernard Diederich, "Interviewing George Louison," Caribbean Review 12, no. 4 (Fall 1983): 17–18.

41. Payne, Sutton, and Thorndike, Grenada, pp. 132–133. For an excellent eyewitness account of the events leading up to "Bloody Wednesday," see Akinyele Sadiq, "Blow by Blow––A Personal Account of the Ravaging of the Revo," The Black Scholar, January/February 1984, pp. 8–20.

42. My description of "Bloody Wednesday" is based primarily upon the eyewitness account of Akinyele Sadiq.

43. Mary Greaves et al., "The Grenada Document––The Bitter, Epic Struggle for the Isle of Spice," Nation, special edition, Barbados, February 1984.

44. DPR–GUC, USIA, Series 2, Document 000091, Bulletin From the Main Political Department 20/10/83, "Their Heroism Is An Example For Us," p. 3.

45. Payne, Sutton, and Thorndike, Grenada, p. 136.

46. Sadiq, "Blow by Blow," p. 16.

47. Greaves et al., "The Grenada Document," p. 25.

48. DPR–GUC, USIA, Series 2, Document 000091, Appeal to the Revolutionary Soldiers and Men of the People's Revolutionary Armed Forces, October 19, 1983.

49. Greaves et al., "The Grenada Document," p. 26.

50. "Statement By The Cuban Party And Revolutionary Government On The Events in Grenada," as cited in The Current Digest of the Soviet Press, vol. 35, no. 43 (November 23, 1983): 3–4.

51. DPR–GUC, USIA, Series 2, Document 00015.

52. Ibid.

53. Payne, Sutton, and Thorndike, Grenada, pp. 183–239.

54. Sunshine and Wheaton, Death of a Revolution, p. 16.

55. For more on Michele Gibbs, see V.S. Naipul, "An Island Betrayed," Harper's, March 1984, pp. 64–65.

56. Jonathan Kwitny, "Oh What A Lovely War!" Mother Jones, June 1984, pp. 28–29.

57. Ibid., p. 30.

Notes to Chapter 5

1. "President's Remarks," October 25, 1983, Department of State Bulletin, December 1983, p. 67.

2. Cecil V. Crabb, Jr., The Doctrines of American Foreign Policy: Their Meaning, Role, and Future (Baton Rouge: Louisiana State University Press, 1982), p. 9, fn. 1.

3. Cf. Walter Lippmann, U.S. Foreign Policy: Shield of the Republic (Boston: Little, Brown & Co., 1943).

4. Quoted in Crabb, Doctrines of American Foreign Policy, p. 38.

5. Cf. Richard H. Immerman, The CIA in Guatemala (Austin: University of Texas Press, 1983).

6. Public Papers of the Presidents: Lyndon B. Johnson, 1965 (Washington, D.C.: Government Printing Office, 1966), vol. 1, p. 461.

7. Ibid., p. 465.

8. Ibid., pp. 471, 472, 473, 474.

9. Crabb, Doctrines of American Foreign Policy, p. 256.

10. Abraham F. Lowenthal, "The Insular Caribbean as a Crucial Test for U.S. Policy," in The Caribbean Challenge: U.S. Policy in a Volatile Region, ed. H. Michael Erisman, (Boulder, Colo.: Westview Press, 1984), p. 191.

Notes to Chapter 6

1. The following discussion of world order politics draws heavily on Richard A. Melanson, Writing History and Making Policy: The Cold War, Vietnam, and Revisionism (Lanham, Md.: University Press of America, 1983), chap. 6.

2. Stanley Hoffmann, Primacy or World Order: American Foreign Policy Since the Cold War (New York: McGraw-Hill, 1978).

3. Ibid., p. 7.

4. Ibid., p. 8.

5. Ibid., pp. 8-9.

6. Ibid., p. 9.

7. Ibid., p. 10.

8. Ibid., p. 23.

9. Ibid., p. 47.

10. Ibid., p. 92.

11. Ibid., p. 94.

12. Ibid., p. 95.

13. Ibid.
14. Ibid., p. 88.
15. See ibid., pp. 162-182.
16. Ibid., p. 111.
17. Ibid., p. 112.
18. Ibid., p. 113.
19. Ibid., p. 114.
20. Stanley Hoffmann, Gulliver's Troubles; or the Setting of American Foreign Policy (New York: McGraw-Hill, 1968).
21. Hoffmann, Primacy or World Order, p. 111.
22. Ibid., p. 118.
23. Ibid.
24. Ibid., p. 121.
25. Ibid.
26. Ibid., p. 122.
27. Ibid., pp. 125, 126.
28. Ibid., pp. 131-132.
29. Ibid., p. 135.
30. Ibid.
31. Ibid., p. 209.
32. Ibid., p. 213.
33. Ibid., p. 224.
34. Ibid.
35. W. Anthony Lake, "Pragmatism and Principle in U.S. Foreign Policy," Boston, Massachusetts, June 13, 1977 (U.S. Department of State: Bureau of Public Affairs), p. 1.
36. Ibid.
37. Ibid.
38. Ibid.
39. Ibid.
40. Sol M. Linowitz et al., The Americas in a Changing World (New York: Quadrangle Books, 1975). This book summarized the Commission's 1974 report.
41. Ibid., p. 11.
42. Ibid., p. 20.
43. Ibid., pp. 60, 61.
44. As summarized by Deputy Assistant Secretary of State for Inter-American Affairs John A. Bushnell before the Subcommittee on Inter-American Affairs of the Committee on Foreign Affairs, House of Representatives, 96th Congress, First Session, July 24, 1979, "Economic and Political Future of the Caribbean" (Washington, D.C.: Government Printing Office, 1979), p. 29.
45. Cf. Philip H. Habib, "Address of the U.S. Ambassador-At-Large to the Miami Conference on the

Caribbean," November 28, 1979, in Department of State,
"U.S. Relations with the Caribbean and Central America"
(U.S. Department of State: Bureau of Public Affairs,
1979), p. 2.

    46. For a more detailed account of these differences,
see Seyom Brown, The Faces of Power: Constancy and Change
in United States Foreign Policy from Truman to Reagan (New
York: Columbia University Press, 1983), pp. 451-463.

    47. Ibid., p. 459.

    48. J. Daniel O'Flaherty, "Finding Jamaica's Way,"
Foreign Policy, 31 (Summer 1978), p. 139.

    49. Brown, Faces of Power, p. 453.

    50. Ibid.

    51. Ibid., p. 454.

    52. Carl H. Gershman, "The Rise and Fall of the New
Foreign-Policy Establishment," Commentary, July 1980, pp.
11-24.

    53. Ibid., p. 24.

    54. Ibid., p. 20.

    55. See Jerry W. Sanders, Peddlers of Crisis: The
Committee on the Present Danger and the Politics of
Containment (Boston: South End Press, 1983).

    56. Speech of October 1, 1979, Weekly Compilation of
Presidential Documents, 15, no. 40, pp. 1802-1806.

    57. Background interview, Washington, D.C., Spring
1981.

    58. Ibid.

    59. Richard R. Fagen, "The End of the Affair,"
Foreign Policy 36 (Fall 1979), p. 189.

    60. Jeane Kirkpatrick, "Dictatorships and Double
Standards," Commentary, November 1979, p. 45.

    61. Ibid., p. 36.

    62. Ibid., p. 40.

    63. Background interview, Washington, D.C., Spring
1981.

    64. Sally A. Shelton at Hearing before the
Subcommittee on Inter-American Affairs of the Committee on
Foreign Affairs, House of Representatives, 97th Congress,
Second Session, June 15, 1982, "United States Policy
Toward Grenada" (Washington, D.C.: Government Printing
Office, 1982), p. 56.

    65. As quoted by Theodore R. Britton, Jr., at
Hearings before the Subcommittees on International
Security and Scientific Affairs and on Western Hemisphere
Affairs of the Committee on Foreign Affairs, House of
Representatives, 98th Congress, First Session, November 2,
1983, "U.S. Military Actions in Grenada: Implications for

U.S. Policy in the Eastern Caribbean" (Washington, D.C.: Government Printing Office, 1984), p. 71.

66. Frank V. Ortiz, "Letter to the Editor," Harper's, June 1984, p. 7.

67. Ibid.

68. Ibid., p. 9.

69. Ibid.

70. Ibid.

71. Ibid.

72. Ibid.

73. Ibid.

74. Ibid.

75. "Economic and Political Future of the Caribbean," pp. 4-6.

76. "U.S. Military Actions in Grenada," pp. 56-58.

77. Washington Post, July 6, 1979, p. Al.

78. Ibid.

79. Ibid.

80. Myles R.R. Frechette, "Soviet-Cuban Impact on the Western Hemisphere," Department of State Bulletin, July 1980, p. 77.

81. For example, Carter NSC staffer Robert A. Pastor told Congress in November 1983 that Bishop "told me that after the incident in 1980 involving the training of the bodyguards of George Odlum, who was deputy prime minister of St. Lucia at that time, he would never again permit the training of Caribbean security officials in Grenada without the express permission of the Head of State." And Ambassador Shelton described as "very thin" evidence that Grenada was training West Indian leftists to subvert neighboring islands. See "U.S. Military Actions in Grenada."

Notes to Chapter 7

1. Norman Podhoretz, "The New American Majority," Commentary, January 1981, p. 21.

2. Norman Podhoretz, "The Future Danger," Commentary, April 1981, p. 29.

3. Carl H. Gershman, "After the Dominoes Fell," Commentary, May 1978, pp. 47-54.

4. Charles Horner, "America Five Years After Defeat," Commentary, April 1980, p. 50.

5. Irving Kristol, "The Trilateral Commission Factor," Wall Street Journal, April 16, 1980, p. 24.

6. Norman Podhoretz, The Present Danger (New York: Simon & Schuster, 1980), p. 90.

7. Kristol, "Trilateral Commission Factor."

8. Podhoretz, "The New American Majority," passim.

9. Podhoretz, "The Future Danger," pp. 38–39.

10. Ibid., p. 39.

11. Ibid.

12. Ibid.

13. Ibid.

14. Ibid., pp. 41–42.

15. The preceding discussion of "neoconservatism" closely follows that in Richard A. Melanson, Writing History and Making Policy: The Cold War, Vietnam, and Revisionism (Lanham, Md.: University Press of America, 1983), chap. 7.

16. William Schneider, "The Public and Foreign Policy," Wall Street Journal, November 7, 1979, p. 26.

17. Robert E. Osgood, "The Revitalization of Containment," America and the World, 1981, Foreign Affairs, 60, no. 5 (1981), p. 471.

18. Ibid., p. 475.

19. Jeffrey Record, "A 3-War Strategy?" Washington Post, March 22, 1982, p. 28.

20. Washington Post, December 14, 1981, pp. A1, A10.

21. Osgood, "Revitalization of Containment," p. 476.

22. Cf. Robert W. Tucker, The Purposes of American Power (New York: Praeger, 1981), chapter V.

23. The Committee of Sante Fe, "A New Inter-American Policy for the Eighties," ed. Lewis Tambs (Washington, D.C.: Council for Inter-American Security, 1980), p. 52.

24. Ibid.

25. Ibid.

26. Ibid., p. 26.

27. Alexander M. Haig, Jr., "Overview of Recent Foreign Policy," Current Policy, no. 344, November 12, 1981 (Washington, D.C.: U.S. Department of State), p. 1.

28. Alexander M. Haig, Jr., Caveat: Realism, Reagan, and Foreign Policy (New York: Macmillan Publishing Co., 1984), p. 122.

29. Ibid.

30. Ibid., p. 129.

31. Ibid., p. 131.

32. Newsweek, March 1, 1982, p. 19.

33. New York Times, March 21, 1982, p. 22.

34. Washington Post, March 24, 1982, p. A8.

35. Washington Post, March 7, 1982, p. A1.

36. Economist, February 13, 1982, p. 26.

37. Robert G. Kaiser, "Is El Salvador Vietnam?" Washington Post, March 7, 1982, p. C5.

38. Washington Post, March 7, 1982, p. A1.

39. Robert A. Pastor, "U.S. Policy Toward the Caribbean: Recurring Problems and Promises," in Latin America and Caribbean Contemporary Record, vol. 1, 1981-82, ed. Jack W. Hopkins (New York: Holmes & Meier, 1983), p. 86.

40. Ronald Reagan, "Caribbean Basin Initiative," Current Policy, no. 370, February 24, 1982 (Washington, D.C.: U.S. Department of State), p. 5.

41. Ibid.

42. Ibid., p. 6.

43. Caleb Rossiter, "The Financial Hit List," International Policy Report, February 1984, p. 4.

44. Ibid.

45. Ibid.

46. Washington Post, February 27, 1983, p. A1.

47. Transafrica Forum 2, nos. 10-11 (November-December 1983), p. 7.

48. Washington Post, February 27, 1983, p. A1.

49. Transafrica Forum, November-December 1983, p. 7.

50. Subcommittee on Inter-American Affairs of the Committee on Foreign Affairs, House of Representatives, 97th Congress, Second Session, June 15, 1982, "United States Policy Toward Grenada" (Washington, D.C.: Government Printing Office, 1982).

51. Ibid., p. 31.

52. "Remarks at Bridgetown, Barbados, April 8, 1982," Weekly Compilation of Presidential Documents, 18, no. 15 (April 19, 1982), p. 463.

53. "Central America and El Salvador, March 10, 1983," Weekly Compilation of Presidential Documents, 19, no. 10 (March 14, 1983), p. 377.

54. "National Security: Address to the Nation, March 23, 1983," Weekly Compilation of Presidential Documents, 19, no. 12 (March 28, 1983), p. 445.

55. Washington Post, February 27, 1983, p. A1.

56. Congressional Record, October 28, 1983, S14884.

57. Washington Post, June 8, 1983, p. A10; New York Times, June 10, 1983, p. 8.

Notes to Chapter 8

1. Mirlande Hippolyte-Manigat, "What Happened in Ocho Rios?" Caribbean Review 12, no. 2 (Spring 1983), p. 14.
2. Ibid.
3. New York Times, November 7, 1983, p. 12.
4. Ibid.
5. Langhorne A. Motley, "The Decision to Assist Grenada," Current Policy, no. 541, January 24, 1984 (Washington, D.C.: U.S. Department of State), p. 2.
6. "Britain's Grenada Shut-Out," Economist, March 10, 1984, p. 31.
7. Ibid.
8. "Second Report from the Foreign Affairs Committee," Session 1983-1984, House of Commons, Grenada (London: HMSO, March 15, 1984), p. xiii.
9. Quoted in Epica Task Force, "Death of a Revolution," Washington, D.C., November 1983, p. 13.
10. "Second Report from the Foreign Affairs Committee," p. xiii.
11. New York Times, October 30, 1983, p. 14.
12. Economist, March 10, 1984, p. 32.
13. New York Times, October 30, 1983, p. 14.
14. "Second Report from the Foreign Affairs Committee," p. xiv.
15. Speech of Prime Minister George Chambers of Trinidad and Tobago to Trinidadian Parliament, November 15, 1983, as reprinted in "Second Report from the Foreign Affairs Committee,"p. xiv.
16. Epica Task Force, "Death of a Revolution," p. 14.
17. "Second Report from the Foreign Affairs Committee," p. xiv.
18. Economist, March 10, 1984, p. 32.
19. Deputy Secretary of State Kenneth W. Dam at Hearings before the Subcommittees on International Security and Scientific Affairs and on Western Hemisphere Affairs of the Committee on Foreign Affairs, House of Representatives, 98th Congress, First Session, November 2, 1983, "U.S. Military Actions in Grenada: Implications for U.S. Policy in the Eastern Caribbean" (Washington, D.C.: Government Printing Office, 1984), p. 11.
20. Economist, March 10, 1984, p. 32.
21. Ibid.
22. New York Times, October 29, 1983, p. 9.
23. Robert A. Pastor in "U.S. Military Actions in Grenada," p. 80.

24. Ibid., pp. 81–92.

25. Geoffrey Bourne in "U.S. Military Actions in Grenada," p. 196.

26. Ibid.

27. Kenneth W. Dam in "U.S. Military Actions in Grenada," p. 11.

28. "Second Report from the Foreign Affairs Committee," p. xvi.

29. Ibid.

30. Economist, March 10, 1984, p. 34.

31. "Secretary Shultz's News Conference, October 25, 1983," Department of State Bulletin, December 1983, pp. 69–72.

32. "Ambassador Middendorf's Statement, OAS, Permanent Council, Oct. 26, 1983," Department of State Bulletin, December 1983, pp. 72–73.

33. Article 52, which appears in Chapter 8 of the Charter on "Regional Arrangements," provides for (in part):

> Nothing in the present Charter precludes the existence of regional arrangements or agencies for dealing with such matters relating to the maintenance of international peace and security as are appropriate for regional action, provided that such arrangements or agencies and their activities are consistent with the Purposes and Principles of the United Nations.

34. Article 22

> Measures adopted for the maintenance of peace and security in accordance with existing treaties do not constitute a violation of the principles set forth in Articles 18 and 20.

Article 28

> If the inviolability or the integrity of the territory or the sovereignty or political independence of any American State should be affected by an armed attack or by an act of aggression that is not an armed attack, or by an extracontinental conflict, or by a conflict between two or more American States, or by any other act or situation that might endanger the peace of America, the American States, in furtherance of the principles of

continental solidarity or collective self-defense,
shall apply the measures and procedures established
in the special treaties on the subject.

35. Article 8: Composition and Functions of the Defence
and Security Committee

1. The Defence and Security Committee shall consist
of the Ministers responsible for Defence and Security
or other Ministers or Plenipotentiaries designated by
Heads of Government of the Member States.
2. Only Member States possess the necessary
competence in respect of matters under consideration
from time to time shall take part in the
deliberations of the Defence and Security Committee.
3. The Defence and Security Committee shall be
responsible to the Authority. It shall take
appropriate action on any matters referred to it by
the Authority and shall have the power to make
recommendations to the Authority. It shall advise
the Authority on matters relating to external defence
and on arrangements for collective security against
external aggression, including mercenary aggression,
with or without the support of internal or national
elements.
4. The Defence and Security Committee shall have
responsibility for co-ordinating the efforts of
Member States for collective defence and the
preservation of peace and security against external
aggression and for the development of close ties
among the Member States of the Organisation in
matters of external defence and security, including
measures to combat the activities of mercenaries,
operating with or without the support of internal or
national elements, in the exercise of the inherent
right of individual or collective self-defence
recognised by Article 51 of the Charter of the United
Nations.
5. The decisions and directives of the Defence and
Security Committee shall be unanimous and shall be
binding on all subordinate institutions of the
Organisation unless otherwise determined by the
Authority.
6. Subject to any directives that the Authority may
give, the Defence and Security Committee shall meet
as and when necessary. It shall determine its own
procedure, including that for convening meetings, for

the conduct of business thereat and at other times,
and for the annual rotation of the Office of Chairman
among its members in accordance with the principle of
alphabetical order of the Member States.

36. "Ambassador Kirkpatrick's Statement, UN Security
Council, Oct. 27, 1983, " Department of State Bulletin,
December 1983, pp. 74-76.
37. "Lebanon and Grenada," Vital Speeches of the Day,
50, no. 3 (November 15, 1983), pp. 66-69.
38. "Ambassador Kirkpatrick's Statement, UN General
Assembly, Nov. 2, 1983," Department of State Bulletin,
December 1983, pp. 76-77.
39. "Deputy Secretary Dam's Remarks, Louisville, Nov.
4, 1983," Department of State Bulletin, December 1983, pp.
79-81.
40. Congressional Record, October 25, 1983, H8579.
41. Ibid., H8580.
42. Ibid., H8582.
43. Congressional Record, October 26, 1983, S14694.
44. Ibid., S14695.
45. Ibid., H8639.
46. Ibid., H8640.
47. Ibid., H8644.
48. Ibid., H8646.
49. Ibid., H8691.
50. Congressional Record, October 27, 1983, H8703.
51. Ibid., H8706.
52. Congressional Record, October 28, 1983, H8846.
53. Ibid., S14870.
54. Ibid., S14877.
55. Ibid., S14895.
56. Ibid., S14879.
57. Ibid.
58. Ibid., S14880.
59. Ibid., S14883.
60. Ibid., S14887.
61. Ibid., S14889.
62. Congressional Record, November 9, 1983, H8849.
63. New York Times, November 9, 1983, p. 6.
64. Washington Post, November 15, 1983, p. A15.
65. New York Times, November 9, 1983, p. 6.
66. Ibid., p. 1.
67. Norman Podhoretz, "The Neo-Conservative Anguish
Over Reagan's Foreign Policy," New York Times Magazine,
May 2, 1982, pp. 88-94.
68. Norman Podhoretz, "Proper Uses of Power," New
York Times, October 30, 1983, p. E19.

69. Ibid.

70. Wall Street Journal, October 26, 1983, p. 28.

71. Editorial from the Columbus Citizen-Journal, November 2, 1983, as reprinted in Congressional Record, November 4, 1983, E5332.

72. Editorial from the Jacksonville Journal, October 30, 1983, as reprinted in Congressional Record, November 1, 1983, E5238.

73. Ronald Steel, "Reveling in Military Power," New York Times, October 30, 1983, p. E19.

74. "Reagan's Credibility," Boston Globe, October 27, 1983, as reprinted in Congressional Record, October 28, 1983, S14878.

75. "Goliath in Grenada," New York Times, October 30, 1983, p. E18.

76. Coalition for a New Foreign and Military Policy, Newsletter, Fall 1983, pp. 8-9.

77. Transafrica, "Press Release," n.d.

78. Carl Rowan, "Grenada's Black Conscience," Washington Post, November 1, 1983, as reprinted in Congressional Record, November 2, 1983, E5278.

79. Morton Kondracke, "Liberals Should Be Cheering U.S. Action in Grenada," Chicago Sun-Times, October 30, 1983, as reprinted in Congressional Record, November 2, 1983, E5278.

80. New York Times, October 28, 1983, p. 6.

81. Ibid., p. 1.

82. New York Times, November 3, 1983, p. 21.

83. New York Times, November 4, 1983, p. 18.

84. New York Times, November 16, 1983, p. 3.

85. New York Times, November 3, 1983, p. 23.

Notes to Chapter 9

1. Gerry Studds in "U.S. Military Actions in Grenada," p. 20.

2. Howard Wolpe in "U.S. Military Actions in Grenada," p. 35.

3. Ibid., p. 19.

4. The following discussion closely follows the model presented by William Schneider, "Conservatism, Not Interventionism: Trends in Foreign Policy Opinion, 1974-1982," in Kenneth A. Oye et al., eds., Eagle Defiant: United States Foreign Policy in the 1980s (Boston: Little, Brown, 1983), pp. 39-43.

5. Ibid., p. 43.

6. Ibid.

7. Ibid., p. 42.

8. Ibid., p. 55.

9. "U.S. Military Actions in Grenada," p. 26.

10. New York Times, July 31, 1984, p. 1.

11. New York Times, August 2, 1984, p. 3.

12. Wayne S. Smith, "The Grenada Complex in Central America," Caribbean Review, 12, no. 4 (fall 1983), p. 34.

Index